CHILDREN OF TVLVS

Essays on the Tiruray People

by

Stuart A. Schlegel

Giraffe Books
Quezon City
1994

National Library of the Philippines CIP Data

Recommended entry:

Schlegel, Stuart A.
    Children of Tulus: essays on the Tiruray
people / by Stuart A. Schlegel. -
Quezon City: Giraffe Books, 1994. 1 v

    1. Tiruray—Philippines—Ethnic identity.
2. Tiruray—Philippines—Social life and
customs.   I. Title.

DS666.T6   1994   305.8'9921   F931000035
ISBN 152 3308 46X
ISBN 978 152 3308 460

To Audrey—with love and thanks.

Young people of Figel settlement, playing gongs at dawn.

Table of Contents

v

Chapter 1

INTRODUCTION

The Tiruray and I

I

This book consists of a number of articles I have written about the Tiruray people of southwestern Mindanao, a people who have been my friends and teachers for over 30 years.

I first met the Tiruray when, as an Episcopal priest not long out of seminary, I was posted at the Mission of St. Francis of Assisi in Upi in 1960. Upi is a municipality in what was then the province of Cotabato, in the portion that is now the province of Maguindanao. The mission had a large central parish church in Upi, where there were some Tiruray communicants, but most of the congregation was made up of Ilocano homesteaders. However, the mission also had some 50 or so "outstation" chapels scattered about in nearby Tiruray communities. One of my tasks was to found St. Francis High School in Upi, and many of the students at this school were from Tiruray families. So, too, were many of the patients at the mission clinic. I quickly recognized what a delightful and engaging people these Tiruray folks were, and I enjoyed working with them very much until I left the mission in 1963 to pursue graduate studies in anthropology at the University of Chicago. My family and I left Upi with some sadness and with a hope of returning, but we wanted a different kind of relationship with the people than we had had as missionaries.

At Chicago, I was able to begin turning my attention to the traditional Tiruray who lived deep in the forests well beyond the Upi valley. There, I had always heard, the Tiruray lived very differently from the acculturated people I had known in and around the mission communities. I proposed a two-year field dissertation research project among the traditional Tiruray, focusing on their legal system and its relationship on the one hand to their social order and on the other to their moral thought. This proposal was accepted by the university and financed by the Foreign Area Fellowship

1

Program of the Social Science Research Council and the American Council of Learned Societies. So, my family and I returned to the Tiruray in early 1966.

A good friend, Simeon Beling, a Tiruray with close contacts with the people in the interior, offered to take me deep into the forest, to a place called Figel, where the old way was being lived and where there was a much admired legal authority. There, a great many hours' hike from the nearest road, he introduced me to the Figel community and explained, as best he could, that I was cheerful, friendly, without the slightest intent to convert anybody to anything, and wished to live with them for two years. To my relief and delight they made me welcome. Simeon left, I stayed, and one of the great experiences of my life began. With my wife and children secure in a small house on the farm of a good friend in Mirab near Upi, where I could come out of the forest and visit once every few weeks, I settled in to spend two years in Figel.

With me in the forest, having hired on as field assistants, were two Tiruray men from the Upi area, Mamerto Martin and Aliman Francisco. They were both acculturated Tiruray, fluent in both English and Tiruray, and had an interest in learning about the "old ways" that was at least as great as my own. They contributed to my studies in countless ways, at the beginning especially helping me struggle to learn the Tiruray language. I knew some Tagalog from my earlier years in Upi, and Tagalog is structurally somewhat similar to Tiruray, but Mamerto's and Aliman's bilingual skills made those early months indescribably easier. Toward the end of my research period, Mamerto worked very energetically with me to produce a Tiruray-English dictionary. He, Aliman and I developed a close friendship in Figel and I have cherished that good time together ever since.

I set out, perhaps rather ambitiously, to gather material on four different aspects of Tiruray life. First, for my dissertation, I wanted to learn about, describe and analyze their traditional legal system. Second, I wanted to study and get some systematic data on both the swidden, hunting, fishing and gathering subsistence system of the traditional people and the peasant agricultural subsistence system of the acculturated Tiruray. Third, I wanted to do a lexicon of the language. And, finally, I wanted to be able to describe the traditional way of life in a general ethnography.

From 1968, when my graduate studies were completed, until the present I have been a professor of anthropology and of Southeast Asian studies at the

University of California, Santa Cruz. In this beautiful setting, I completed and published all of those four projects except the last. In 1960, *Tiruray Justice: Traditional Tiruray Morality and Law* was published by the University of California Press, and some years later it was republished by the Institute of Philippine Studies of the Ateneo de Manila University in a Philippine paperback edition. My *Tiruray-English Lexicon* was also brought out by University of California Press the following year. *Tiruray Subsistence: From Shifting Cultivation to Plow Agriculture* appeared in 1979, published by the Ateneo de Manila Press. A somewhat more detailed and technical version of this work was at that time made available in Xerox form in the Rizal Library at the Ateneo.[1] I am presently at work on the ethnographic study, which will for the first time make generally available the rich data which I have on Tiruray spirituality and world-view.

In addition to these book-length treatises, I have written a number of articles on various aspects of Tiruray thinking and social life. Out of these, I have chosen the papers which are reprinted in this volume. As with my books, whenever possible I have published these in the Philippines. The Philippines has a splendid social science infrastructure, including a variety of scholarly presses and journals, in support of a large number of outstanding Filipino anthropologists and other social scientists. Publishing my materials in this scholarly context—in the country from which the data were derived and the work was done—has always seemed to me to be not only appropriate and sensible but indeed a matter of honor.

As one's scholarly articles inevitably are, the papers collected here first appeared in a scattered variety of journals, books, and collections of essays. Each necessarily started out with a bit about who and where the Tiruray are. I have therefore edited them to remove as much of that sort of repetition as I could without hurting the flow of thought. Where some repetition necessarily remains, I ask the reader's forbearance. In some cases I have updated the essays, and I have put all of the Tiruray words into a consistent orthography. I have re-footnoted them all, again to avoid needless repetition.

In the chapters that follow, I set forth a bit of information about each of the articles and how it came to be written. They contain a considerable amount of ethnographic detail, and so perhaps begin to make good on the last of my early publishing goals.

What is so true, but what may well not show through the scholarly sort of prose that follows, is that living among the Tiruray has changed my life in many very important ways. Their moral system is elegant, with its basic openness of one person to another and to the other's needs and wants, and their spirituality with great beauty conceives of the world—both spirit and human—as a fundamentally egalitarian network of partners, interdependent with each other and with nature. These aspects of Tiruray life have moved me deeply and have indelibly affected my own sense of how life can and should be lived. I owe the Tiruray much more than I could ever put into words.

But enough about me. Let me now introduce the Tiruray to those who have not yet had the privilege of knowing them.

II

The Tiruray (in their own language, "Teduray") are a hill people who live in relative though rapidly decreasing isolation in the northern part of the Cotabato Cordillera, a range of mountains which curves along the south-western coast of Mindanao, facing the Celebes Sea, in the province of Maguindanao. The mountains and valleys of this range are neither very rugged nor very high, and are covered with dense tropical evergreen forest, wherever recent plow agriculture and logging have not replaced the trees with farms or savanna grassland.[2]

Traditionally Tiruray were adapted to the forests, and made their living through shifting cultivation, hunting, fishing, and gathering, but in recent decades a large number have been greatly acculturated and have adopted a typical Filipino lowland peasant way of life in the areas where the forest cover has been removed.[3] Only in disappearing pockets of isolation, deep in the mountains or far up the Tran Grande River—their traditional southern boundary—are Tiruray communities still to be found living in what is, essentially, the old way. From there as one moves toward the coastline to the west, toward the great Cotabato basin to the east, or toward the extremes of the mountains near Cotabato City to the north, one encounters Tiruray who have known more than half a century of intense contact with, first American and then Filipino, military, educational, and missionary enterprises and with peasant homesteaders, both Christian and Muslim. Some people from these areas have moved deeper into the mountains, seeking refuge from all the changes, but most have stayed. These have necessarily given up swidden cultivation and become plow farmers, they have been drawn deeply into the cash-and-credit market economy typical of Filipino peasant life, they have become Christians, and have adopted western dress. Most have learned to speak the national language. In my writing, I typically refer to the people who live the old way as "traditional Tiruray," and to the acculturated people as "peasant Tiruray."

The Tiruray, numbering some 25,000-30,000 persons, are Malay in physical appearance and speak a language which, although not mutually intelligible with those of neighboring ethnic groups, is structurally very similar to them and to the other Philippine languages of the Malayo-Polynesian family.[4] Their nearest ethnic neighbors to the north and east are the Muslim Maguindanaon people, and farther south in the mountains are such other animist groups as the Cotabato Manobo and the T'boli. Also to be found in the Cotabato lowlands and the acculturated areas of the hills, of course, are homesteaders from the Visayas and Luzon and, in the towns, some Chinese.

Origins of the different ethnic groups in the Philippines have for a long time yielded great controversy over slight data. Linguistically and racially, the Tiruray are clearly related to the other Philippine peoples and to the rest of the Malay populations of Southeast Asia. Like the other hill peoples of the archipelago, they may be viewed, at least in part, as surviving representatives of the sort of cultures that were widely distributed in the Philippines prior to the coming of strong Spanish and Islamic influences.

By the 15th century C.E., the lowland populations around the Cotabato Cordillera had been converted to the Muslim faith and formed into the Maguindanaon confederation.[5] They were not, however, able to conquer or convert the Tiruray and the other hill tribes. In the last decades of the 19th century, when the Spanish, after centuries of warfare with the Muslims, were finally able to establish a garrison in Cotabato City, the Jesuits opened a school and mission for the Tiruray in the Tamantaka area near Awang at the foot of what they called the "Tiruray Mountains."[6] Several families were baptized, but Spanish presence in the area was short-lived and replaced early in the 20th century by American occupation.

One of the early Americans in the area, a Philippine Constabulary officer named Irving Edwards, took a special interest in the Tiruray and married a young Tiruray woman. He lived among them until his death in the late 1950s, devoting himself over the decades, in a variety of official and unofficial capacities, to the furthering of schools and of what he took to be "progress" among the Tiruray. In 1916, Edwards established a public school at Awang, and, in 1919, he opened an agricultural school in Upi and had built a winding road from the lowlands up to the new school. The road now goes considerably deeper into the mountains and is scheduled eventually to link up with Lebak along the coast, south of the Tiruray area.

In the 1920s many additional schools were constructed in areas of Tiruray occupation and numerous homesteaders from Luzon, mostly Ilocanos, began to enter the hills. These were joined by some immigrants from the Visayas and by a number of Maguindanaon Muslims. The number of the latter in the Tiruray area increased greatly after World War II, and political control of the area has tended to be in Maguindanaon hands since the late 1940's.

Acculturated Tiruray wear the same generally Western work and dress clothes as other Filipino peasants. Their traditional clothing, however, is more distinctive and colorful. Originally made from bark, the clothes have for a long time been cut from cloth which, since the Tiruray do not weave, they obtain through trade with the Maguindanaon. Traditionally, Tiruray men wear a closely fitted pair of trousers and a long-sleeved tunic. The women wear a tight blouse, buttoned at the front, with a sarong skirt. They also wear a series of brass bracelets and anklets, as well as brass earrings, and, for dressy occasions, one or more necklaces made of glass beads and gold. Men, when dressed formally, always carry a wavy-bladed kris. Traditional women further decorate themselves with white face powder, red lip stain, and a kind of temporary facial tattooing which results from making many small blood-blisters in a pattern on the forehead. Traditionally both sexes wear their hair long, uncut since early childhood. The women gather their hair into a bun at the back, and the men wind it around their head and secure it under a bandanna. In the old way, also, all Tiruray had their teeth filed and blackened at puberty. This and the women's blood-blistering constitute their only forms of body-mutilation. More acculturated Tiruray wear their hair in western styles.

Traditional Tiruray houses are constructed of wood and bamboo, roofed with grass, and are quite small—generally about 3 x 5 meters—intended to hold a single nuclear family. They are built up on posts about two meters off the ground, with a notched log ladder which can be pulled into the house at night for security. There are typically no windows, and a single door which is hinged at the bottom. The center pole of the roof is decorated with various ornaments to ward off malign spirits. The entire house is held together by rattan or vine lashing. Cooking typically is done under the house, using iron pots over a wood fire.

Food is divided conceptually into four categories: starch staples including rice, corn, yam, taro and others; viands or side dishes which include meat, fish, and a great variety of vegetables; spices such as salt, onion, and garlic; and snacks which would include fruits, coffee, and rice cakes. The starch staple is the most highly valued part of the meal, and the various starches eaten by the Tiruray are culturally ranked, with rice at the top and with the wild yam at the bottom constituting a virtual famine food. Tiruray are fond of drinking coffee and, from the market, tea—but no intoxicants are used in the traditional way of life except for the mild stimulant of chewing betel quid, which is done by all traditional persons past puberty. Acculturated Tiruray, especially the men, tend to give up chewing betel and in its place smoke cigarettes or cigars. Many drink tuba and some use the harder liquors.

Traditional Tiruray purchase or trade for certain items from the market, notably iron tools, cloth, and salt, but for the most part they subsist on the proceeds from swidden cultivation, from hunting and fishing, and from extensive gathering of wild foods.

The cycle of slash-and-burn, or swidden, activities follows a yearly sequence and is timed by careful reference to the position in the night sky of several constellations. In late December or early January, the men ritually mark their swidden sites for the coming year, and begin the heavy work of slashing away the dense jungle undergrowth and felling the massive trees. The men of a neighborhood work in each household's site in turn, until all are ready to be burned, generally by March or April. The swiddens are then planted by the neighborhood men and women, working together on each field in order, first in corn and then in several varieties of rice. A great variety of other crops—tubers, vegetables, fruit, spices, and such non-edibles as cotton—are also planted at various times in and around the borders of the field. By May or June the first corn crops are harvested by the women of the neighborhood, again taking the fields in turn, and stored on drying racks. The rice is ready for harvest by August or September. The rice stalks are cleared away and a second corn crop is then normally planted in the swidden. The various crops are harvested as they mature and are needed, but the field is not further planted. Each household will establish a new swidden elsewhere the following year, leaving the old field to fallow for many years so that the forest vegetation may be reestablished.

Land tenure among traditional Tiruray consists of right of use and not formal ownership. The forests around the settlements are considered an ample good and each family may work as much land as they feel able, locating their swidden wherever the land is not actually being used by someone else.

The tools used by traditional farmers are quite simple: a slashing bolo (*fais*), a shorter all-purpose bolo (*badung*), an ax for telling large trees (*fatuk*), a weeding knife (*susud*), and a small harvesting blade (*langgaman*). The iron blades and the iron ax head of these tools are obtained from the market, but the handles are carved and lashed on by the worker himself. Sharpened poles are also used: a long narrow one for dibbling (*ohok*) and shorter ones for digging (*tudok, kedor*).

When the main crops have been planted, the work of weeding is done by the women, each on her own household's swidden, and the men are free to devote most of their time to hunting, fishing, and gathering wild foods from the forest. Many kinds of traps, including spring snares (*kotor, ambirut*) and spears (*feliyad*), spiked pits (*kanseb*), and log falls (*diran*), are utilized, and a very broad subsistence base of wild plant and animal foods are regularly exploited. Traditional Tiruray are expert with the bow (*bohor*) and arrow (*banting*), the hunting spear (*sebat*), and the blowgun (*lefuk*). In recent years they have also begun using homemade shotguns (*faletik*) constructed from galvanized iron pipe. Hunting dogs are kept and trained to locate and corner game.

Some Tiruray live near the sea coast, and all others traditionally lived close to rivers or streams. Using a variety of methods—hooks and line (*duray*), spears (*serafang*), woven traps (*siyuk, takef, sukub*), poisons, etc.—they extract a good supply of fish, eels, crustaceans, and other aquatic food resources. Except for the road from the lowlands near Cotabato City to way past Upi, only trails connect the various Tiruray hamlets, and all transport is by foot.

The settlement system of traditional Tiruray reflects their cooperative scheme of shifting cultivation. The largest social unit with discrete boundaries is the "neighborhood" (*inged*) and consists of 20 or 30 families which regularly assist each other in their swidden activities and rituals. All who live in a given neighborhood are said to be "of one house" (*setifon*), the literal meaning of which seems to reflect an earlier period when neighbors all shared a single large house. At the present time, however, they live in single family dwellings divided among several "settlements" (*denongon*), small dispersed hamlets of one to 20 houses—three to six being most common. Settlements are named after prominent geographical features nearby and do not have the stability of location or household composition which is typical of the larger neighborhood. The residential unit and fundamental social building block is the "household." Usually, the household is composed of a single nuclear family (*kureng*), though polygynous households are occasionally encountered. There is no limit to the number of wives a Tiruray man may have, but he must be able to care for each of his families equally well; in practice, the great majority of households are monogamous. Relations between households may be by kinship, brideprice contract, or work cooperation, but each one is independent and economically self-determining. When children marry they are considered to have formed a new family and household with full responsibility of feeding and provisioning itself.

The peasant Tiruray, living where the forests have been cut down, have had to abandon their traditional system of shifting cultivation, and have become for the most part plow-farming tenants on other people's land. The marked environmental changes have resulted in a major shift in their entire subsistence system. Acculturated Tiruray grow or gather much less of their daily diet—most of their produce are sold in the market and a large percentage of their food is purchased there. With the jungle cover cleared away, and with the rivers in settled areas badly over-exploited, hunting, fishing, and gathering have virtually been eliminated from the Tiruray way of life. Market relations are, of course, greatly expanded over the very peripheral use made by the traditional Tiruray of the marketplace. The traditional people are familiar with cash and use it in the market but in virtually no other way.

The principal crops grown by peasant Tiruray on their plowed fields and gardens are dry rice, corn, and such cash crops as tomatoes and onions. The tools used are those typical of Filipino plow farmers everywhere: the carabao- or bull-drawn iron plows (*dadu*), harrows (*fakaras*), and dragging sleds (*kangga*), the threshing platform (*tagikan*), and, of course, the bolo (*fais*) and the weeding knife (*susud*).

The kinship system is the same for both traditional and acculturated Tiruray. Every individual is the center point of a personal kindred which, reckoned bilaterally (through both mother's and father's side) from that person, includes all the descendants of his/her four pairs of great grandparents, and thus reaches laterally to include all second cousins. No one may marry within the kindred, as to do so would be considered incest (*sumbang*). A person's kindred have important responsibilities toward him or her, and are mobilized on the person's behalf in disputes (whether settled legally or by feuding), at the establishment of a family through marriage and the giving of brideprice, or at the dissolution of a marriage through death or divorce. If a man is involved in a feud, he expects all in his kindred to come to his assistance and he has, similarly, placed them all in danger of attack. Should the dispute be solved legally instead of by feuding, the person's kindred will share in paying the fine if he/she is at fault or in the distribution of the fine if the person is found to have been in the right. At marriage, the groom's kindred are called on to contribute brideprice items (*tamuk*), while the bride's kindred share in the receiving of the brideprice. When someone dies, his/her kindred are summoned to share in the seven days of funeral rites and in their cost.

Terminologically, the kinship system is bilateral. It gives emphasis to the importance of the nuclear family by singling out with specific reference terms the blood kinsmen of the family into which a person is born and of the family which he/she creates by marriage, as follows: father (*eboh*), mother (*ideng*), older sibling (*ofò*), younger sibling (*tuwarey*), child (*engà*). Otherwise, all blood relatives within a person's kindred of his/her grandparent's generation and above and all of his/her grandchildren's generation and below are referred to as grandparent or grandchild (both *bébê*). All other kindred males in the father's generation are called uncle (*momò*), and all other kindred females of the mother's generation are called aunt (*inà*). All kindred elders are collectively known as elders (*lukes*). Kindred persons in one's own generation, other than siblings, are called cousins (*dumon*). All kindred persons in one's child's generation, except the immediate children themselves, are referred to as nephew or niece (both *onok*).

With regard to relatives by marriage, a person's spouse—either husband or wife—is referred to as *bawag*, and one's spouse's parents are called *terimà*, a term extended to all kindred elders of the spouse. The spouse of a person's child or grandchild is referred to as child-in-law (*awas*), and his/her parents as co-parent-in-law (*belai*), this term also being extended to include all kindred elders. In a polygynous household, the first wife is referred to as the "senior wife" (*tafay bawag*), and each other wife is termed a "co-wife" (*duwoy*).

In a person's own generation, the terms of reference for relatives by

10

marriage make a distinction according to whether or not the relationship is between males. A man speaks of his wife's brothers or male cousins and of his sister's or female cousin's husband as his sibling-in-law (*efēl*); he refers to his wife's sisters and female cousins and to his brother's or cousin's wives as *ibò*. A woman refers to any of her husband's siblings or any of her sibling's spouses as *ibò*. The term co-sibling-in-law (*idos*) is used to refer to one joined to a person by two marriage links; e.g., it is used between men who are married to sisters.

Parents, in direct address, are called by their referential term and all other elders, whether related or not, are addressed by the kinship term appropriate to their sex and generation: grandparent, uncle, or aunt. The use of an elder's personal name is strictly avoided, but one may address one's siblings or children and any other kindred peer or junior by their names. Spouses are also addressed by personal names. All peers related by marriage are addressed by use of the referential terms, and all others of one's own generation by their teknonym (Father-of-X or Mother-of-X) or by the general expression for friend (*adih* between males, or *awê* between females).

The division of daily labor in the fields between men's work and women's work makes it virtually mandatory that each adult be married to an active spouse, and in terms of behavior the closest relationship of all is between a man and his wife. Among the Tiruray, one's spouse has sole right to sexual access; there are no mistresses and no prostitution. It is the great importance of the married couple to each other which yields the deep concern in Tiruray society for the establishment and maintenance of viable marriages and which makes elopement with a married person such a serious offense. The first wife must consent to her husband's taking any additional wives, and when this occurs she is the leader of the others, assigning them to their share of household and field work.

Parents are completely responsible for their children and do not ask for help in their care from kinsmen, who are felt to be occupied with their own concerns. As soon as children are old enough to help their parents they are put to work, girls helping their mothers and boys doing male tasks. By the time of adolescence they have absorbed the skills needed to function as Tiruray adults. Traditional Tiruray have no other form of schooling. Peasant Tiruray, however, frequently send their children to government schools if they exist in the area where they live.

Siblings are close in companionship when they are young, but age difference is of great importance, and they must be respectful at all times to their older brothers and sisters. They are also close, of course, to their parents, but kindred elders of other nuclear families, e.g., uncles or grandparents, are not particularly close emotionally. Being nonkindred, people go to great lengths to be especially kind to and considerate of their in-laws.

It is a cardinal rule of Tiruray ethics that no one should act in any way that would abuse and anger another person, as it is believed that anyone who is hurt or angered by a nonkinsman may very likely respond with violence and precipitate a feud. Behavioral customs (*adat*) are thus viewed as being rules of respect, and in any situation where custom is not clear, one must behave so as to be respectful of the feelings of all other persons. One who ignores the imperative to respect one's fellows and who intentionally or imprudently abuses someone bears the responsibility (*salà*) for the consequences. The wronged person, in turn, has what is considered an understandable desire for retaliation (*benal*). Properly one with *benal* should endorse his case to a legal authority (*kefeduwan*) for adjudication, but it is feared that he/she may instead involve his/her kindred in blood revenge (*bonò*) against the offender and his/her kindred.

The legal authority and the religious shaman are the two principal leadership roles in Tiruray society. The legal authorities settle various kinds of cases in a special very formal discussion called *tiyawan*. These may concern either an agreement to be formally established (e.g., a marriage agreement) or a dispute to be authoritatively settled. The role of a legal authority is an achieved and nonprofessional specialization open to anyone, man or woman, who learns to speak in the highly metaphorical rhetoric of *tiyawan* and who is accepted by his/her fellows as a trustworthy representative. To the Tiruray, "justice" aims at a situation in which all persons' feelings are properly respected. The legal authority's primary dedication is to the achievement of justice by seeking, through *tiyawan*, a settlement in which all fault is accepted and all hurts are recognized and satisfied by an appropriate fine. Legal authorities represent a certain individual and his kindred but do not contend on anyone's behalf in the manner of a trial lawyer in Western adversary proceedings. They do not attempt to "win," and anyone who does so is severely censured by the others. Representation of a "side" takes the form of willingness to accept fault on behalf of that side if necessary. All legal authorities are committed, as a group, to seek just decisions which result in all feelings being made good.

Two types of *tiyawan* are distinguished: "hot" *tiyawan*, where a dispute is involved, and "good" *tiyawan* where the issue does not include hurt feelings, as with making marriage arrangements. The legal authority, when not involved in *tiyawan*, lives the normal life of any other traditional Tiruray person, working in the swiddens and around the home. The Tiruray are fundamentally egalitarian, and the legal authorities are not political chiefs or headmen in any way. Indeed there is no formal institutionalization of power in Tiruray society. Among acculturated Tiruray, the role of the legal authority is almost entirely diminished, and peasant Tiruray are constituents of the normal representatives of municipal Philippine law and politics, mostly non-Tiruray.

The second major leader of traditional Tiruray society is the shaman (*beliyan*). Tiruray cosmological and mythical beliefs comprise a rich and complex imagery focused primarily on various sorts of spirits. The universe is conceived of as being populated with a vast number of different types of "people" (*etew*), some of which, the "humans" (*keilawan*), can be seen and others of which, the "spirits (*meginalew*), cannot be seen without a special charisma. Some spirits are named individuals, but most are organized in tribes living in different cosmic regions (*bangel*) and possessed of differing amounts of spiritual authority (*barakat*). In general, they go about their business, co-inhabiting the universe with the humans. Some are by nature cruel and malignant in their relations with humans, as, for example the *busaw*, a tribe of giant spirits who generally live in caves. Others, such as *Tulus*, the creator of the universe and greatest authority of all spirits, or *Tulus'* messengers, the *telaki*, are naturally kind to the humans. But most tribes of spirits are, like human societies, composed of individuals who are quite friendly if they are not angered, but who can inflict harm on any person who offends them.

The Tiruray view their relations with the spirits as being just like their relations with other humans, with the added difficulty that the spirits are invisible to the ordinary person. The cruel, dangerous ones should be avoided if possible and guarded against by charms and amulets. With the other spirits, one merely strives to have good interpersonal relations. In daily life, altercations do arise, however, and the spirits retaliate by making the human offender sick. This is the general Tiruray view of the origin of illness. In such a situation, the services of a shaman are needed. The shaman, who like the legal authority may be either a man or a woman, has the particular gift from

13

the spirit world of being able to see and talk to spirits. He or she is then able to seek out an offended spirit and bring the issue to the spirit's shaman for settlement through the legal discussion of *tiyawan*. The shaman is, in fact, a special kind of legal authority—one who settles disputes between spirits and humans. The various spirit tribes are seen as having their own legal authorities to handle the affairs among their own kind, and they have their own shamans to settle disputes between their spirit followers and other kinds of spirits or humans. What the Tiruray do, in terms of interpersonal relations, is to extend both their moral prescriptions and their legal institutions to the spiritual, cosmic level.

Aside from his healing functions, the shaman is also the ritual leader at a series of communal sacred meals (*kanduli*) which are observed by traditional Tiruray four times each year, marking off significant points in the swidden cycle. These meals involve the continual passing back and forth among a neighborhood's families of rice from a special ritual plot within each one's swidden field, so that when the meal is actually eaten some rice from every swidden is eaten by each neighbor who worked on that field. A bit of the commingled rice is offered to the spirit of food as well. The *kanduli* is a powerful ritual statement of the interdependence and cooperation which exists between neighbor and neighbor, and between humans and spirits, in the enterprises of growing food and, indeed, of all of life.

Among acculturated, peasant Tiruray, the role of the shaman, like that of the legal authority, has greatly decreased through the transformation of the subsistence system and the general acceptance of Christianity. In 1926, at the invitation of Captain Edwards, the Philippine Episcopal Church began extensive missionary work among the Tiruray, establishing chapels in many of their communities in the areas of rapid social and cultural change. Episcopal work has remained strong among the Tiruray, and since the end of World War II has been joined by vigorous Roman Catholic and Protestant efforts. Many Tiruray families have taken ôn Christianity as a part of their new peasant Filipino way of life, just as they have adopted Western dress, begun using the national language, and started to send their children to public and parochial schools. Various government and religiously sponsored clinics have been established and are used by many of the acculturated Tiruray, although belief in spirits rather than germs as the cause of disease remains strong and folk healers continue to play a major role among the Tiruray as they do among many rural Filipinos.

14

The two principal art forms among the Tiruray are music and basket weaving. Traditional Tiruray music is rapidly being lost but consisted of instrumental, vocal, and dance forms. Tiruray musical instruments included tuned percussion beams (*kagul*), the reed lip flute (*falendag*) and the smaller ring flute (*suling*), the bamboo jaw harp (*kubing*), several types of bamboo zythers (*togò belotokan* and *teganggù*), a drum (*togò tefuken*), and a set of five small tuned gongs with shallow boss (*agung*). All of these instruments are played frequently for entertainment and the gongs have numerous roles in the various ritual events of traditional Tiruray life.

The types of vocal music include a long epic chant (*berinarew*) describing the exploits of an ancient Tiruray culture hero, *Lagey Lingkuwos*, which requires over 12 full nights to sing in its entirety, several forms of impromptu singing discourse, either in monologue or dialogue (*siyasid, balikatà, seringon,* and *linggeng*), love songs (*lindogan*) and sung riddles (*bayuk*). These, like the musical instruments and like Tiruray dancing, are seldom performed by acculturated people and Tiruray music in general may be said to be rapidly dying out.

Basket weaving is done in a number of decorative styles to produce various forms of containers, winnowing baskets, and fish traps. This art, like music, was in great decline among the Tiruray until recent decades when certain adaptations of traditional designs have come into demand for the Manila tourist trade and for export. The establishment of a ready market and the allied increase in sale value of Tiruray weaving has greatly stimulated the learning and production of basketwork art, for home use as well as for sale.

Most Tiruray view the profound changes their society is undergoing with a certain sadness, and with a deep sense of pride in the culture of their forebears. But the transformation of their way of life seems now inevitable and irreversible. With it, come profound changes in the traditional authority roles. As the older religious and legal authorities fade from importance, their place is being taken by a new set of educated leaders—Tiruray lawyers, school teachers, government officials, agricultural experts and the like. It is these people who will lead the Tiruray people as they draw ever further away from their traditional forest isolation and into the new ways, opportunities, and challenges of participation in the mainstream of Philippine life.

Notes

[1]Schlegel (1977).

[2]For a somewhat more extensive discussion of the people, what is known of their history, and the area, see Schlegel (1970b, 1979).

[3]A number of the chapters of this book deal with Tiruray subsistence systems. A full account is in Schlegel (1977, 1979).

[4]Conklin (1952, 1955).

[5]For an extensive discussion, see Majul (1973).

[6]Saleeby (1905:15).

Chapter 2

TIRURAY-MAGUINDANAON ETHNIC RELATIONS

An Ethnohistorical Puzzle

This paper was prepared for a conference on Mindanao held in 1971 in Cotabato City, and it was then published in Manila by Solidarity (Vol. VII, No. 4) in April of 1972. I had long been intrigued by the puzzle it describes, and this paper was my attempt to unscramble the known data to try to make more sense of them than seemed to be present in the commonly held beliefs about the relations between the Tiruray and their lowland Muslim neighbors.

I

The Maguindanaon people are Muslim, lowland, wet-rice growing neighbors of the Tiruray, who live in the adjacent great Cotabato Basin, formed by the drainage of the Pulangi, or Rio Grande, River. Both people share the belief that they are descendants of a common stock, that until the relatively recent coming of Islam to Mindanao, roughly five centuries ago, the Tiruray and the Maguindanaon were one single people.

The folk stories of both Tiruray and Maguindanaon include a common tale of the coming of Sharif Kabungsuwan, the founder of Islam in Mindanao, to the mouth of the Rio Grande, of his being met there and made welcome by two brothers named Tabunaway and Mamalu, who were leaders of the "people of Maguindanao." Sharif Kabungsuwan insists that the people of Maguindanao accept Islam. In both versions of the story, Tabunaway accepts the Muslim faith, is circumcised and forswears the eating of pork. But his brother, Mamalu, it is told, refuses. He runs away to the mountains with his recalcitrant pagan followers, and these become the Tiruray of today. Tabunaway remains a follower of Islam and Sharif Kabungsuwan, and his people are the Maguindanaon of today.

In short, the stories of both people agree that they were once a single ethnic group, but that they divided into two with the coming of Islam and its subsequent acceptance by one group and rejection by the other. These stories are faithfully believed by both people today, who insist that, until the coming of Sharif Kabungsuwan, the Tiruray and the Maguindanaon were indeed one ethnic entity; that although different in religious faith, they are of the same blood.

Now, what is so interesting about this tradition on origins is not that it is held in common by two peoples in almost identical terms, nor that it is taken for granted to be true history by both ethnolinguistic groups—for, after all, it is also accepted as factual by most historians who have touched on the subject.[1] What is interesting is that—in the face of such unanimity—the story is almost certainly not true. Certain aspects of the tale may be factual, and surely are, but the central message—that the Tiruray came into being from a fission within the Maguindanaon spurred by the preaching of Islam in Mindanao—this central message is clearly false.

That the Maguindanaon and the Tiruray are exceedingly different in culture is quickly apparent to anyone who knows them both with any intimacy. This is not merely a matter of religion. The Maguindanaon find their cultural relatives most readily among the other lowland Filipino groups of wet-rice farmers; the Tiruray are most closely related to the other two swidden farming, mountain and rain-forest dwelling groups in the Cotabato Cordillera, the T'Boli and the Bilaan. These relationships—and the long-standing separateness of the Tiruray and the Maguindanaon—are most dramatically manifested in their respective languages. Thomas and Healy, who have done lexicostatistical analysis of the Philippine language families, quite correctly place the Tiruray with the T'Boli and the Bilaan as members of the Southern Mindanao branch, while they include Maguindanaon in the Philippine Superstock branch—which means, by their calculations, that the family which includes the Tiruray and that which includes the Maguindanaon separated from each other as long ago as 1300 BC.[2] Even if one has little confidence in the precision of lexicostatistical dating, the divergence of these two languages—and with them the two ethnic groups that use them—clearly occurred a long, long time before the arrival of Sharif Kabungsuwan at the mouth of the Rio Grande, somewhere around the beginning of the 16th century.

Herein, then, lies what I have called "an ethnohistorical puzzle." What was the relationship of old between the Tiruray and the Maguindanaon, if not what they both believe it to have been? And how, then, did this common tradition come into being?

In trying to answer questions such as these, one must necessarily rely on a certain amount of conjecture. There are some things, however, which may be known with fair certainty. We know, for example, that for centuries the Maguindanaon and the Tiruray have maintained important trade relationships. And it seems clear that certain Tiruray (those from the Awang area at the foot of the mountains) and certain Maguindanaon (those of the Maguindanao vicinity proper, which is to say those living around the mouth of the Pulangi, or Rio Grande, in the area that is today known as Cotabato City) were traditionally military allies.

It is worth looking in some detail at the trade relations which have obtained until fairly recent times between the Tiruray and the Maguindanaon. Prior to the coming of American rule, the Maguindanaon were seldom allowed to penetrate the hill country of the Tiruray. Partly because the Maguindanaon were known to be slave takers, and partly because the Tiruray—like many relatively isolated tribal groups—were, in general, suspicious of people of different customs than their own, the Tiruray made a sort of fortress out of their mountainous homeland and would simply not allow others—primarily the Maguindanaon, of course—to come up. The only exception to this policy of exclusion was in the case of certain, ritually approved, traders and peddlers. It was through these persons, whose privilege of access was part of established trade pacts made between particular Tiruray neighborhoods and particular Maguindanaon datus, that the principal contact existed between the two ethnic groups.

These trade pacts were not general in their nature, but—as I said—were between specific groups of the Tiruray and particular groups of the Maguindanaon. They were established by a small ritual which asserted symbolically that, for purposes of trade, the contracting individuals would act toward each other in the manner of brothers rather than with the muted but chronic hostility which normally existed between individuals of these two societies. The ritual, used by the Maguindanaon in establishing trade pacts with many other ethnic groups as well as with the Tiruray, is called in the Tiruray dialect *seketas téél* or "cutting rattan together." Wishing to enter into trade with each other, the datu of a certain Maguindanaon place and the *kefeduwan* (or legal authority) of a certain Tiruray place would each take hold of the end of a strip of rattan and, laying the rattan upon a log, would chop it into two with a kris, while swearing to be "as brothers"—to treat each other henceforth not as hostile but, for purposes of trade, as being "of one father, one mother." The oath taken proclaimed that, from then on, should either one betray their special relationship, "may his life be cut off as this piece of rattan is being cut." Having performed this ritual, the datu—or, more commonly, one of his followers engaged in trade and peddling—could safely enter the mountains and carry out trade with this particular community. The *seketas téél* ceremony, however, did not give unlimited access to the Maguindanaon trader to roam the Tiruray mountains—it was quite specifically a pact with one place, with the followers of one particular Tiruray *kefeduwan*. Other Tiruray groups made their own pacts with some Maguindanaon group for purposes of carrying out trade. Having established the pact through cutting rattan, the datu would commonly assign some *gelal* (or "Muslim title") to his Tiruray trade partner, and such titles as *Ulubalang, Datu Kafitan,* or *Datu sa Falaw,* as used by Tiruray leaders today, originated in this manner. They are not indigenous Tiruray titles but come from the Maguindanaon datus in the creation of trade pacts.

The trade which went on between the Tiruray and the Maguindanaon was significant, in fact essential, to both parties. Tiruray traditionally neither weave cloth nor do blacksmithing; they got their cloth for clothing and their iron tools for swidden agriculture from the Maguindanaon through this trade. Salt, so fundamental to the Tiruray diet, always had come from the Maguindanaon, as had the various goods used by the Tiruray for brideprice and legal settlements: krises, necklaces, brass boxes for betel quid ingredients, gongs, spears, and the like. All of these intrinsically necessary items to Tiruray life and culture were obtained through the trade pacts from the lowland Maguindanaon. In return, down the mountains flowed goods needed by the Maguindanaon. Of major importance have been products of the tropical rain forests in the mountains, particularly rattan. Until recently, too, the Maguindanaon have not grown their own tobacco, but have traded with the Tiruray for this product of their mountain swiddens. Similarly, beeswax from the Tiruray forests went in trade to the Maguindanaon, who valued it for further trading with the Chinese and others.[3]

The Maguindanaon acted as middlemen for further trade of many items of Tiruray origin to Sulu and to the Chinese. In the 19th century, for example, the three most valuable products in the trade of Sulu were mother-of-pearl, gutta percha, and almaciga, the last two being forest products from the Mindanao highlands. Gutta percha is the sap of the tree which the Tiruray call *tefedus* (*Palaquium ahernanum* Merr). When the transatlantic cable was being built in the 1860's and 1870's, there was a huge demand for gutta percha, which was used as insulation for the cable. Singapore was the major market for this product. The gutta percha was originally collected by the Tiruray (and other mountain peoples trading with the Maguindanaon), and traded to the Muslims in return for iron tools, cloth, salt, and the like. From the Maguindanaon, it went in trade to Sulu and from there to Sandakan or Lubuan and thence on to Singapore, where it was known as "North Borneo gutta percha."[4]

Almaciga—the sap of another tree known to the Tiruray as *lunay solò* (*Agathis philippinensis* Warb)—is used in making copal varnish. It and gutta percha were highly valued by the Spanish, who used them in shipbuilding. Almaciga, too, which originated with mountain forest groups such as the Tiruray, would go in trade to the Maguindanaon, and from them on through various channels to the Spanish.[5]

In short, the trade between the Tiruray and the Maguindanaon, established through the ritual of cutting rattan, and cast in the metaphor of brotherhood, has been of critical importance to both groups. While certain exotic items such as almaciga and gutta percha have entered into this trade at different periods of history, the bedrock items have been rattan, beeswax, tobacco, and other swidden and forest items flowing down the mountains from the Tiruray to the Maguindanaon, and iron tools, clothing, pots, and salt going up in return. Such trade patterns—and the charter ritual of cutting rattan—doubtless go back far in time, well into the mists of prehistory.

The other aspect of the relationship between at least some Tiruray and some Maguindanaon was the military alliance which brought the Tiruray of Awang to the aid of the Maguindanaon from around what is today Cotabato City, that is to say, the "people of Maguindanao" proper. Awang is located at the very foot of the mountains south of Cotabato City, somewhat near the Tamantaka River branch of the Rio Grande, and the Awang Tiruray have long been closer and less hostile to the lowland Muslims than the majority of the Tiruray who live in the hills. Bits and pieces of stories, folk tales, and legends make reference to this military cooperation, and I have been told that in the conflict which has gone on for centuries between the Muslims of the lower valley (around Cotabato City) and those of the upper valley (the mid-basin interior areas), the Awang Tiruray would traditionally fight alongside the lower valley forces. Therefore, when the old Maguindanaon tarsila reports that "all the men of Maguindanao" went forth to meet the forces of Sharif Kabungsuwan, "all the men of Maguindanao" may very well have included Awang Tiruray.[6]

III

If the first section of this paper posed the puzzle involved in Tiruray-Maguindanaon ethnic relations, and the second section set forth what we can *know* about them, this third section will suggest some *guesses* that might be made. Here I propose to set aside the sober analysis and description of historical data, and engage in some, perhaps fanciful, speculation. Much scholarship, of course, does precisely this much of the time, but it is well to be quite open about it, lest what is set forth as conjecture be taken as the reporting of fact. I do not *know* what the true meaning is of the stories of Tabunaway and Mamalu. But I have some conjecture to suggest.

The story, again, is common to both the Tiruray and the Maguindanaon and runs something like this: Sharif Kabungsuwan, a Muslim nobleman from Jahore, set out with a host of followers and in due time arrived in Mindanao, at the mouth of the Rio Grande River. Tabunaway, the leader of the people in that area called Maguindanao, and Mamalu, his brother, were fishing there at the mouth of the river. They met Kabungsuwan and his forces, who insisted that the people of Maguindanao must accept Islam. Tabunaway and Mamalu agreed and Sharif Kabungsuwan established himself as the first Sultan of Maguindanao. Later, Mamalu changed his mind and refused to accept Islam. He and his followers then ran off to the mountains, where they are today known as the Tiruray. Tabunaway remained true to the Muslim faith, and the descendants of him, his followers, and Sharif Kabungsuwan are those people today known as the Maguindanaon.[7]

Now for some conjecture. Suppose that Mamalu was not a Maguindanaon at all but was a Tiruray, related to Tabunaway not as a blood brother but as a trade pact brother, one who in cutting rattan had sworn to be as of "one mother, one father." Suppose that while Tabunaway was the headman of the Maguindanaon, Mamalu was the leading *kefeduwan* of the Tiruray at Awang. They were brothers in trade and were military allies. They were thus—as the stories tell—at the joint head of their forces, when "all the men of Maguin-

22

danao" were called forth to meet Sharif Kabungsuwan. The rest of the tale would make good sense. Due either to threat of superior arms or perhaps superior charisma, they agreed to Kabungsuwan's instruction that all must become Muslim, and they so informed their followers. But, whereas Tabunaway was a Maguindanaon datu and could *order* his people to accept Islam, Mamalu as a Tiruray *kefeduwan* had no such power over his people. The *kefeduwan* in Tiruray culture is not a datu; he is a legal authority—a kind of judge—whose influence over his people is moral and judicial, not one of power. The Tiruray follow their *kefeduwan* because they believe *kefeduwan* to give justice, and not because they have the sort of institutionalized power common to the ruling class in Maguindanaon culture.[8] Thus the Maguindanaon followed Tabunaway and became Muslims; the Tiruray were quite unwilling to give up eating pork and to be circumcised, and they could not be forced. In the spreading of the Islamic faith into the interior, the Tiruray, like the T'Boli, the Bilaan, and the Manubu, were able in their mountainous redoubt to defend their traditional religious system from conversion.

Now, not too much stress need be placed on the idea—perhaps whimsical—that Mamalu was a Tiruray and a trader, rather than a blood brother of Tabunaway. Quite possibly Mamalu was the consanguineal sibling of Tabunaway and, refusing for whatever reasons of his own to become—or at least to remain—Muslim, he left the Maguindanaon fold and joined the Tiruray community. This, too, is certainly a possible interpretation of the tradition. I would like, however, to stay a bit longer with the supposition that Mamalu was a Tiruray, because it allows a key to understanding yet another of the stories that come down through the ages about these two "brothers"—the story of the birth of Putri Tunina.

In this tale, Tabunaway and Mamalu were together cutting bamboo to use in building a fish corral. In cutting down the last young stalk of a particular clump of bamboo, Mamalu found—in it, the stories say—a young girl child, who was Putri Tunina. He took and showed the child to Tabunaway, who replied that Mamalu should adopt her because he was childless. The girl grew up and ultimately became one of the wives of Sharif Kabungsuwan and the maternal founder of an important line of Maguindanaon royalty. Reference is made to this origin of Putri Tunina in no less than six of the tarsila translated by Saleeby,[9] and twice emphasis is placed on the fact that Mamalu *found* her, took and offered her to Tabunaway, and was told by Tabunaway

23

to raise her himself because he, Mamalu, was childless.[10] Suppose again that Mamalu was, in fact, a Tiruray. When, years later, Putri Tunina became the wife of Kabungsuwan, and when the Tiruray—who had raised her—were recalcitrant pagans rather than good Muslims, would it not have become crucial to insist that Putri Tunina was not actually a Tiruray, that she had only been adopted into the Tiruray, and that her foster father was, in fact, childless? It is interesting to note that a Bilaan woman—the only other woman of pagan stock mentioned in the tarsilas translated by Saleeby as marrying a Maguindanaon nobleman—was also ascribed a miraculous birth, not in this case from a bamboo stalk, but from a crow's egg.[11]

Again, of course, this is nothing more than sheer conjecture; its veridical status is plainly that "it ain't necessarily so." But it, at least, makes more sense than granting that some 3000-plus years of linguistic differentiation have occurred between the Tiruray and the Maguindanaon since the turn of the 16th century A.D.!

IV

In conclusion, whatever the ethnic status of Mamalu, certain things can be taken, I think, as sure. The Tiruray and the Maguindanaon were *not* "one people" at the time of the coming of Islam. The linguistic evidence of a far greater historical period of ethnic separateness is simply coercive. In all probability, the Tiruray—like the T'Boli and the Bilaan whom they resemble so much in language and culture—were mountain people since primordial times, while the Maguindanaon were lowland folk. Almost certainly, since long before the time of Sharif Kabungsuwan, the two groups were related by trade and the barter of goods, through *seketas téél* pacts cast in the idiom of brotherhood. And the Awang Tiruray and the Maguindanaon of the delta of the Rio Grande were doubtless a particular instance of this general trade situation, as well, perhaps, as being military allies in the regional disputes and conflicts of the Maguindanaon.

Notes

[1]Until Majul (1973), the classic Maguindanaon history was Saleeby's, which reports as fact the content of the common origin tradition; see Saleeby (1905: 55-56). Doubtless, following Saleeby in this matter are others such as Costa (1968:49) and de los Angeles (1964: 9).

[2]Thomas and Healy (1964: 21-23).

[3]Corte (1887: 351-352); Montano (1887: 41); Sawyer (1900: 150, 332, 345, 373-374); Wickberg (1965: 92).

[4]Sawyer (1900: 142); Sherman (1903: 7-8, 15-16); Wickberg (1965: 91-92).

[5]Sawyer (1900: 142, 314, 345); Wickberg (1965: 91-92).

[6]Saleeby (1904: 24).

[7]Parts of this story are recorded in tarsila translated by Saleeby (1905: 23-24, 29-31, 54). The rest is from Tiruray and Maguindanaon oral tradition.

[8]Nowhere in Tiruray social relations is power—the capacity to *force* compliance—institutionalized. There are, of course, many forms of authority—the capacity to *obtain* compliance. The matter is discussed, in the context of a full account of Tiruray law and legal leadership, in Schlegel (1970b).

[9]Saleeby (1905: 24, 26, 27, 30-31, 34, 37).

[10]Saleeby (1905: 31, 37).

[11]Saleeby (1905: 34, 37).

Chapter 3

TIRURAY MORALITY

This essay first appeared as a chapter in Tiruray Justice: Traditional Tiruray Morality and Law, *my 1970 book on the Tiruray legal system and the morality from which it emerges. It was reproduced a year later by the* Philippine Sociological Review *(Vol. 19, Nos. 1-2, pp. 99-130). The essay was intended to set forth the very elegant system of moral understandings of the Tiruray people, but also, following the work of English jurisprudential scholar H. L. A. Hart, to show that it, like any code of morality, suffers from certain inherent operational defects. With Hart, I argue in my book that it is from these problematic areas of the morality that the legal system arises. The essay has been so very graciously received over the years, that it seems appropriate to include it in this collection.*

I spent most of the morning speaking with an old man about the customs (*adat*) surrounding a wedding ceremony. He asked at one point whether I had ever seen a Maguindanaon wedding and explained that they have a very different set of customs which comes out of their written law (*kitab*). "The Maguindanaon have their Koran," he said, "but we cannot read or write; our law is the *adat*."[1]

To the Tiruray, in one fundamental sense of the word, the *adat* of a people is their customs, the things they customarily do, the activities that mark them as a distinctive cultural entity. The Maguindanaon have their *adat*; the Americans have theirs; the Tiruray, theirs. Early in my fieldwork among the Tiruray, I learned that such questions as "Why do you do that?" or "Why is it like that?" or "Why is it done in that fashion?" were all one-way, dead-end streets leading to the inevitable reply, "It is the *adat*." They do what they do, in the way they do it, because it is the Tiruray custom to do it, and in that way. Why do Tiruray press hands one way when departing, whereas Americans shake hands a different way when they leave? Because each has his own *adat*.

Adat, however, has another fundamental meaning: respect. In this sense, it can be used not only as a noun but as a verb, meaning to pay respect to

26

someone or something. The two senses, custom and respect, are by no means discrete for the Tiruray; they are aspects of a single idea. The customs aim at respect. Respect is what customs are for. It is, in fact, what customs are—*adat*. One can speak of an individual's *adat* (or a family's) with the same combined meaning, both of someone's characteristic behavior and of the quality of his respect for the feelings of other people. Frequently, I have heard it said that a particular marriage is a difficult one because one of the couple has a bad *adat*, even though the person comes from a family known for its good *adat*. When the marriage was arranged, it is implied, there was nothing in the respectful, considerate ways of the errant spouse's parents and kinsmen to warn the prospective in-laws of the bad manners, hot temper, snobbery, or whatever—the disrespect of others' feelings—that was to be revealed in the newlywed.

There is still a third significant element in the notion of *adat*. It is normative; it includes the idea of "ought." A tribe's, family's, or individual's *adat* may be contrasted to its *tufu*, another term which has the English sense of custom or habit. If a man wears a mustache, that is his *tufu*. One who goes regularly at a certain time each morning to check his pig has developed a *tufu* to do that. Some families have the *tufu* to give or to ask for working animals as part of the brideprice; other families have the *tufu* not to; still others are indifferent to the question—they have no *tufu* on that matter either way. The critical difference between *tufu* and *adat* is that the latter has a normative content, whereas the former has none. A man's habits in the care of his pig or the wearing of a mustache are his own concern; a family may decide for itself whether it wishes to give or to ask for carabaos. *Adat* is not involved in the custom, as it is not one which bears upon respect for other people, and no moral obligation is implied.

Of course, *adat* is certainly involved in how people deal with someone's particular *tufu*. The decision to wear a mustache is *tufu*; not to make a derogatory comment about someone else's mustache is *adat*.

Balaud, the most renowned legal authority in the Figel area, told a story about the importance of respecting the *tufu*. There was a family, whose *tufu* was to ask for carabaos as part of the brideprice. They were arranging a marriage between their daughter and the boy of a family whose *tufu* was not to give animals. What happened was that they asked for one animal, and the boy's side gave one, but the girl's side immediately gave one kris, which they called a *teleb sogo*, "to cover over the footprints," which is to say, to hide the carabao's having been given. That way neither side was forced to break its *tufu*. The girl's side considered the carabao as part of the brideprice; the boy's side did not, but looked upon it as a gift. It was remembered, but not formally counted in their reckoning of the settlement. Several years later, the girl ran away with another man, and the brideprice had to be returned. A carabao was returned of course, but it was called a *ruranan tamuk*, "to carry the brideprice items." Thus the woman's side considered that they returned the carabao, but the other side looked upon that animal as having merely borne their goods back to them. "That is the way," Balaud said, "we show *adat*; one must always observe the *adat*."

For the Tiruray, then, the *adat* is not only (like *tufu*) what they, as Tiruray, do and how they do it (their customs with regard to weddings, newcomers, labor exchange, and the like), but it is also (unlike *tufu*) what they ought to do and how they ought to do it. The *adat* sets standards of conduct; it places obligations—all of which are seen in terms of interpersonal respect.

As I have mentioned, an aspect of the Tiruray world view underlies this overwhelming concern for respectful behavior. Like that of all peoples, Tiruray culture sets forth a world in which everyone understands one's self to live, a world whose nature is taken for granted.[2] Thus, to the Tiruray there are certain "facts" about the nature of this world, about mankind, and about social life which they understand as being simply and self-evidently true. One such fact is that people are, by nature, potentially violent. People are capable of exploding under provocation into a fury of bloodshed and vengeance. Why this should be so is not at issue here; to the Tiruray it is so, and people just *are* that way.

Furthermore, one is especially likely to burst into violence when outraged by a nonrelative; one is, by nature, less apt to feel hatred toward a kinsman in the first place and, if he should do so, is far more able to contain his inherent propensity to lash out violently. Thus it is a fact of life to the Tiruray that the world of interfamilial social relations is one of danger, potential bloodshed, and continual risk, and that amidst one's kinsmen there are mutual assistance and a context of relative safety. A father may attempt to give moral advice or a mild scolding to his son, but the world "being as it is," only a madman would scold a nonkinsman and incur the inevitable retaliatory consequences.

However much an anthropologist or a sociologist may demonstrate that other people in other lands do not understand human nature in this way, to the Tiruray themselves those propositions about the nature of people and society are simply true. They are objective realities of the Tiruray common-sense world. To behave in violation of their normative implications would not merely show bad taste, it would flout the fundamental canons of common sense so thoroughly as to suggest utter insanity.[3]

For the Tiruray, as for the participants in any culturally given and shared world view, their taken-for-granted world is their paramount reality—the foundation of their everyday awareness and the matrix from which common sense is established as the natural attitude toward day-to-day affairs, that is, as the primary model for pragmatic action in the world.[4] It is the peculiar function of common sense that it embraces the apparent givenness of the seemingly real in both its cognitive and normative aspects, and thereby sets forth a model for prudent behavior in daily life—a model which is rooted both in that which "clearly is" and in that which "clearly ought to be." The violent propensities of human nature, the security that prevails among kinsmen, and the perils of social intercourse outside one's family are, to Tiruray common sense, not matters for speculation. They are cognitive facts. And, similarly, the conviction that only an appropriately related elder ought to engage in scolding someone—and then only with utmost care—is no mere rubric of etiquette but a normative fact, a moral truth proceeding from what the Tiruray understand to be the very nature of the world and of people in the world.

Thus, respect for others is the Tiruray's most basic moral obligation—the essence of one's tribal custom and the guiding intention of behavior felt to be most distinctively Tiruray. Thus, too, a world in which the sensitivities of all are respected by all is the society's most compelling moral goal. Only such a social situation can be assessed as good, as right, as being "the way it should be"—as being, in the fundamentally important Tiruray concept which sums up all such ideas, *fiyo*.

A thing is *fiyo* when it is just the way it ought to be. A woman who has physical beauty according to Tiruray canons (light skin, shiny long black hair, thick ankles, a narrow waist) is, with regard to her appearance, *fiyo*. More generally, a woman, however plain, who works hard, who is kind, who is modest, who thus meets the more important and serious canons involved in judging female quality, is also *fiyo*. The weather is *fiyo* when it is clear so that one can do one's work. A decision is *fiyo* when it is made with sensitivity and sense. One who has been sick is *fiyo* again upon recovery. A *fiyo* homemade shotgun is one that shoots regularly and accurately. A meal is *fiyo* if it tastes good and is filling. Ubiquitous in Tiruray discourse, the term can range over a vast number of connotations for which English has separate words, such as proper, delicious, attractive, adequate, convincing, right, and good. Its opposite, *tété*—as commonly used and as widely applied as *fiyo*—denotes anything that is bad, wicked, ugly, defective, or, in sum, anything that is in an important way not as it should be, that is fundamentally, profoundly amiss, that is not *fiyo*.

The "good world" is one, then, in which as much as possible is *fiyo*. The Tiruray realize, of course, that there are limits and bounds to the human capacity to bring about the good and that not every aspect of existence can be always *fiyo*. Good weather is bound to alternate with bad. In a forest existence, there inevitably are times when the stomach is too empty and the muscles are too tired. They fully expect that death will inflict grief and that childbirth will bring pain. Life's hardships are beyond human control. But many misfortunes are not; they are believed to have a personal cause. People (whether humans or spirits) are apt to react with violence against anyone who injures them in body or in feelings. Thus, in one vastly significant area of life, human behavior can and must be channeled. People must be obliged to respect each other's normally placid, but inherently dangerous, feelings. It is a basic premise of Tiruray common sense that only in a social order of mutual forbearance, a moral order laying upon both humans and spirits the obligation of interpersonal respect can one hope for even the most minimally *fiyo* world.

Much of the variety of day-to-day interpersonal contact can be structured by established tribal custom so that, in a straightforward manner, one can be respectful of one's fellow's feelings by adherence to the customs. Much, but not all. Respect for each individual's feelings is the overriding goal of the *adat*, not merely scrupulous observance of tribal custom, however important the latter may seem as a means of achieving the moral goal. Thus, *adat* (as respect) daily requires everyone to make decisions about right behavior in situations where the *adat* (as specific Tiruray custom) is silent. In these uncharted situations, the individual must determine for himself or herself what course of action is morally right, what is *adat* for him or her at that moment and in that set of circumstances.

Respecting the feelings of others is characteristically spoken of in terms of not giving anyone a *tété fedew*, literally, a "bad gall bladder." The notion of a person's *fedew* is utterly central to Tiruray moral and legal thought and must be considered with care.

The Tiruray word *fedew*, like the English word "heart," on one level names an organ of the body, but also, like heart, *fedew* is widely extended to embrace a cluster of figurative, metaphorical meanings. The *fedew* in this extended sense is one's state of mind or rational feelings, one's condition of desiring or intending. Some examples may help to clarify the concept of *fedew*.

"What is your *fedew*?" asks of a person his specific desire, decision, or intention about a particular matter, as, "What is your *fedew*; will you go on Wednesday or Friday?" or "It is my *fedew* to sleep in Tagisa before proceeding."

"How does your *fedew* feel?" inquires into someone's mental reaction to an event and evokes such replies as, "My *fedew* is quite all right (*fiyo*)," meaning, "I am glad," "I am satisfied," "I don't mind," or "my *fedew* is very bad," which may indicate that the speaker is lonely or very sick and worried about his family or that he is hurt and angry because of some insult. This sense of the word appears in statements of necessary conditions for making one's *fedew* good again or in the gentle introduction of a kinsman to the offering of advice: "Don't have a bad *fedew* if I have something to tell you."

Feelings which are referred to the *fedew* are ones which involve active thinking—conscious mental processes. It is a mind at ease, free from disturbance, which is *fiyo*. In contrast, one which is distracted from its practical, day-to-day concerns and obsessed with thoughts of worry, fear, anger, hatred, and revenge is *tété*, not as it should be, bad.

Two general kinds of bad *fedew* are distinguished, according to whether the cause was fate or the action of a person. The first, *embukù fedew*, might be glossed as a "painful" *fedew*. One is lonesome, sad, in grief, worried, or bothered with haunting envy. One feels ashamed, in the presence of someone else, of his poor house, or his embarrassing error. He feels vaguely suspicious that something is amiss, without knowing who or what the cause is. In such cases (each having its own descriptive term, as *memala*, "embarrassed"; *embukù*, "lonely," "grieving"; *melidù*, "worried"), the *fedew* is said to be generally *embukù*, "painful." In such instances, although the person has

31

a bad *fedew*, he does not feel anger or hatred or a drive toward vengeance. His painful *fedew* is caused by his fate in a difficult and uncertain world; it is bad, but it is not "hurt"—the second kind of bad *fedew*—through the actions of some other person.

When a *fedew* is "hurt" (*demawet fedew*), it is because the person feels that he has been abused in some way. However successful he may be in containing and controlling his rage, even in outwardly concealing it, that a person so injured will feel a deep moral outrage and hatred toward the one who wronged him and that he will inevitably wish revenge is never questioned.

> We spoke for a while about shame. He told me that it is very different to be "ashamed" (*memala*—really more like the English "embarrassed") and to be "put to shame" (*fenmala*). "You can be ashamed without feeling hurt and angry, although it is very painful. But anyone who is put to shame will be very hurt and terribly angry. If a big shot came to our town, and perhaps was a relative—a distant cousin, say, who was a big shot now in the city—so he came to eat at my house, of course I would be ashamed because my house is very small, poor, very humble. My *fedew* would be bad. But I would do the best I could to receive him. We would butcher a chicken, and be sure and obtain some rice to eat. Then, if he were to refuse my food—perhaps even comment that he feared getting sick—I would also be very hurt, so my *fedew* would be bad in a much worse way. I would be put to shame and very hot with anger. Of course, especially if it is my relative, I would try to hold it, but I know I would want to hit him, or do something even worse.

An ordinary person cannot help feeling embarrassed at the rustic hospitality he can offer to a prestigious, renowned, or affluent visitor, but he can expect that his guest will not insult him or put him to public embarrassment. The latter would be a clear violation of moral principle and a radically different matter. His otherwise "painful" *fedew* would then be "hurt." He might or might not show an immediate overt reaction, but his hurt *fedew* would certainly be angry, and it would cry out for revenge. It would harbor henceforth a deep grudge; it would be a hating *fedew*. Any act is wrong which either intentionally or imprudently leads to such a bad *fedew*.

A bad *fedew* is—simply—not *fiyo*; it is not "as it should be." The painful *fedew* and the hurt *fedew* differ essentially in their origins and therefore in their potential danger to social harmony and well-being. The one is caused by somebody and thus brings the bad *fedew* into a hating relationship with another person, a situation fraught, as the Tiruray see it, with danger and violence. Painful feelings are part of the unavoidable ups and downs of life. There is much that one can do through religious belief and ritual to live with them and to render them meaningful, but little that one can do to avoid them. In contrast, a bad *fedew* caused by human foolishness can and ought to be avoided. It is this "ought" which is conceived to be the rationale for, the meaning and end of, the customs (*adat*). It defines respect—one ought never cause a bad *fedew*—and thus permits substance to be given to that most fundamental principle of Tiruray moral thought.

My traveling companion (a graduate of the agricultural high school, more given perhaps to systematic thought than most) and I chatted at length along the way about *keaḍ*, "exercising care not to cause anyone a bad *fedew*." As he saw it, there are three main things to respect: a person's belongings (*entingayen*), his standing (*tindeg*), and his feelings as such (*fedew*). Disrespect for any of these, he felt, is what incites a bad *fedew*.

A person's *entingayen*, his "belongings" or "possessions," are all that are his, all of which he is *géfé*. To be *géfé* of something is to have exclusive rights over its present use. In peasant areas, the actual owner, holding title to a tract of land, is the *géfé* of the land; but, if he has a tenant to whom he has assigned his land to work, his tenant is the *géfé* of the plowed field which he is working. Traditional Tiruray have no concept of permanent land ownership, but the man who cuts a particular swidden is its *géfé* and the "owner" of all that is grown upon it. When it returns to fallow, it returns to the public domain. A man is the *géfé* of his own house, of his wife, of his work animals, of whatever property is his at any given time, of a wedding that he is celebrating for his daughter, of a legal proceeding that concerns his hurt *fedew*, in short, of any object, person, or event in which he has not only an economic and emotional interest, but a personal, legitimate oversight. Such things (his clothing, his family, his rituals, his property, his fields) are his for so long as his rights over them continue; they are collectively his *entingayen*, and he is the *géfé* of each and of all. And, my companion urged, one cannot respect the person without respecting those rights.

Stealing (*menakaw*) *is* very bad and will surely cause a bad *fedew*. Getting property is hard, and what's yours is yours. It should not be taken. You take someone's property without his permission and without giving him anything—he will surely be very hot. How can people live together who do that? Rice and corn will not just grow unless they are planted. Things are owned. The *géfe* is the *géfe*. If you really need something or need help, just ask. Tiruray are kind; they will share. But if you take without asking, you don't respect the person. You lower his standing. He will be terribly angry.

Not respecting one's belongings thus touches another of the suggested danger areas, one's *tindeg*, "standing." The following situations all involve the notion of standing:

There was much discussion about a religious leader from a community just over the mountains to the northeast. It seems that he called for all of his followers to gather together, and a large number did not come. They say he has a very bad *fedew* to those who did not come, since they did not respect his standing. Even though he is not doing anything, he is very hating. He will keep it in mind, and if they continue to act that way he will not help them when they need him.

We had gone several kilometers along extremely mucky trails, when we came to a house, and stopped to take a drink of water. The owner asked us to come up, and I was about to do so—without thinking about the mud all over my shoes—when (my companion on the hike) stopped me gently and pointed to my feet. I removed my shoes. Later, I asked him about it, and he explained that among the Tiruray to enter someone's house with muddy feet is against the customs; it is as though his house is the home of a pig rather than a person, as though you think of him as not caring for his home; it would lower his standing.

He said the rape not only lowered his daughter's standing and put her to shame, but also his own and his whole family's standing; if

34

the man wanted his daughter, he should have told his old folks and they could have come and arranged for a marriage in the right way.

A person's standing is, in a broad sense, his or her social position. It includes one's relative age and authority, one's relative dignity and honor, one's social esteem. Everyone has his or her standing. Families or individuals have "higher" or "lower" standing, in the sense of their general reputations; a son who does foolish things is said to lower the standing of his family, by acting in a way more base than his relatives and forefathers have been known to act. But, in another sense, a person's standing is his or her "good name" —one's personal, individual honor and standing among one's fellows. And everyone has a right to having his or her standing treated with respect. However humble one's family, each person has his or her own good name and the right to it. A person can lower her own standing—can sully her own good name—by her own actions, but she will be deeply offended if anyone else would do that to her.

The idea of standing is clearly manifested in the distinction between the Tiruray concepts of "despising" and of "correcting" or "advising."

Because of the harvest, Benito (a brother of one of the wives in the Figel neighborhood) and Tenganga (their first cousin) were in Figel for a few days. Benito kept complaining that Tenganga was lacking in dignity. He was saying that whenever there was a gathering Tenganga did not sit formally but was always darting around. He gave as his opinion that when a fellow is ugly, he should at least have dignity. When these words reached Tenganga, he became furious at his cousin. He went up to him and demanded, "Why do you talk about me, despising me? I will give you a good beating for your lies about me." Benito replied, "Come on and see if you can. Besides, it is all true—you are ugly and you are a fool." So they began to fight.

When he learned what was going on, their uncle (a considerably older man) ran over and separated them. He told them to sit down where they were, and he asked them what happened. Once they were a bit cooler, he called them aside and told them privately that both were foolish. He told Tenganga that he too felt that he did not show much dignity in his blatant lack of formality; he then told

35

Benito that he was hardly showing dignity himself in publicly despising his cousin. He advised them both that if they wanted to fight each other they should go ahead *inside* his house, among their own kin, who could see how foolish they were without having to suffer public shame, but that outside the house they had better act more sensibly, or they would end up offending some nonrelative and then would be in real trouble.

I asked the uncle, when he later described to me how he had corrected his nephews, whether they would not feel that he was despising them. He replied, "An elder close relative may give a person advice, warnings, scoldings—he can be quite frank. He has the right to do that; he has the standing. But, otherwise, to say such things to a person would be to despise him and would surely cause him a bad *fedew*. For example, if you were to tell me that you do not like my clothes (he was wearing the traditional Tiruray dress), it would be very bad. A person may wear what he likes to wear. You would be despising me, and I would have a very bad *fedew*. If you said that thing in front of others and despised me publicly, it would be far worse. My *fedew* would not only be hurt, but shamed."

I asked whether a person would be hurt if it was his father who criticized his manner of dress. "No, not if he told him in a nice way. That would be correcting, not despising. Even if the person disagreed with his father, he would not feel that he was hating him, but only trying to give him good advice." I then wondered what would happen if a close friend tried to offer some good advice. He looked surprised at the question. "No one would ever do that. Only relatives who are older give you advice. We never try to advise nonrelatives; we have no standing to do that. It would most certainly be considered despising." Could a nephew ever advise his uncle, for example, not to gamble? There was continued curious surprise at such naive questions: "No, no. He could never do that. The uncle would feel that his nephew did not respect his standing and would be very hurt. It is against our custom."

Several terms used in advising or scolding display the great concern for respect and the fear about the consequences of disrespect. One who is insensitive to the feelings of others is said to be not *semegafa*, and elders tell

36

children frequently that if they are not *semegafa* they will be hated, they will find themselves in danger, they will cause great trouble for everyone. A person who does as he pleases without *any* thought for the feelings of others is called *lemigisligis,* and it is said that a true *lemigisligis* seldom lives to grow old. He ignores his acts of disrespect, so his acts are foolhardy; they should make him ashamed and worried, but they actually leave him unconcerned. They do not lead him to learn proper behavior, to make sensible, decent estimates of his moral obligations in the situations of daily life. Such estimates are difficult enough for the earnest person; one who ignores signs and clues that might help is either utterly foolish or mad.

An individual's estimate of a situation is the *karang* of his *fedew*. He can have a *karang* of whether it will rain or whether it is a good day to hunt pigs. One's estimate is, of course, crucial to his effort to behave morally. Many judgments must be made concerning a situation—what is required, what is reasonable, what will hurt, and so forth. It is the *fedew* which, in reaching its estimate of a situation, takes a position regarding moral obligation and the demands of respect.

My traveling companion's assessment of the general areas of moral tenderness—one's property, one's self-esteem, and one's social position—is no formal analysis; his categories are certainly not exclusive (to steal one's wife is also to hurt his feelings and to lower his standing), nor, probably, are they exhaustive. But if he is not a systematic philosopher, he is a morally earnest person faced with the daily problem of specifying in particular instances what is involved in respect. His categories do indicate, more than does the notion of *fedew* alone, how one proceeds to behave respectfully in order not to cause a bad *fedew*. One applies a set of ideas—ideas which to Tiruray seem sheer common sense, simply features of the way things are—of what constitutes a good *fedew* and of what is apt to turn it bad. One employs one's general knowledge of the sorts of sensitivity to which any *fedew* is given and looks for specific clues to understand any particular sensitivities of the particular *fedew* with which he is confronted.

Communication of such clues—both sending and receiving the signals—is critically important, and a vast array of concepts in Tiruray thought are employed for this. Of the myriad, a few examples from two classes may be taken as typical. Both are classes of noun forms derived from adjectives which specify something—an object, a person, a situation—in which a specific *fedew* is deeply involved emotionally. Each, by setting forth some piece of public

37

information about that *fedew*, serves to identify its claims upon or sensitivities regarding respect.

The first set of terms signals that someone is probably holding in strong and explosive desires; that he should be "handled with care" because his *fedew* is already in some internal turmoil and less than usually able to contain any subsequent pressure. Moreover, they identify the focus of the engaged *fedew* and warn that for the person in question it too must be treated with prudent care. Something which is causing a person profound envy, for example, is said by that person to be his "envy object," the *keingaran* of his *fedew*. Similarly, there are terms for that which is filling a *fedew* with thoughts of hatred (the *kerarekon fedew*), or which has brought someone close to the end of his patience, has rendered him "fed up" (the *kesemunon fedew*), or is the object of his serious suspicions or jealousy (the *kedalewon fedew*). These concepts provide plain public warnings about a given *fedew* in a given set of circumstances.

Another class of *fedew*-signals serves to publish an individual's claims to reasonable and specific respect from his fellows for particular concerns of his own. A plan of action that a person is known to have, some intention to do something, is said to be the *bantak* of her *fedew*. The intellect (*itungen*) considers the plan, thinks through the details. It is, however, the *fedew* which feels commitment to it, and others ought to give reasonable respect to a person's plans and not complicate or obstruct them needlessly. A *bantak* is, therefore, publicly known information about a *fedew*'s engagement. If you know that a man's *fedew* has a certain intention, you know something substantive about respecting that man; not causing him a bad *fedew* is given content in terms of respect for his plan of action. Conversely, of course, failure to respect his plans is specified and identified as a failure to respect his *fedew*.

Similarly, a *keikaan* of someone's *fedew* is its known personal aversion, something that the individual really dislikes. Not all persons have the same aversion, nor do all have the same quantity of personal dislikes. One fellow's personal aversions may include a whole roster of relatively minor "pet peeves"; another's may be some single, intensely felt hatred. Whatever and however many the known *keikaan* of an individual, those who deal with him socially are extremely careful about them, lest they set off a bad *fedew*.

The same is true about a known *ketayan*, that which a *fedew* especially likes or desires. In general, Tiruray feel morally obliged to grant people respect for their purely individual tastes and idiosyncrasies, where they are within reasonable limits. Of course, an aversion that was utterly disruptive of normal social expectations, such as a dislike for meeting one's reciprocal labor obligations, or an equivalent personal wish, such as a desire for another man's wife, would hardly be considered by one's companions to create moral obligation. But it is also true that no one would seriously and publicly present such an outlandish suggestion as the aversion or the desire of his *fedew*. Both in asserting their own *fedew* and in attending to others', the Tiruray are common participants in a general cultural consensus concerning the reasonable and sensible limits of personal demands.

The precise boundaries of reason and good sense in any given concrete situation are, however, an inevitable source of difficulty. Despite acute efforts to be morally sensitive, situations often do arise in which there can be honest and deeply felt differences of opinion about whether a particular personal plan of action has been given its due respect, whether someone's desire is beyond the limits of propriety, or the extent to which an individual's peculiar antipathy should morally obligate his neighbors to suffer sustained inconvenience.

Some guidance is provided by folk stories, such as this humorous episode in the escapades of Inoterigo, a marvelous female of "long ago":

> When Inoterigo wanted to catch some nice fish for her supper, she would go to the mouth of the river and, plugging her anus with an egg, would drink up all the water. When the river bed was dry, she could easily fill her basket with fish. Then she would vomit back the water and go home. One day, when she was fishing in this manner and had drunk up all the water from the river, a young man named Tibugel happened to pass by. He asked Inoterigo for some of her fish—because she had gotten them all but she would not give him any, saying that it was her *fedew*'s dislike (*keikaan*) to share any of her catch. So Tibugel went home. At his house, he had a pet wild rooster, which he dispatched to the river. The rooster found Inoterigo bent over, picking up fish from the river bed, and pecked the egg in her anus. The egg broke and the water all rushed out of Inoterigo. The rooster ran home to Tibugel. Inoterigo repented her foolishness and from then on would always share her fish.

Tibugel had rejected Inoterigo's personal aversion as unreasonable; she had recognized the justice of his effective, if whimsical, rebuke. The story and others like it make the point that there are limits beyond which moral obligation is not established; but they cannot spell out for specific cases precisely what those limits are.

The "dislike," the "plan," and the "desire" are examples of a large class of concepts which publish the presumably reasonable demands of a particular *fedew* in a particular situation. A *fedew* may also have that for which it is profoundly craving, for which it is longing. It may have its overriding concern, its absolute first priority. All such ideas give, in an overt and accessible manner, meaning and content to the general moral imperative to respect one's fellows, to avoid causing anyone a bad *fedew*. Concepts of this sort are necessary: tribal custom can organize vast amounts, but not all, of interpersonal behavior. And they are effective: in most cases, most of the time, claims to respect so published are felt to be well within bounds and to constitute binding moral obligations. But it is also true that in some cases, some of the time, they necessarily raise the question "at the boundary" of what is reasonable respect and what are unreasonable demands.

The Tiruray sense of moral obligation to respect each other's *fedew* underlies and finds expression in a normative terminology, words which might be glossed as "right," "good," "rights," "fault," "wrong," "bad," "transgressor," "wrongdoer," all of which have within their meanings a characteristic sense of *ought*—required, observed, or violated. The *arus* way of doing something, for example, is the best way to do it, in the sense of the most expedient, straightforward way; the *fatut* way of doing it is the morally proper way, the way that is good (*fiyo*), that is in keeping with custom (*adat*), the way that will not hurt anyone's *fedew*. A course of action may well be recommended as both *arus* (the most practical) and *fatut* (the decent) approach, but the two evaluations are not the same. If a theft were planned and carried out with logic, finesse, and success, the thief might well be credited with having done his wrong in an *arus* way. But it would not have been *fatut*; stealing is wrong, however elegantly done, and the victim will have a thoroughly outraged bad *fedew*. The former is devoid of normative content; the latter specifically applies it.

A person whose actions have caused a bad *fedew* is said to be *dufang*, the fundamental pejorative in moral evaluation. In its various linguistic forms, the term may mean the one who makes the trouble, the wrong act itself,

40

the doing of it, or the one against whom it is done. But in each instance the word specifies a situation in which someone has violated his or her moral obligation to respect another, he has caused a hurt *fedew*, he has done wrong. By definition and by the whole logic of Tiruray morality, *dufang* is serious and dangerous. Acculturated English-speaking Tiruray translate it as "foolish," but the gloss is too mild unless understood in the sense of being utterly reckless. To act "foolishly" is to enrage a *fedew*. It is, thus, certain to upset normal social relations, and it is very possible to incur violent, bloody turmoil for oneself and for society. Whenever one must in the course of normal activities do something which could imply disrespect, like walking in front of someone, passing between two people, or interrupting a conversation, custom and respect (*adat*) call for the expression *tabiyà*, which, rather like "excuse me," signals that no disrespect is intended.

He warned me about hiking along the river—one must be careful not to offend. "You may pass where a woman is bathing. If she sees you coming and knows that there is no other trail, she will take cover and not be hurt. But, it may be that she is facing the other way and cannot see your coming; you should call out, "*Tabiyà*, you will be seen!" Then she can cover herself. If you happen to see a naked woman—for example, if you happen upon her unexpectedly when crossing a river—you must be quick to say, "You were seen; *tabiyà*!" If you do not say that, she will think that you were intentionally peeping. Once you say that, even though she will be embarrassed that her body was seen, she will not be angry at you because she will know that it was an accident and that you did not *dufang* her."

To *dufang* is to act either with intention to do wrong or with excessive imprudence. If a group of men are working together slashing a swidden site, and the bolo blade of one breaks, flies, and cuts the flesh of a companion, there is no bad *fedew*. Although by custom the one who caused blood to flow will give his injured associate a token gift, he was not "foolish"; there was no intention to cause harm. If a woman was forced into having extramarital sexual intercourse, she did not *dufang* her husband, although her abuser certainly did. Should a man pick up someone else's property by mistake and return it, there is no "foolishness," because there was no intention to

41

steal. The issue here is whether the act is intentional or not; it is not whether the person doing it expects to be caught:

Moilag and Mobayaw (two legal leaders) were chatting in Moilag's house one morning, where they were awaiting Motinengka, who was expected to arrive sometime that day to ask to marry Ideng Surut, the divorced daughter of Mobayaw. Their conversation turned to how ugly they felt Motinengka to be, since his teeth were not kept properly blackened, but were merely yellow from betel chewing. Laughingly, they compared his teeth and general appearance to that of the man-eating giant, the *busaw*. Unfortunately, at that moment, Motinengka happened by the house, and overheard what the two men were saying. He was extremely angry, and, entering the house with his spear high as though ready to thrust, he confronted the two men and growled that he may have yellow teeth, but he has not yet eaten any human being. He accused them of despising him and asked them to judge themselves. They immediately accepted their fault and placed 60 plates and two krises before Motinengka, to restore his good *fedew*. With that, he cooled off and lowered his spear; soon afterwards he returned to his own place, and he sought a wife elsewhere.

Even where there is no intention to hurt, a reasonable exercise of prudence is required by *adat*, and one whose carelessness runs him afoul of someone's feelings is also culpable.

On arrival at Figel (my research site, after having been away for over a week), I learned that Mosew had a very bad *fedew* toward a youth from Tuwol. The young man had been here overnight and had been showing around his newly acquired homemade shotgun. To demonstrate the gun, he fired once into the bushes to the east of the settlement. It was dusk, and already quite dark, and he did not see Mosew walking nearby. Mosew said he was badly frightened by the nearness of the report and was almost hit by the flying pellets. He had been really upset, and, although the boy from Tuwol had earnestly insisted that he did not realize anyone was there, Mosew says that he cannot forget such foolishness.

(Several days later) Udoy, a legal authority (*kefeduwan*) from Tuwol, came and said that the foolishness had not been intentional but that he agreed that Mosew had the right to ask whatever he wished. Mosew said that he had been genuinely outraged by the youth's foolishness, but that he would ask for only one spear.

Whenever an offense occurs and a *fedew* is made bad, the matter of *salà* (fault or responsibility) and the matter of *benal* (understandable demands for retaliation, for acceptable compensation) are immediately raised. A person is *mensalà*, he "has the fault" or "bears the responsibility" when a *fedew* is made bad by his "foolish" behavior. If the one who has been hurt is a close relative, he may be expected under ordinary circumstances to hold his feelings in check until his anger toward his kinsman subsides or until an elder can correct the errant one. But, if the one hurt is not a close blood relative and his *fedew* was made angry, he cannot be expected to do nothing. He is hurt; his *fedew* hates and craves revenge, and that craving for revenge and retaliation is, to the Tiruray, "human nature" and understandable. Given the hurt he has been forced to endure, it is his inevitable and natural inclination to seek redress; this is his *benal*. That he can be expected to strike out in vengeance against the person who committed the foolishness against him is simply and, to Tiruray common sense, obviously the consequence of "foolish" (*dufang*) behavior. However dislocating it is to the general social order, and however dangerous it may be for all his relatives, the individual "foolish" enough to hurt a *fedew* cannot expect that suffering will not follow. He is the *mensalà*; his victim has his *benal*.

I asked whether the *toow béén* (a particularly poisonous jungle snake) was considered "cruel" (*mediyabu*), and was told a fascinating bit of Tiruray "history." The *toow béén* was the very first of all the snakes and was born to a Tiruray father and mother, twin to a baby boy. The boy and his snake brother always played together, and they slept on the same mat in the house. One day the boy fell dead, but the snake cured him by getting grasses and rubbing his body. The father, however, was worried and told the snake, "You had better separate from your twin. You are a snake, and the houses are for humans. The proper place for snakes is in the forest." So the boy and the snake made an agreement, promising never to harm

43

each other since they were of the same blood. Henceforth, they would live, each in his own place, and neither would go to the house of the other. A human might always go through the forest, and the *toow béén* would not kill him, unless he steps upon his nest; similarly, the human would not kill the snake, unless the *toow béén* should break the agreement and come to the house of the human. Of course, if either trespasses their agreement—if the human steps on the snake's nest in the forest, or if the snake is found in someone's home—then the trespasser clearly has the fault (*salà*), and the other will as clearly have the *benal* to kill him. Thus, to this day, on the whole, people and this variety of venomous snake leave each other alone. When the snake is "foolish" (*dufang*) enough to go where he should not be, of course the people try to kill him. Similarly, when a human is bitten by that snake in the forest, you know that it is not because the snake was cruel, but because he had the *benal*. The *toow béén* would not kill anyone who did not break the agreement. It is not cruel to attack someone who has offended you. The *busaw* (a kind of malign spirit) are the cruel ones, because they would eat you, even though you do nothing to offend them. They attack you without *benal*.

One evening, one of the older men of Ranao (a nearby neighborhood) spent some time with me out under the stars, explaining and telling stories about the constellations which he saw in the night sky. It was a beautiful, warm night, and the talk drifted from one subject to another, finally settling on difficulties that arise among neighbors and how they should be handled so that they would not lead to serious trouble.

"My cousin and I were once living very near each other," he told me, "and quite far from the spring where we were getting our water. So our wives and daughters had to carry water a great distance every day. My cousin's wife fell into the habit of just getting water at our house, rather than carrying it all the way from the spring. She did not do it every time, of course, but still much too often. Pretty soon my wife had a bad *fedew* to her cousin-in-law, and although she held her anger within her *fedew*, she complained bitterly to me that my cousin's wife was not respecting what was ours. I planned to speak

44

to my cousin and urge him to provide his own house with water, so that our wives would not fight. This is what happens when wives are not related—they easily quarrel. But when I went to see my cousin, I did not have the courage to bring out my advice, so we only talked about hunting. I went to see him another time, but still could not bring this out, for fear that he might be resentful of my words. So I went to see our uncle, who lived fairly nearby, and I told him my problem. He agreed that my wife might not be able to hold it much longer, and promised to speak to my cousin. Things did not change, though, so we built a different house farther away from my cousin's house and there was no further trouble."

It sometimes happens that a person is very ready to call for help with his field, but, when asked to reciprocate, always seems to have something else to do. People will soon have a bad *fedew* to that person. They will just hold it and not do or say anything directly to him, although they will certainly talk about what he does when he is not around. At first, everyone may help him all the more—to emphasize what is right; then they will just stop helping him. They will hold on to their anger, because he is their *dumon*, "relative," "neighbor." But when he calls them for help they will all say that they have other things to do.

"Holding" *(getingkel)*—literally, "able to hold steady"—is one possible response of a bad *fedew* toward the one at fault. As in the two instances above, to hold *fedew* is the characteristic response to *dufang*, "foolish," behavior among close relatives. To a somewhat less predictable extent, it may be expected among non-kinsmen neighbors who are close day-to-day associates. In general, a cool restraint of those violent, vengeful urges considered so natural to hurt *fedew* is thought to be as clearly worthy of praise as it is difficult of achievement. Anger is conceived as engulfing the *fedew* in a rising crest of hatred. It can be contained to a point. Then it will break forth in *benal*, in desire for vengeance. There is an obligation to hold anger at petty irritations, but Tiruray believe that beyond a certain point it is only a morally heroic *fedew* which might be capable of bearing the resentment and hatred. Everyone should hold himself as much as possible. People should not just get hot right away whenever they are displeased, especially with close relatives. But there are limits; some things are just too much, and anger is bound to come out. Here, as with such ideas as the aversion of the *fedew*, the central point is quite clear—people deserve reasonable respect for their aversions and they are also expected to bear a reasonable amount of annoyance. But the matter of how much is too much, of where the boundaries of reason and sense lie, is inevitably problematic. That people can hold only so much is an empirical observation without normative content. That they should hold on to their rage to a certain extent, and that no one should push anyone else past that point, is an entirely normative matter. Judging what constitutes that reasonable extent is a profoundly sensitive operation.

The violence which is so feared is, indeed, another possible reaction to being morally abused. A bad *fedew*, pushed beyond its capacity to hold, will have the understandable *benal* to see vindication of its honor, and it may very well go looking for blood revenge. Such killing because of moral outrage, called *bonò*, is strictly distinguished from murder, *lifut*, which is killing without any such reason. *Bonò* is feared and considered wrong, but it is recognized as a dangerous possibility, a potential explosion of moral outrage in search of retaliation. One can only hold so much before one's self-esteem and standing require some vindication. Should a foolish person lower a man's standing—should he challenge his very manhood, for example, by making love to his wife—he has, in a sense, called that man's standing into public question. Were the man to do nothing in return, he would accept that lower standing. A bad *fedew* wants to purge the pain, assuage the anger, and seek vindication. One such way—extreme and wrong to the Tiruray, but completely understandable to them—is to kill.

Sigayan, author of *The Customs of the Tiruray People*, speaking of Awang Tiruray custom as he knew it in the mid-19th century, gives this description of revenge killing:

> Now the way they kill, if there is somebody with whom they are angry or against whom they have a grudge, is this: they go after revenge. When it is still daytime, they set out hiking to the place of the one they hate. Then, when they are at that place, and it is night, they shoot him with their bow and arrow, or else they might spear him as he sleeps. The avengers hide, for they do this killing with stealth. Once they have killed, they move away a bit—but they do not proceed home. They stay near the one whom they stabbed, in order to make sure from the sounds in the house whether the man died

or not. When they hear someone shout out, "Who stabbed?" they, still being close by, reply, "We did; we came on behalf of . . . our friend." After that the killers go home, for they are satisfied.[5]

Moensay, an elderly *kefeduwan*, now living beyond the Tran in the Basak homesteading area, who frequently returns to his old haunts near Figel and the traditional tribal atmosphere which he finds vastly more congenial, told me this story, so similar in detail to Sigayan's:

He said that before the coming of the Japanese [the great chronological bench mark of recent times—he probably means the 30s, but possibly the 20s], his aunt, Amung, was caught by her husband, Liwas, having sexual intercourse with Samberan, a cousin of Liwas. The infuriated husband lunged at them with his field knife, but there was much scrambling about and confusion, and the illicit lovers were able to run away. Liwas reported what had happened to his uncle, who was an important *kefeduwan* and the leader of his family and who was known by the title Datu Kafitan. He sent messengers at once to call for the principal elders closely related to Amung, two *kefeduwan*, named Minted and Maselà. They arrived within several hours, and asked to settle the case nicely—agreeing that Amung had the *salà* (the fault of Samberan, at this point, not being their concern) and offering to return the entire brideprice. Datu Kafitan could not locate Liwas, however. Later that night, four men—Liwas and three relatives—appeared at the place of Amung's parents and, with a bolo, repeatedly stabbed Amung's father through the slat floor of his elevated house. He was dead within a few hours. In the morning, when Maselà and Minted arrived, and when they learned that Liwas had taken blood revenge for his bad *fedew*, they called together all of the close kinsmen of Amung's father. Some were told to proceed with the burial, but most prepared to avenge his death. The same day a large group left to *bonò*. That night they slept by the river, near the settlement of Liwas, and early in the morning they ambushed Bilù and Buluntù, two first cousins of Liwas, who had gone to gather bamboo. Both were killed. Datu Kafitan called for Maselà and Minted to come and adjudicate the matter before there was more loss of life, and it was settled without any

47

further killing.

Another well remembered example:

He [a middle-aged man] said that his grandfather had gone to *bonò* as a young man, when his older brother's wife had eloped with a man from beyond Bantek [in the mountains about 15 kilometers south of Upi]. His grandfather's brother was very hot and called his relatives together, saying that they should go at once to seek blood revenge. A large group went to the place of the eloper, where they killed five of his close relatives. Nothing more happened for over a year, and then the men of that place came and killed almost 20 of his grandparent's kindred.

Several salient features of revenge killing appear in these accounts which contribute to its bloody and disruptive character and therefore to the general fear in which it is held in this society. *Bonò* is usually by stealth, striking without warning, which necessitates an extreme and often long-lasting vigilance. It spreads beyond the exact individuals involved in the original "foolish" act to endanger entire kindreds, and it rapidly escalates from a single act of revenge into a widening and self-perpetuating feud.

Tales tell of fabulously brave *alek,* "heroes," who, fearing no one, would seek revenge openly. Instead of stabbing his opponent through the floor of his house or falling upon him by ambush, a "hero" would place two stakes along a trail he knew the opponent would pass, marking off an area in which they would fight. Seeing this warning, the person could draw his kris and prepare to defend himself before entering the area. When fully ready to fight, he would spring into the marked-off stretch of trail, shouting "Who is challenging me?" at which time the avenger would come from his hiding place. This way of challenging openly is called "cutting short one's hiding" (*kemereb feràà*) and is said to be rare—characteristic of heroes but not of ordinary men and ordinary revenge. Usually, as in the stories told above, the revenge is "hidden" *(mono senirung)* and thus is an effective leveler—the famous fighter is no more frightening when he seeks revenge than is any other man. So long as there is the possibility that someone may have a hating *fedew* toward an individual, the individual must fear the sudden arrows from along the path, a sudden spear thrust through the floor when he is asleep, the blast of a homemade shotgun fired from concealment. Sharpened spurs of bamboo must be set into the ground all around the home. Watchfulness and care must be constant. Life is reduced to siege.

Not only is the offender himself thrown into danger and fear, but anyone in his entire kindred is apt to be killed in revenge for what he did. The responsibility (*salà*) is borne by all close relatives of the actual one responsible (the *mensalà*) for the bad *fedew*. One of the most immediate and most vexed rebukes that an offending individual can expect from his elders is that he has placed his relatives in grave danger. From the time the wrong is committed until it is settled by successful adjudication, there is anxiety among all the close kinsmen. Similarly, any close relative of the one hurt and craving vindication is expected to share in his sense of pain and *benal* and may well join him in a revenge killing raid.

Killing in revenge leads to further killing in counter-revenge. However human and understandable it may be in the Tiruray scheme, it is still wrong to them. It causes bad *fedew*, and it establishes new threats. Even though the one killed in revenge may have precipitated his own death by foolishly hurting someone's *fedew*—even though he clearly had the fault (*salà*)—still his relatives will be expected to avenge him. Thus vengeance turns into feuding, not only extending outward to include the full kindreds of each person involved, but perpetuating itself forward in time as each killing to satisfy honor creates a new expectation for killing in return.

The explosion of a hurt *fedew* into *bonò* may be instantaneous if the offender is at hand, as when Liwas found his wife Amung in the act of cuckolding him with Samberan and (albeit unsuccessfully) tried to stab them both on the spot.

I caught a ride with the mayor in his jeep and learned of a *bonò* killing that had occurred a few weeks ago in Mangga. The son of Monggò of that place had run away with the wife of Serumfong of Benuan near Kuya. The trouble was settled by adjudication, but Monggò did not send the peace offering when he was supposed to, so Serumfong went to his house to get it. While they were eating, Monggò began to grossly insult Serumfong, who is a short fellow with only stumps of fingers on one hand as a result of leprosy years ago. Monggò said that he was deformed and small, that he doubted that he need even bother giving such a cripple a peace offering, that he doubted that he could kill if he wanted to. Serumfong said nothing, but continued eating and tried to hold his anger. Monggò got a homemade shotgun and rudely threw it at Serumfong saying, "Here, here is your peace offering." Serumfong apparently ignored the taunt and just placed the gun on his lap and went on eating. Unseen, however, he slipped in a shell, and when Monggò insulted him again he shot him, blowing him to bits with a 12-gauge shell at close range. Then he ran away, and turned himself in to the mayor at Nuro. The mayor said that he had called for the relatives from both sides and had been promised that the matter would be settled without further bloodshed. Monggò's brother (an important *kefeduwan*) had investigated the situation and had accepted that his brother had been gravely at fault; he had agreed to settle the matter to the satisfaction of all by way of *tiyawan*.

In this case, *bonò* had not drawn the kindred of the one upon whom vengeance had been taken into counter-revenge and feuding; rather, cooler heads had prevailed, and the issues involved had been submitted to adjudication. This is the third of the major responses to a hurt *fedew*, and the moral response to a desire for retaliation (*benal*). If one cannot hold until the anger seeps away, but feels that his *fedew* must have some acceptable recompense for what it has suffered, he should still settle the issue in the proper way—he should inform the legal authority (*kefeduwan*), so that in formal adjudication (*tiyawan*) they might decide the fault (*salà*) and the proper restitution (*benal*) officially, assess the appropriate fines, and thus restore his good *fedew*. Formal adjudication is a deeply serious matter and the context of one of the two most distinctive forms of leadership among the Tiruray. Just as morality is the society's primary defense against the ravages of a bad *fedew*, so *tiyawan* are the final line of defense against the outbreak of violence.

Tiruray moral ideas define what, for them, is good, and they guide behavior that, for them, is right. Similarly, they define what is bad and identify conduct that is wrong and "foolish." They establish an ultimate moral standard—respect—and they tie it to a pervasive moral symbol, the *fedew*. They set forth the responsibility of the wrongdoer for the consequences of his disrespect, stressing that human nature is such that the consequences could be bloody indeed. They institutionalize the obligation of respect into specific customs and into a general, variable standard: the *adat*, in both of its senses. It is in terms of these ideas that the Tiruray person attempts to behave in a respectful and responsible manner.

All of these seek to work out in practice the normative aspects of Tiruray common sense, which constitute the imperatives of Tiruray morality. Throughout, however, it is clear that this moral code suffers from certain limitations which are generic to moral systems.

The first inherent difficulty of any moral system derives from the diffuse sources of the social pressure which support moral obligations and render them difficult and inefficient to maintain.[6] A system of straightforward moral imperatives and prescriptions making up the oughts for social life is, by itself, poorly equipped to deal with real or supposed breaches of the standards. For example, a person ought not to steal the rice from your granary, and yet you return home to find that someone has helped himself. What follows? Is it now proper for you to steal some rice back from the one you know—or think you know—did it? Suppose the individual you "know" to have done it denies that he did. How do you know that you know? Granted some clear moral obligation (not to steal) and granted some clear violation (something was stolen), the inefficiency problem inherent in any moral system is that collective morality, individually applied, cannot establish with authority either what happened or what should be done. Such pressing issues as determination of the offender, of the punishment due him, of how it should be administered, of the satisfaction due the offended, and of how it should be claimed are left to the individuals involved and whatever support they can muster to their points of view. Suppose someone does not respect his companion's personal aversion (his *keikaan*), perhaps by foolishly mentioning the name of some individual for whom his companion has a deep hatred. What precisely is the proper satisfaction of his angered companion's *fedew*? Surely this is not sufficient grounds for a bloody feud. Morality recognizes a desire for restitution; that is, it recognizes *benal*; but *benal* to do what?

A second generic difficulty in moral systems springs from the general nature of moral obligations. They are not specific to certain individuals in certain situations, but rather refer to classes of acts and classes of persons; their application necessarily requires that specific cases be identifiable as particular instances of general classes. Sometimes this is quite simple. A thief, sneaking in from another village with intent to rob a granary, looking furtively about, selecting a dark night when the owner is away, and so forth, is an instance of stealing, a plain and clear case of the general concept. But, along with its

51

core of settled meaning, there is in every general concept a more blurred, fuzzy edge where some of the features of the classic core case are present but others are either not there or are different. You were gone, and someone took the grain without asking because he needed it right then. He had planned to ask you, had you been home. Did he steal it or did he borrow it? The issue here is not the same as in the first case discussed. It is not "Is X the one who stole?" or "What should be done with X in view of his being a thief?" It is rather the very different question, "Is what X did to be considered stealing?" One ought not wantonly endanger another's life. But, when the youth from Tuwol tested out his home-made shotgun, not knowing that Mosew was walking nearby in the cool of the evening, was his act—however unintentional—sufficiently imprudent to constitute "foolishness"? Was it simply an unfortunate accident and a narrow escape for Mosew, or did the boy wrong him? A moral standard cannot, itself, determine whether it is applicable to a particular act. It can only direct the determining individuals to its unambiguous core examples; the individual must himself or herself then classify it as falling under the standard or not, according to his or her interpretation and assessment of the resemblances and the variations taken to be critical.[7]

Still a third problem arises in trying to live according to a system of morality. Moral standards are part of a culture's view of reality. They are taken for granted as being rooted in the very nature of the world itself, and thus as being inherently immune to conscious human modification. Received moralities are felt to be eternal verities, which means that they find change difficult to incorporate. There is no way to introduce a new moral rule, however needed; no authoritative procedure is felt competent to eliminate an existing moral rule, however dysfunctional it may have become. Both situations defy the logic of the givenness of moral obligations. A man, for example, should not scold another man, unless they are closely related, for it will constitute, to the Tiruray, despising. But, suppose the first person has become a municipal policeman and he has spoken concerning the breaking of a law. Tiruray custom knows nothing of municipal police forces or of Philippine laws. Do these new things in peasant Tiruray life alter the obligation of the Tiruray policeman not to interfere in the schemes and activities of another person—for surely that is the rule of Tiruray custom? The oughts are seen by participants in a morality as facts of life, inexorable and unalterable. The idea of a "new morality" is invariably offensive and threatening to those whose common sense incorporates an older system.

These three difficulties in living according to a conventional morality—the maintenance inefficiency, the generality, and the unalterability of moral obligations—comprise a set of cultural strains inherent in any moral system *per se*.[8] In this sense, the difficulties may be viewed as tending toward law. In any society they call for the establishment of a certain set of sociocultural institutions to serve as practical and adaptive elaborations upon the moral bare bones of normative common sense. These are the legal institutions of a society.

The problem of generality—whether in a particular case a particular obligation did or did not exist—may result, in one society, in authoritative reference to a set of statutes and, in another society, in autonomic ordeals. Maintenance inefficiency may be dealt with among one people by investing their chiefs with absolute adjudicatory authority and punitive power, among others by the development of a complex system of courts and prisons. The unalterability of moral obligation may underlie the emergence of institutions as substantively different as a legislature and an infallible papacy. The problems and their attendant strain toward institutional elaboration are generic; the substantive content of resulting ideas and structures is not.

Institutionalized in different ways in different societies, and internalized to varying degrees in various individuals within any specific society, "the legal" may thus be seen as being related to and emerging from a matrix of "the moral" in the occurrence of this particular cluster of cultural responses.[9]

Notes

[1]Throughout this chapter, indented extracts not otherwise identified, come more or less directly from my field notes. Most of what was recorded in the Tiruray vernacular I have translated into English, and I have made a few editorial improvements in the original prose.

[2]The term "world" is here understood in the phenomenological sense. For extended discussions of the world as one's phenomenal, taken-for-granted sphere of reality, see Schutz (1962) and Berger and Luckmann (1966).

[3]The fundamental role of common sense has been profoundly analyzed by Schutz; see especially (1962:3-47).

[4]The term "paramount reality" is from Schultz; see (1962: 207ff). My discussion has been importantly influenced by Geertz; see especially (1958, 1964a, 1964b, 1966).

[5]Tenorio (1892); see chapter 12, p. 186, of this book.

[6]This discussion of the difficulties inherent in the operation of a morality derives from Hart's analysis of the "defects" in any regime of primary rules alone. See Hart (1961: 89ff).

[7]The literature on the problem of the general and the particular is, of course, immense. For discussions of the problem as it applies directly to moral and legal reasoning, see Hart (1961: 121ff); Stone (1961: 137ff).

[8]The idea of "cultural strains" is taken from Geertz; see (1964a: 64).

[9]The rest of the book, *Tiruray Justice*, describes the legal institutions in Tiruray life which exist to deal authoritatively with precisely such difficulties in their recognition and in the observance of moral demands.

Chapter 4

THE TRADITIONAL TIRURAY ZODIAC

The Celestial Calendar of a Swidden and Foraging People

It has been known for a long time that traditional Southeast Asian people, prior to the coming of Western or other calendars, made use of the night sky to locate themselves in the cycle of the year's seasonal changes. I was fascinated by how the Tiruray did this, as well as by the very interesting set of constellations which they recognized in their zodiac, and I set out to learn from them about their celestial calendar. Many a night I spent lying on my back beside one or another of the old men of Figel, as they spun for me tales about the characters and events they saw in the heavens. They taught me how their constellations were named, how they moved and how they were located at various times of the year. And they explained how all of these told them of where they were in the year. I wrote a preliminary article on this which was published in the Philippine Journal of Science *in 1967 (vol. 96, no. 3, pp. 116-142). The present essay is an expanded version of that paper, which goes into far more detail about the people's use of the night sky in cultivation and foraging activities. It appeared in 1987 in the* Philippine Quarterly of Culture and Society *(vol. 15, pp. 12-26).*

Introduction

Historically based upon swidden farming and foraging in the surrounding forests and nearby rivers or streams, Tiruray society is today undergoing rapid transition to sedentary agricultural practices and a Filipino peasant way of life as government-authorized logging operations transform their environment. Only in disappearing pockets of isolation, deep in the mountains or far up the Tran Grande, are Tiruray communities still to be found living in what is essentially the old way. From these, as one moves toward the edges of Tirurayland—toward the great Cotabato basin to the east, or towards the extremes of the mountains near Cotabato City to the north—one meets Tiruray who are increasingly acculturated and peasantized. For such people, many aspects of the old lore of their people, the knowledge and beliefs of their old folks, are becoming less and less known and relevant to their daily life.

One such aspect of vanishing traditional Tiruray lore—their use of the night sky as a reliable seasonal calendar—is the subject of this chapter.

Traditional Tiruray Subsistence

Today, the more acculturated Tiruray farmers plow their own or, more commonly, their landlord's established fields, repeatedly preparing, planting, and harvesting the same plots of land. Like their ancestors, however, the still remote and traditional Tiruray of today follow an entirely different mode of life. The subsistence economy of the traditional people consists of shifting swidden cultivation, hunting, fishing and gathering of wild resources from the forests and streams, and some trade in non-Tiruray markets.

The cycle of shifting cultivation activities is broadly similar to many other "slash-and-burn" regimes found elsewhere in the humid tropics. The first stage in the process of temporarily replacing the native forest vegetation with humanly selected cultivates is site selection. From the end of the previous year's harvesting until approximately mid-December, the men of a neighborhood range the surrounding forests, primarily to hunt and gather, and also to select sites for their next swiddens. Each family looks for a suitable place according to certain well-defined criteria: vegetation type, soil type, land topography, distance from the residential settlements, etc. Traditional Tiruray have no sense of private or corporate land ownership; all sites are occupied by right of usufruct only for as long as the crops introduced continue to bear. Selected sites are discussed informally among neighborhood men; then, in late December, they are ritually marked.

The next main stage in the shifting cultivation cycle consists of cutting away the natural vegetation and includes two main activities. First, about January, the lower underbrush growth is slashed. This is done cooperatively, the men of a neighborhood working together in each of their swidden sites in turn until all have been slashed. Next, again by similar cooperative effort, the sites are one after another felled of the large forest trees. This general-

56

ly occurs during February and March and involves labor which is both quite heavy and dangerous. Once all the neighborhood sites are cleared, they are allowed to dry for a number of weeks, then are burned—again by the men—generally in late March and early April.

Planting of new vegetation, its care, and its harvesting make up the next stage of the cycle and involves neighborhood women as well as men. Corn is planted in the swiddens first; usually it is April by this time. Rice is planted once the corn has begun to sprout. The swiddens are again worked in turn, the neighborhood men dibbling and the women laying the seed. As these grains grow, each family plants a wide variety of fruits, vegetables, spices, and the like in their swidden amidst the rice and corn. Finally a second corn crop is planted by the women, after the main rice crop has been harvested, usually in July through September. Care of the planted swidden occupies the women many hours in weeding and the men significant portions of time in fencing, building scarecrows, and guarding against wild pigs, monkeys, and rice birds. Harvesting corn is done by the woman, each in her own swidden, but harvesting, hauling, threshing, and drying rice requires the efforts of both men and women and is, again, a neighborhood cooperative effort taking the swiddens one after the other.

After the second corn crop is harvested, a variety of residual productive plants continue to be harvested for some time, but there is no further working of the site; it is allowed to lie fallow so that natural reforestation may occur. New swiddens, in the following year's cycle, are cut in another place.

The activities of the swidden cultivation cycle form only one part of the total subsistence activities of traditional Tiruray. The surrounding rain forest contains much wild game which is hunted and many wild plants which are gathered. Similarly, the rivers and larger streams abound in fish, eels, crustaceans, and the like. Traditional Tiruray are shifting cultivators, to be sure, but they are also hunters, fishers, and gatherers, and these activities produce a significant portion of their subsistence base.

All adult males hunt and fish regularly, and in certain seasons—especially June to December—when their major swidden labor is finished for the year, hunting and fishing are their main activities. The most highly prized games are wild deer and wild pig, though monkeys and a great variety of forest fowl are also taken. Many different methods, traps, snares, and weapons are employed, mostly by single individuals, though in some cases several men will go hunting together, and certain hunting techniques are specifically group activities.

Fishing contrasts with hunting in that it is done by both men and women. Again, a large variety of techniques, traps, and devices are employed and a considerable number of different aquatic resources are taken from the rivers and streams. They form, with the meat from hunting, a significant portion of the traditional Tiruray diet.

Finally, with regard to resources taken from wild sources, one could hardly overstate the importance to the food base of wild flora gathered by men and women from the forest. The forest contains a variety of nourishing edibles: starches, vegetables, seeds, nuts, and fruits, as well as other goods needed for daily life from firewood to medicines.

The last element in the traditional Tiruray subsistence system is a limited trade at non-Tiruray markets. Although the great majority of goods needed and used are either grown or foraged for, certain items come from outside the indigenous Tiruray world and are purchased at a coastal market. Traditional Tiruray do not weave or smith, so clothing and iron tools must be purchased, as well as salt, cooking pots, beddings, ceremonial exchange items, and the like. These are purchased with cash, received typically in the same market visit in exchange for forest products, especially rattan and tree resins.

Marketing occurs very sporadically, and a hike to the coast to visit a lowlands market takes place only when a family has some specific market need. Foraging for food in the forest and stream is, in a sense, continuous. Various forest plants bear edible parts at various times in the year, and there is a large number available for exploitation at any given time. The swidden cultivation cycle, however, is regular and seasonal and makes great demands on man- and woman-power at specific times. This, in effect, gives a seasonal quality also to the exploitation of wild resources beyond their own intrinsic seasonality. Traditional Tiruray, faced with potential conflicts in scheduling between cultivation demands and foraging, will always resolve them in favor of the less flexible swidden cycle. Partly this is because the variety of wild food available is so great and partly because so many of them are not particularly seasonable.

The swidden process annually runs through a well-defined series of phases and activities, steps which cannot occur at random times but which must be carefully and accurately keyed to the seasonal variations in temperature, winds, and rainfall. To determine these seasons, the traditional Tiruray use the stars of the night sky.

The Tiruray Constellations

Kufukufu

Different peoples see different things when they look up at the stars. The first of the constellations, or star groupings, to march northwestward in a line across the Tiruray skies is a mass of stars that is known to Western astronomy as the Pleiades. A cluster of stars visible to the unaided eye in the upper western quadrant of the "standard"[1] constellation of Taurus, this group has been noticed and variously named by many different peoples. They were mentioned by Chinese more than 4000 years ago; they were worshipped by such diverse people as the Aztecs and the Hindus, the Egyptians and the Japanese. To the Ancient Greeks, the Pleiades were sisters, the daughters of Atlas and Pleione.

Figure 1: *Kufukufu*[2]

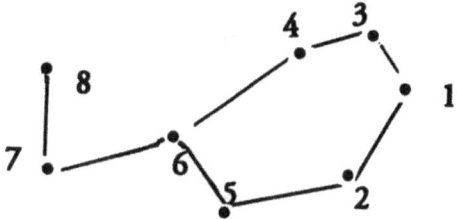

No.	Name	RA	(1950)	Dec		mag
1. 16 Tauri (Celango)		3^h	41.8^m	$+24.0°$	8'	5.4
2. 17 Tauri (Electra)		3	41.9	23.0	57	3.8
3. 19 Tauri (Toygeta)		3	42.2	24.0	19	4.4
4. 20 Tauri (Maia)		3	42.8	24.0	13	4.0
5. 23 Tauri (Merope)		3	43.4	23.0	48	4.3
6. Eta Tauri (Alcyone)		3	44.5	23.0	57	3.0
7. 27 Tauri (Atlas)		3	46.2	23.0	54	3.8
8. 28 Tauri (Pleione)		3	46.2	23.0	59	5.2

To the Tiruray, this cluster of stars is called by the name *Kufukufu*, and it is conceptualized as a swarm of flies in the heavens, buzzing around the carcass of a wild pig, which has been killed by a celestial hunter. *Kufukufu* is the first of six Tiruray constellations.

Bakà

Ancient Greeks, placing the sisters into a larger scene, considered the Pleiades to be the right shoulder of a great bull (Taurus), and considered the gleaming V-shaped group of stars to their southeast—the Hyades—to be its face, the group's brightest star, Aldebaran, to be the bull's eye. To the Tiruray, the Hyades—which they call *Bakà* ("jawbone")—is also part of a face, and it is also related to *Kufukufu*; for *Bakà* is the jaw of the rotting carcass of the wild pig, around which the flies of *Kufukufu* are swarming.

Figure 2: *Bakà*

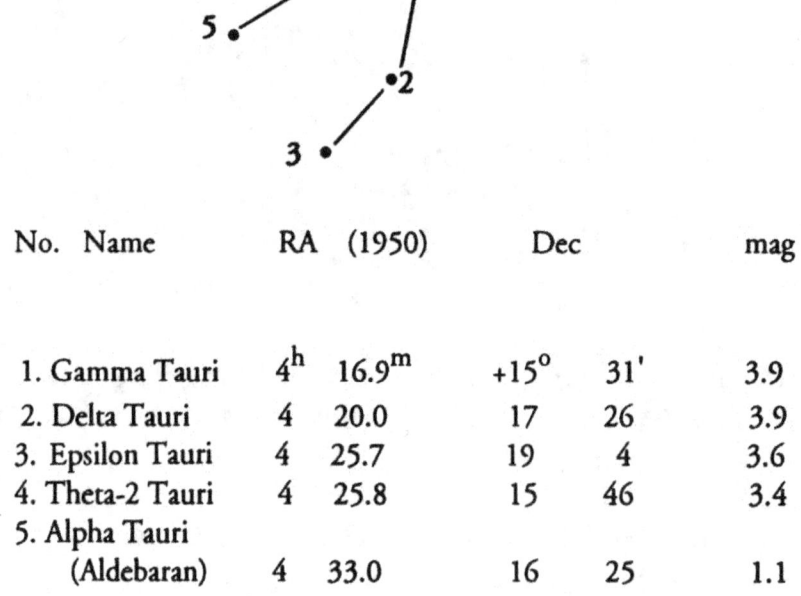

No. Name	RA	(1950)	Dec		mag
1. Gamma Tauri	4^h	16.9^m	$+15°$	$31'$	3.9
2. Delta Tauri	4	20.0	17	26	3.9
3. Epsilon Tauri	4	25.7	19	4	3.6
4. Theta-2 Tauri	4	25.8	15	46	3.4
5. Alpha Tauri (Aldebaran)	4	33.0	16	25	1.1

Seretar

To minds in many different cultures, this striking group of stars has seemed to form a mighty man in the sky. To the Greeks, he was the powerful hunter, Orion, who moved amidst the heavens flourishing a club in one hand and a lion skin in the other. Egyptians believed him to be Osiris. The Arabians saw in him a nameless giant. To the Tiruray, he is *Seretar* (literally, "neatly arranged"), the lucky hunter who was able to kill the wild pig. The hunter himself is formed by the three conspicuously "neatly arranged" stars of what we call "Orion's Belt." To each side of *Seretar's* body are his impressive arms: his left arm the great red variable supergiant, Betelgeuse; his right arm, Rigel, one of the brightest stars in absolute magnitude in the celestial Southern Hemisphere. At the side of *Seretar* hangs his working knife in its woven rattan sheath. Like the Chinese, who saw three kings, the Tiruray do not include in *Seretar* all of the stars of the standard Orion.

Figure 3: *Seretar*

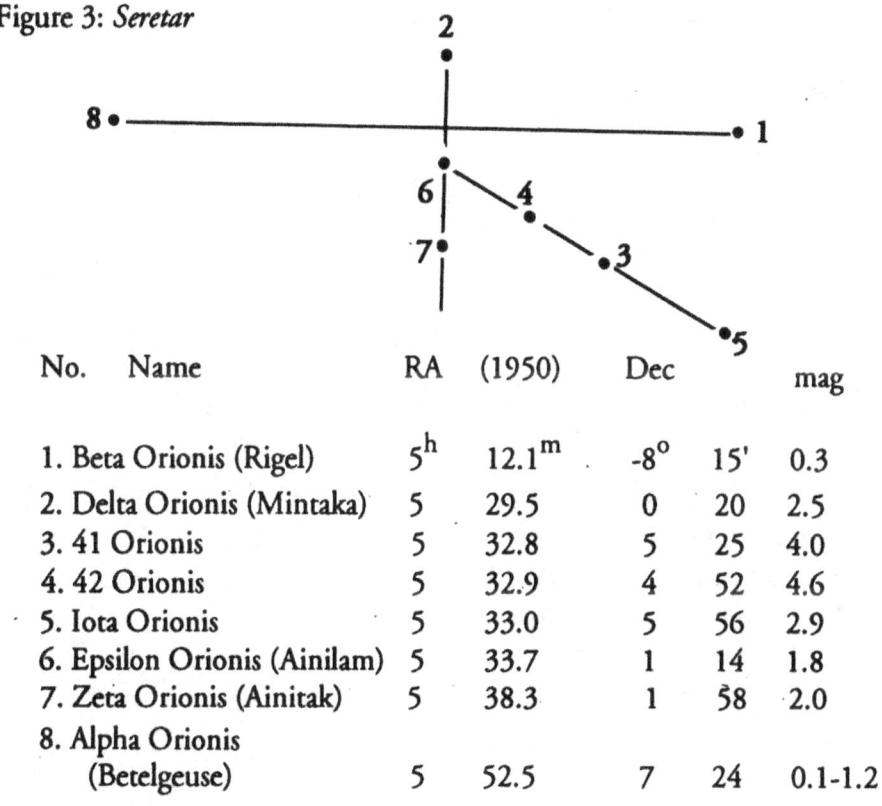

No.	Name	RA	(1950)	Dec		mag
1.	Beta Orionis (Rigel)	5^h	12.1^m	-8°	15'	0.3
2.	Delta Orionis (Mintaka)	5	29.5	0	20	2.5
3.	41 Orionis	5	32.8	5	25	4.0
4.	42 Orionis	5	32.9	4	52	4.6
5.	Iota Orionis	5	33.0	5	56	2.9
6.	Epsilon Orionis (Ainilam)	5	33.7	1	14	1.8
7.	Zeta Orionis (Ainitak)	5	38.3	1	58	2.0
8.	Alpha Orionis (Betelgeuse)	5	52.5	7	24	0.1-1.2

Fegeferafad

Following the hunter, *Seretar*, the Tiruray see an even more splendid man, whom they call *Fegeferafad*, and whose head is the brilliant, golden yellow star, Procyon. Nearby, just four degrees northwest, the smaller Gomeisa is a rooster's long sickle feather, worn proudly by *Fegeferafad* in his bandanna as a symbol of his bravery and might—it means that he has defended his family's honor. These two stars, in the ancient West, were said to be a dog—sometimes a water-dog standing by a great river in the sky (the Milky Way), sometimes a hunting dog following its master, Orion. But to the Tiruray, they are not a constellation in themselves but are part of the far larger *Fegeferafad*, whose left arm is formed by the two brightest stars in Orion's bigger dog, and whose right arm is what we see as a pair of young twins, Castor and Pollux.

Figure 4: *Fegeferafad*

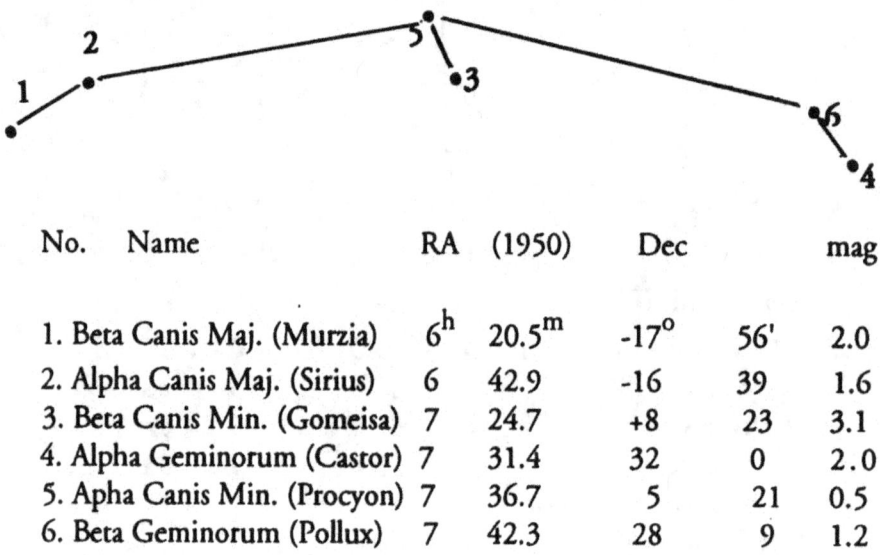

No.	Name	RA	(1950)	Dec		mag
1. Beta Canis Maj. (Murzia)		6^h	20.5^m	$-17°$	56'	2.0
2. Alpha Canis Maj. (Sirius)		6	42.9	-16	39	1.6
3. Beta Canis Min. (Gomeisa)		7	24.7	+8	23	3.1
4. Alpha Geminorum (Castor)		7	31.4	32	0	2.0
5. Apha Canis Min. (Procyon)		7	36.7	5	21	0.5
6. Beta Geminorum (Pollux)		7	42.3	28	9	1.2

Singkad and Kenogon

The four constellations that have been introduced above are considered by the Tiruray to be evening stars, because early in the year they look for them to be high in the heavens at star-break every night. In contrast, *Singkad* and *Kenogon* are the morning stars, for one rises early in order to check their position, just before they fade with the coming of dawn.

Singkad (a Tiruray personal name) is another string of three stars in a line: the striking, first magnitude Altair and its two companions, Alshain and Tarazed—all part of the standard constellation Aquila, a great bird of prey to the Greeks, Persians, Romans, Hebrews, and Arabs. To the Tiruray, *Singkad* is a man on his way to work his swidden. With him, approximately ten degrees northeast in the sky, is his wife, *Kenogon* (literally "maiden," but also a common personal name). She is a dainty lady, formed by a small group of five faint stars which are in the standard Delphinius—the Dolphin, or Job's Coffin. The faintest star of the five, the one closest to *Singkad*, is the comb of *Kenogon's* hair knot; the other four are her body.

Figure 5: *Singkad and Kenogon*

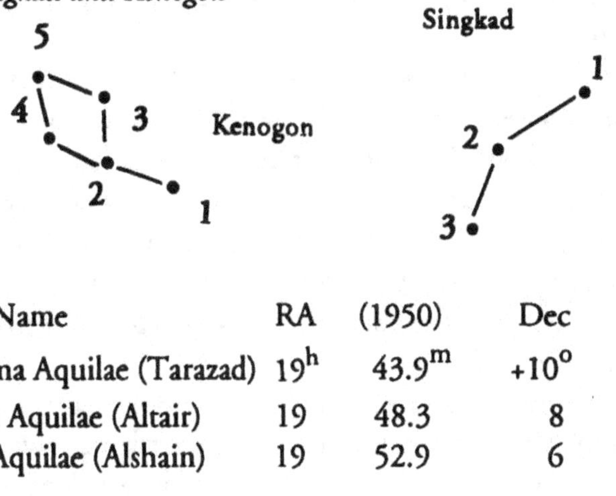

Singkad:

No. Name	RA	(1950)	Dec		mag
1. Gamma Aquilae (Tarazad)	19^h	43.9^m	+10°	29'	2.8
2. Alpha Aquilae (Altair)	19	48.3	8	44	0.9
3. Beta Aquilae (Alshain)	19	52.9	6	17	3.9

Kenogon:

No. Name	RA	(1950)	Dec		mag
1. Zeta Delphinius	20^h	33.0^m	+14°	31'	4.6
2. Beta Delphinius (Roranev)	20	35.2	14	26	3.8
3. Alpha Delphinius (Sualocin)	20	37.3	15	44	3.9
4. Delta Delphinius	20	41.1	14	54	4.5
5. Gamma Delphinius	20	44.3	15	57	4.5

The Origin of the Constellations

The Tiruray believe that their creator spirit, *Tulus*, made the world and then, in order that its forests might be properly made into swiddens, *Tulus* created human beings.[3] So long as there is a world, it is the proper work of humanity to farm its forests; and, as the *Berinarew*, the great Tiruray epic, puts it: "So long as a forested world exists, *Tulus* wants there to be people to care for it."

The Tiruray also believe that should a religious leader have sufficient wit, authority, and goodness, he could lead all of his followers "beyond the sky" to live in the land of *Tulus*. None in recent memory have had such charisma, but in the heroic days of Tiruray mythology there were those who could and did lead their followers away from their earthly labors in the forest to live in quiet and companionable ease beyond the sky. The greatest legendary hero of them all, *Lagey Lingkuwos*, in fact, led to heaven every single one of the existing human beings—and part of that tale relates the story of the origin of the constellations.

In the days of *Lagey Lingkuwos*, people had a difficult time with their farming. They wanted to please *Tulus* by farming well, but they were never sure when the winds would be right for burning; they had trouble predicting the arrival of the rainy season, and thus were unsure when they should plant; and they lacked a way of calling for the various good or bad omens. Farming was, therefore, a matter of guesswork with regard to timing, and the swidden cycle for those people was seldom properly keyed to the yearly seasons as it so clearly needed to be.

Lagey Lingkuwos was aware of this serious problem and was determined to do something about it. Near his place was a settlement where six people lived. They were, like all people, cultivators and foragers. And, like all human beings at that time, they were followers of *Lagey Lingkuwos*. Three were young, unmarried men—all first cousins—whose names were *Kufukufu*, *Bakà* and *Seretar*. Each lived in his own house, near the houses of their two uncles: the widower, *Keluguy*, who was the legal leader of the settlement, and *Singkad*, the group's only married man who lived with his wife *Kenogon*. As a pet, these people had a variety of forest dove, which the Tiruray call *lemugen*.[4]

When it came time for *Lagey Lingkuwos* to lead his followers to the place of *Tulus*, beyond the sky, he asked two special favors of the six people. Knowing that *Tulus* would not leave the world without human beings to make swiddens in the forests, and wanting the next creation to have an easier time than the last, he asked those six followers to leave their pet bird behind in the forest, where its call could become the needed giver of omens. He further asked them to live in the sky for as long as there should be a world and people to work it. They agreed to both requests of their leader, and so it is today that the *lemugen's* call gives the farmer much needed omens, and the six constellations move across the night sky, assisting this new creation of people to properly anchor their subsistence cycle in the annual round of seasons. The Tiruray say that the six seem, like themselves, to be always processing to work in their swiddens—the three young cousins ahead, followed by their uncle and headman. *Singkad* comes next, prudently keeping himself between his attractive wife and their legal leader, *Keluguy*, whom Tiruray never refer to by name—to do so would be too disrespectful—but call by his nickname, *Fegeferafad.*[5]

The Calendric Use of the Stars

Once rice has been harvested from the swidden field, usually sometime between early July and late September, the remaining work in that field—planting and harvesting a second corn crop as well as harvesting the many non-grains that have been planted—becomes largely women's work. The man is free for several months to range far and wide in the forests, hunting and gathering wild foods. During these months, he keeps a sharp eye open for a good place to make his next year's swidden. When he marks his new field and begins to cut away the forest, another year's cycle of activities has begun.

Many of the activities and phases of the cycle are timed quite naturally by reference to preceding activities. Harvesting of any of the cultivated plants, for instance, takes place when the plant has ripened properly and thus is, in timing, a function of the time that particular cultivate was planted. Similarly, the felling of the large trees in the prospective swidden follows immediately upon the finishing of the slashing of the underbrush, which itself follows directly the ceremony of ritually marking the field.

Other key events in the agricultural cycle, however, are not of that kind and require the most sensitive sort of timing. Burning must occur at a time when there has been a long dry spell to thoroughly dry all the cut vegetation and when there are lively winds to ensure a complete burn. The Tiruray greatly prefer, in fact, to burn late in the hot season, when the winds are reaching their maximum strength. Yet, if they delay too long, the weather will turn cool and the hard rains will begin.

Besides burning, two other critical timing decisions must be made. The process of clearing the forest growth away from the chosen site is initiated by the ritual marking and first ritual slashing of the field. If this is done too soon, the field will be slashed and the big trees cut down too far ahead of the proper time for burning. New growth of weeds and shoots will be too well established to allow a clean, adequate burn of the site. On the other hand, if marking is delayed past a critical point, there will not be sufficient time for the arduous work of clearing before the date for burning comes and goes.

The first planting of corn simply follows directly the burning of the field; the second corn planting likewise follows the rice harvest, whenever that occurs. But the planting of the rice presents the Tiruray farmer with the year's most difficult calendric decision. Rice must be planted before the rains start, so that the field will be dry for dibbling and seeding, but it cannot be planted too long before; newly planted rice requires lots of rain if it is to grow well. If planted too far in advance of the coming of the rain, the seed will fail to germinate, will fall prey to ants, or will give forth only a stunted stock. If planting is after the rainy season has fully begun, not only is seeding itself very difficult but, as the Tiruray put it, "the weeds will grow faster and better and will defeat the rice."

Thus, at three crucial points, the swidden cycle requires that it be properly meshed with the annual seasonal changes in temperature, winds, and rains. These changes are actually quite predictable in the Tiruray area each year. February, March, and often much of April are hot and dry; the middle of this time is especially windy and ideal for burning. With late April a period of milder weather and occasional showers begins, lasting until May, when the rains become heavy and frequent; thus the weeks of April are optimum times for planting rice. The rains continue to be strong and almost daily until about August; from then until the end of January it may rain, but less often and less heavily.

The Tiruray are well aware of these seasons and their regularity, but they do not know or classify them, as was just done above, by the months of our calendar. They know them by the position of those six followers that *Lagey Lingkuwos* left for them in the sky above. They know them by the stars.

The Tiruray have a colorful way of designating the zenith of the night sky. Any star or constellation which has reached its culmination, which is to say its highest celestial point or upper transit, is said to be *kemudà* or "riding the horse." If it is within a circle around the zenith of about twenty degrees diameter, they say that it is in the *rangà*, the "chicken's nest." It is characteristic of each of the Tiruray constellations that at a certain time of each year it enters "the chicken's nest" and is soon afterwards "riding the horse." The time of a constellation's being *kemudà* is reckoned by where it is at star-break if it is an evening star, or at star-fade if it is a morning star. In terms of the months of the year, these times are:

1. *Kufukufu*   late February
2. *Bakà*   early to mid March
3. *Seretar*   late March
4. *Fegeferafad* late April
5. *Singkad*   late April
6. *Kenogon*   late May

The cultivator knows that it is time to mark and begin clearing his field when he sees that *Seretar's* body is about twenty degrees above the horizon at star-break. *Kufukufu* and *Bakà* are, of course, higher in the sky—although none of the constellations have yet begun to enter the nest. There are other calendric indicators of the marking season: the first traces of *megenihan*, a relatively strong wind from the east, begin to be felt, and the wild forest tree *Kegùkù*[6] begins to flower. But these are much less determinative. Late in December or early in January the traditional Tiruray communities hold their marking ritual festival, and commence the new year's cycle of cultivation, when they see the hunter *Seretar* in full view at star-break.

Burning time comes when the days are hot and dry and the winds strong. The farmer weighs many technical considerations in selecting the exact day for the burning. The winds should be straight and fast. The day should be either Saturday or, better, Monday, as those days belong to the spirit of fire. Two or three neighbors must be available to help with the burn, in return for which they will be helped to burn their fields. But, above all, the sun must be hot and the vegetative debris thoroughly dry. The hottest days come between the time that *Kufukufu* "rides the horse" and the time that *Seretar* takes his place on the "horse's back," roughly between the latter part of

February and the end of March.

Since traditional Tiruray feel that they face no decision more grave than that of when to plant their rice, they approach it with care and solemnity. First, they decide the season and then, applying different criteria, they decide the exact day. They say that planting is theoretically possible from the time that *Kufukufu* "rides the horse" (late in February)—though no one ever plants so early—to as late as the time when *Kenogon* is "on horseback" (late May). Planting rice is best, however, when *Seretar* is somewhere in "the chicken's nest" (from approximately mid-March until mid-April). Because of this, most try to burn before *Seretar* "enters the nest" so that they can get their first crop of corn in and growing and still get their rice planted before *Seretar* "leaves the nest."

Having set the general season, the constellations are one of two celestial factors to be considered in choosing the exact day of planting. In this respect, they warn of a particularly bad time. Whenever the feather of *Fegeferafad* is "on the horse," planting would lead to sure disaster—for those days are believed to belong to the rats, to the rice birds, to rice bugs, and to all the various worms and larvae that attack rice. So long as the feather is not *kemudà*, the stars say no more about the precise day for planting. For additional guidance, the Tiruray consult the waxing and waning of the moon, which advises them of the days which are bad because of various inauspicious connotations.

There is room among the Tiruray, as among most people, for those persons who feel that they have developed their own "system," or for whom some particular point in a range of possible choices seems especially right. Some persons maintain that the precise time when *Bakà* and *Seretar* are both at opposite edges of "the chicken's nest" is the time of times to plant rice. Thus they cant their cycle in the direction of early planting. Another old man says that, for him, the best of all times to plant rice is very, very late—when *Seretar* is already "out of the nest" and *Fegeferafad* is "on the horse."

Other factors played their inevitable role—sickness, accidents, unexpected summonses to a distant burial, laziness—but, on the whole, the people of the community I worked in followed the stars and heeded the night sky's advice during the 1966 cycle. The following data, taken from my field records, show the actual range of the critically timed swidden activities of the 28 families of the Figel neighborhood:

Marking   18 Dec '65-12 Feb '66

Burning	14 Mar '66-30 Apr '66
Planting rice	25 Mar '66-16 May '66

Thus, with few exceptions, everyone got things done within the general period that they had to be done, and while some individuals timed their work much better than others, no one committed any truly disastrous errors in scheduling their swidden activities.

Hunting, fishing, and gathering of wild resources are not so much scheduled as done whenever possible. As mentioned earlier, the rhythm of foraging activities is dictated less by seasonalities of available foods than by work demands of the swidden cycle. The most heavily exploited aquatic game—fish, eels, shrimp, crabs—are available throughout the year. The most popular forest plants—wild yams, legumes, and edible ferns—are not seasonal. The favorite hunting prey—wild pig, deer, and most fowl—are continuously available. Nevertheless, there is a seasonal character to foraging.

Men are most busy with swidden chores during the dry season, December through April, when they mark, cut, and burn their fields. Once the rains begin and planting is finished, women do most of the day-to-day swidden work of care for the growing crops. This means that the men are free to do most of their hunting, fishing, and gathering from June through November, during the rainy season, while women do most of their fishing and gathering early in the swidden cycle during the dry season.

Certain foraging activities are seasonal in nature. For example, the eggs of a large forest bird known as *tawen*[7] are found only in February through May and are therefore gathered almost exclusively by women. Similarly, most species of forest mushrooms are maximally available during the rainy season, and they are gathered principally by men as they hunt. Most fish, eels, and crustaceans are not periodic, but there is a marked seasonal character to the condition of the water in rivers and streams. The water is quite low and clear in the dry months, but with the coming of heavy rains in late April the waterways flood and become very muddy and unclear. Thus the women and children, who do much of the dry season fishing, are most likely to use the methods which are appropriate to clear, quiet water, such as certain traps, some kinds of poison, and fishing with the bare hands (which the Tiruray call "true fishing"). Men, who do most of their fishing in the rainy season, use other methods—such as hook and line, or large stationary weirs—appropriate to rushing, muddy water.

69

Conclusion

In sum, traditional Tiruray are not only swidden cultivators, they are avid hunters, fishers, and gatherers. But since the swidden cycle has become established among them, most of whatever seasonality was characteristic of their foraging has disappeared. The main calendric decisions are made now with regard to cultivation requirements, and hunting, fishing, and gathering, although still very significant aspects of the Tiruray subsistence system, are fit in around those requirements.

The calendric decisions themselves are made by observation of the stars, of the distinctive constellations of the Tiruray zodiac and where they are in the celestial field. Traditional Tiruray are generally aware of what month the lowlanders reckon the world to be in, even, if they have recently been to market along the coast, perhaps what day of the month. But the calendar they use to make their critical decisions—when to mark, when to burn, especially when to plant rice—this calendar is not the one that hangs on the market vendor's wall. It is the one that hangs in the night sky, where their compassionate legendary hero placed it so long ago.

Notes

[1]The recommendations regarding constellation boundaries made by the 1930 report of the Delporte Commission of the International Astronomical Union have since been considered standard in international astronomy.

[2]Citations of Right Ascension (RA), Declination (Dec), and visual magnitude (mag) are for the reference year of 1950. I want to acknowledge with gratitude the staff of the Lick Observatory at the University of California at Santa Cruz, especially Professor S. Vasilevskis, for assistance in making the stellar identifications presented in this essay.

[3]Tiruray folklore is not everywhere the same in detail, but the general outlines, themes and personalities are largely held in common. The version

of the story here presented is that told by the people of Figel.

[4]Phapitreron leueofis (Temminck).

[5]Once in the sky, the three cousins become elements in another picture, that of the hunter, the slain pig, and the flies—but this is a different matter to the Tiruray and suggests no contradiction.

[6]Eugenia calubkob C.R. Rob.

[7]Megapodius freycinet Gaimard.

Chapter 5

TIRURAY GARDENS

From Use-Right to Private Ownership

This little essay emerged from a number of conversations I had in the mid-1970s with Prof. Joseph Spencer, one of the great authorities on Philippine cultural geography and a University of California colleague of mine. We were discussing the shift in traditional societies to notions of private ownership, and I suggested to him that the Tiruray material on gardening, in the context of their attitudes toward use-right and property and their conservative ideas regarding swidden cultivation, might give a clue—even an example—of how such a shift could take place. We thought of preparing a rather long comparative piece together on the transition worldwide to the notion of private ownership, but after a few stabs at drafts, Prof. Spencer said he was too busy with other things and that I should go ahead and tell the Tiruray story. The present essay appeared in the Philippine Quarterly of Culture and Society *in 1981 (Vol. 9, No. 1, pp. 5-8).*

To describe the Tiruray understanding of use-rights and property, it is necessary to introduce a Tiruray concept. The central term in their language pertaining to property is *géfé*.[1] To be *géfé* of something is to have exclusive rights over its present use. A person's belongings—his *entingayen*—include all the things one calls one's own, in the sense that one stands to them in the relation of *géfé*. A man is thus said to be *géfé* of his house, of his wife, of his tools, of a wedding he is celebrating for his daughter, or of a legal proceeding which concerns him directly. In short, he is *géfé* of any object, person, or even a ceremony in which he not only has an economic and emotional interest, but also has legitimate personal oversight. Such things (his clothing, his family and his rituals) are "his" so long as his rights over them continue. The word may be glossed into English as "legitimate user" or, more simply and loosely, as "owner," but the essence of the Tiruary concept is right-of-use.

Tenure of land among traditional Tiruray employs this concept directly in the sense of right of usufruct. A swidden site belongs to a man who is its

72

géfé until the harvest is completed and the site no longer bears cultivated produce, after which time he is no longer *géfé* over that site. Population density among traditional Tiruray is quite low, so that land is ample and not thought of as a scarce good, and every family is entitled to as much land as the family feels able to work. Land selected by an individual for a swidden becomes that family's to use for a crop cycle, once it has been publicly and properly claimed and marked. A great deal of cooperative work by neighbors will take place in the course of a cropping cycle on each field cropped by the community, but each family must plan and organize their particular field and the family has sole rights to the produce. The family is thus *géfé* of that particular plot in terms of an exclusive private right of use. Some planted crops do yield useful products during the early regeneration cycle, and the *géfé* of that plot is alone entitled to harvest them so long as he continues to do so.

Thus, traditional Tiruray do not conceive of themselves as formally holding any private possessory right over specific swidden sites beyond the produce from a single cropping cycle. Among the Tiruray, use-rights are not inherited by children or other descendants. Land no longer harvested reverts to the public domain and has the same free-good status as any wild forest area. Individuals may hunt freely anywhere in the wild forests around the neighborhood, and there is no need to avoid lands that formerly were utilized as primary cultivation sites. When the forest growth has been sufficiently restored to be reworked, anyone may select the site without regard for the former *géfé*. With regard to swidden land, in short, the Tiruray employ a pure concept of right of usufruct.

In addition to the swiddens annually cleared and planted, each traditional Tiruray family maintains a garden near its house. In these gardens, they grow such crops as taro, manioc, and sweet potatoes. Most of these crops are also grown, though sparingly, in the swidden; the Tiruray consider that their extended cropping there would have drastic implications for forest regeneration, so such plantings are not long maintained in swiddens. Traditional Tiruray are greatly concerned that land used for swiddens should lie fallow under fully natural regeneration for a sufficient number of years so that the regrowth of jungle forest will mature properly. Many aspects of their particular system of shifting cultivation—size of plots, length of cropping cycle, length of fallow, and types of crops planted—proceed directly from their concern that forest growth should fully reclaim the land following its cropping cycle. They know and fear the terminal succession to grassland resulting from too short fallow or incomplete forest regeneration.

Gardens, on the other hand, are viewed as a very different kind of commitment of land. Recognizing that the concentrated planting of such root crops as taro, manioc, and sweet potatoes can, and will, eliminate effective reversion of land to forest, the Tiruray view their gardens as long-term plots, to be treated differently from their swiddens. Tiruray gardens are located both within the hamlet and close to it, but the sites are selected with care, very carefully managed, and kept in continuous production for many years.

The concept of use-right over these gardens is no different from that concerning any other thing over which a family is *géfé*. A family has the use of land for a garden under exactly the same concept as for any other land over which the family is *géfé*. There is no change in the concept of tenure with regard to garden land, but rather a subtle shift in the way the land is used. No new terminology has been introduced to distinguish short-term *cyclic* use of land for swiddens from long-term *continuous* use of land in gardens, but clearly the concept of use-right is being stretched to cover a rather different order of landholding—something that, in effect, results in a private possessory right. It is recognized by the Tiruray that the maximal concentrated planting of root crops over a continued period of time will effectively commit the plot, that it will eliminate the possibility of the plot's returning to forest and to free public use, and that it will leave the individual who planted it as permanent *géfé*. Thus, importantly, when a man dies, his wife continues to be *géfé* over garden land (as she does of his tools or other personal effects); she does not retain rights over swidden land after it is fully harvested. The difference is that her use of the garden is permanent and continuous.

In this regard, it is significant to note how traditional Tiruray are responding conceptually to the first beginnings of permanent field plow farming among them. Even in the traditional neighborhood of Figel, a few men have started rather tentatively to use the carabao to plow small fields and to plant commercial corn in addition to working their swiddens. When this began to occur, the plowed fields (maximally planted and temporally permanent) were immediately and intuitively classed by the community as a kind of garden and referred to by the same term. The plowed fields, like the gardens, were seen as removed from the public domain.

There is a very important point to these observations. It might seem "logically" that the shift in tenure system from that associated with shifting cultivation to that associated with permanent field cropping must involve a change in a basic pattern of thought. But the Tiruray example suggests this may not necessarily be the case. Regularly in permanent gardens and quite recently in permanent plowed fields, the Tiruray have readily applied the same basic concept which they utilize in dealing with their primary fields: the *géfé* has rights to the plot for so long as he is using it. *It is not the cultural idea of géfé which is undergoing a shift, but rather the way land is being used in practice.* Yet the transition is clearly observable here from a classic pattern of usufruct to what is, at least in embryo, the practice of private possession of permanent fields.

I suggest that the Tiruray case is of considerable interest to a study of the development of permanent field agriculture out of shifting cultivation. First of all, it gives a documentation of this development actually in the process of taking place, and such empirical data are uncommon. Secondly, it indicates the significance of the garden as an aspect of the total subsistence system, an aspect which has all too often been neglected in the literature.[2] But, especially, the Tiruray material is very suggestive with regard to understanding the emergence of an idea of private property.

Contrary to what might be readily assumed in the abstract, it suggests that the critical innovation may well not be a shift in cultural ideas about land tenure, but one in the technological practice on the land. A garden, and by extension a plowed field, is used on a permanent basis by its *géfé*, and thus the *géfé* has become not merely its user but also its possessor, meaning in the modern context, of course, its "owner."

Notes

[1]See also Schlegel (1970), where the context of this concept in Tiruray legal and moral thought is elaborated.

[2]See Spencer (1966: 145-148).

75

Chapter 6

FROM TRIBAL TO PEASANT

Two Tiruray Communities

Since the Tiruray far in the interior of the remaining forest were still traditional in their way of life, living much in the old tribal ways Tiruray had historically lived, whereas the Tiruray in the Upi Valley and northwards were so profoundly acculturated into Filipino peasant life, it seemed to me that these people were a living example of a very significant social transformation which had occurred at one time or another over much of the globe. I had been doing systematic study of several Tiruray communities, both within the rainforest and outside it in the very acculturated areas. So it seemed logical to describe how that shift from tribal organization to peasant organization looked on the ground as it appeared in the Tiruray case. The present essay first appeared in the collection Studies in Third World Societies *in 1976 (vol. 1, no. 1, pp. 73-95. It has since been translated into Spanish and included in a volume on* Los Indígenas de Las Islas Filipinas, *edited by Mario Zamora and others.*

I

The term "peasant," as a contrast to "tribal," has long if imprecisely been used in anthropological writing to refer to rural societies which are imbedded in some larger social whole. Kroeber[1] gives the classic sense of the term: peasants are rural yet live in relation to market systems, to some larger system of social stratification, to urban centers—even metropolitan capitals. "They constitute part-societies with part cultures." Tribal societies have their own religions, their own political systems, their own languages. People in peasant societies, in contrast, retain some loyalty to their distinctive ethnic identity, but profess the religion of some enveloping "great tradition," are constituent elements of some larger political integration, and, usually, must speak some language other than their own to get along in the larger social whole of which their society is merely a part.

This use of the term "peasant" is being roundly criticized as obscuring more than it reveals, as submerging vast differences under too facile a rubric, and, in general, as virtually prohibiting intelligible generalizations.[2] Yet the descriptive distinction which it makes between tribal societies and peasant societies—however inadequate for a sophisticated global economic taxonomy—does underline a real and fundamental difference among Philippine ethnic groups. If we take the situation at the turn of the 20th century as a baseline, a number of Philippine societies were at that time clearly "tribal." The Bontoc and Kalinga, for example, in the north, the Hanunóo and the Sulud in the Visayas, and the Subanun and Bagobo in Mindanao—all were quite separate cultures with their own customs and languages, their own political, legal, and religious systems, their own internal sense of unity and their conviction that "other people" were precisely that: other, distinct, utterly foreign. In contrast, there were the various societies of Luzon and the Visayas which had been brought together into a kind of unity through centuries of common Spanish rule, societies such as the Tagalog, the Ilocano, the Cebuano, the Ilonggo. These were all indeed what Kroeber calls "peasant"—part-societies and part-cultures. Pre-Spanish animism continued to infuse their religious beliefs, but the people of these hispanized societies were all, nonetheless, Catholic Christians. Local politics had many indigenous qualities, but the arena in which they took place was nationwide, multi-ethnic, and centered in Manila. Official legal affairs were carried out in local branches of a national court system, which was neither Tagalog nor Cebuano but Filipino. In short, these societies, tribal in pre-Spanish times, had been welded by Spanish colonial rule into a common Filipino peasantry of "lowland Christians." Those ethnic groups not brought under Spanish hegemony—mostly hill tribes in mountains which the Spanish could not effectively penetrate—remained tribally distinct, at least until American times. Muslim expansion played a similar role in the Southern Philippines.

The Tiruray are a society which is right now caught up in this very shift from tribal to peasant, a society which in recent decades is being transformed from an isolated and independent tribe into a sector of Filipino peasantry. This essay will look at two Tiruray communities—one on each side of this shift—and the sort of life lived in each.

In what might be called "traditional times"—before the advent of Western military and cultural influence in the early 20th century—the Tiruray lived in nearly complete isolation in their forest-covered mountains. They had no significant contact with other forest-dwelling tribes farther south in the Cotabato Cordillera and only highly formalized trade relations with the Muslim Magindanaon who occupied the lowlands to the north and east of the Tiruray hills.[3]

Today, although severe acculturation has changed the way of life in much of the Tiruray region, there still remain areas deep in the mountains where the traditional life is virtually intact. One such community is Figel. Located some 20 kilometers up the winding Tran Grande River from the coast of the Celebes Sea, in the midst of dense tropical rain forest, Figel is quite isolated from the forces of change engulfing so much of Tiruray society. It, and a few other places like it, represent what remains of traditional Tiruray culture.

Four discrete social groups may be identified among traditional Tiruray: the neighborhood, the settlement, the household, and the nuclear family. The family is determined by kin ties, the household and the settlement are spatially identified, and the neighborhood is a matter of ongoing social ties related to cooperation in day-to-day subsistence work.

The neighborhood (*inged*) is the largest social unit with discrete boundaries. A neighborhood consists of a number of families, usually living in several settlements, which regularly assist each other in their farming activities and rituals. The neighborhood is, in short, a subsistence cooperation group. The various neighborhoods which remain viable in traditional terms in the Tran area are scattered through the mountains, some 10 to 20 kilometers apart, so that a considerable portion of forest land exists between them. Any Tiruray can easily name the various households and settlements which comprise his own neighborhood. It is not a distinctive attribute of a traditional Tiruray neighborhood that its members should all be linked by consanguineal or affinal kin ties, but, in fact, it is most commonly the case that almost all are.

Neighborhoods vary widely in overall population, and in the number of settlements, households, and families that they include. In Figel there are seven settlements, comprised of 31 families living in 29 households—a total of 126 people.

The history of Figel as a community is quite typical of how such traditional neighborhoods come into being. About 1800, a man known as Moembot came to the narrow place (*figel*) in the Tran Grande River where Figel's main settlement stands today. He brought his family with him and over the years many of his descendants have remained and have brought in spouses from elsewhere.[4] Today there are three heads of families who are fourth-generation male descendants of Moembot. Nine present heads of families are fifth-generation male descendants and two family heads are married to fifth-generation female descendants. Five heads of families are male descendants of the sixth generation and two are married to sixth-generation females. These families all consider Figel to be their ancestral home and speak of themselves as "people of Figel." Other descendants of Moembot, both male and female, have married or migrated to other places. Thus, they are not part of the Figel neighborhood.

The principal leader of the Figel community is a man known as Balaud, a renowned legal authority, whose father had married into Figel. In 1951, Abad—a first cousin of Balaud through their fathers—came to Figel and settled near him. He had left his home place farther north, in the area which was being drastically acculturated, in order to escape the many changes both in the physical and the social environment. With regard to Abad, of course, the Figel people were mostly in-laws. A few years later, another first cousin of Abad and Balaud followed for the same reason and settled in the Figel neighborhood. In 1958, another family—step-parents of Abad's wife—arrived and settled in. These moves were all regarded as permanent, and the persons involved were thereafter considered to be people of Figel.

In 1965, Buntung, one of the major religious leaders of Figel, came there to live—also to escape the changes occurring in the Tiruray way of life in his previous home place. He is the husband of a woman whose daughter by a previous marriage had married a man from Figel. With Buntung came three other families: two married sons and a married stepson.

Finally, a few months later, still another family came to Figel to flee from troubles and changes. In this case, the wife is the sister of a woman married to a fifth-generation Figel man.

Thus, no families in Figel neighborhood are completely unrelated to anyone else—although in many cases the relationships that exist are quite minor. No consanguineal or affinal relationship at all is required. There is no rule or attitude prohibiting a totally unrelated family from settling among

79

Figel people. Should one wish to do so, and were it prepared to share in the cooperative activities on the swiddens of its Figel neighbors, it would be welcomed and counted among the people of Figel.

The persons living in any neighborhood do not normally reside in a single central village, but in settlements (*dengonon*), small dispersed hamlets of from one to ten or more houses. Every swidden farmer must necessarily associate his family with others in a neighborhood, to be part of the needed cooperative work group, but he need not live in the company of other families in a settlement. Of the seven settlements that comprised Figel neighborhood at the time of my census in 1966, two had only one family, one three, one four, two had six, and one had eight. In general, any family is free to establish its residence in any settlement it wishes, and no rules exist to structure a settlement according to any kinship principle. Nonetheless, commonly there will be some relationship, either affinal or consanguineal, linking the families that settle together in the same hamlet.

Settlements are generally sited near a source of water, and are regularly named after prominent nearby geographical features. Figel, as noted, means a narrow place in the river. A neighborhood generally takes its name from its principal settlement. If asked where they are from, the Tiruray always reply with the name of their neighborhood, not that of their settlement. The latter do not have the stability of location or family composition that a neighborhood has, and tend to shift around as the people look for better spots or abandon a location which has come to be associated with illness or death. Neighborhoods, and not settlements, are the important and relatively stable territorial units .

Much sharing goes on among the households of a settlement. Fish caught in the river in any number are always shared with all one's settlement-mate families, as are snack foods such as fruit or roasted corn. Chickens, eggs, and rice—on the other hand—are never shared, except in ritual meals or with visitors, as they symbolize the discreteness of every household. In contrast, the flesh of a deer or wild pig caught in hunting is always shared throughout the entire neighborhood, with each household receiving a carefully measured equal share, these catches symbolizing the cooperative unity of the neighborhood—a unity also expressed in the rice exchanges characteristic of neighborhood ritual feasts.

The Tiruray residential unit is the household. Houses in traditional settlements are generally loosely grouped within a small clearing; they are of wood and bamboo construction, roofed with grass, and average in size approximately three by five meters. In most cases, the household is composed of a single nuclear family which eats from the same pot (the word for family being *kureng*, "pot"). In some cases—there was one such in the Figel neighborhood in 1966—an unmarried and dependent elder is included in the family. Polygyny is accepted though uncommon. A polygynous household contains a man who is a member of as many pots—families—as he has wives. Only two of the 29 Figel neighborhood households were polygynous; in both cases, the man had "inherited" his second wife through the operation of a system of spouse replacement at death. There is no limit to the number of wives a man may have, and thus the number of families to which he may belong, but he must care for them all satisfactorily and equally well. Polyandry is unknown.

Rarely, a single house will contain two households; there were three such cases in the Figel neighborhood. Such arrangements are always considered to be temporary and irregular. As in the three Figel cases, they usually occur when a couple are newly married and still have not put up their own dwelling, or when a newly arrived household has been unable yet to erect its own house.

When children marry they are in a new family and eat from a new "pot." Relations between households may be by kinship or brideprice contract or swidden cooperation, but the households are very much independent, self-determining units. When a father and his married son cooperate in working on their respective swiddens, they are doing so merely as neighbors. In the case where there is more than one wife, the senior (first) wife is the spokesperson for all the other women with regard to economic tasks, responsibilities, and rights within their household.

Aside from his membership in such discrete social groups as the family, household, settlement, and neighborhood, every Tiruray is the center point of a personal kindred which, reckoned bilaterally from Ego, includes all the descendants of his four pairs of great-grandparents and thus reaches laterally to include all of Ego's second cousins. Spouses married into one's kindred are not included in it. The kindred has important responsibilities and its members are mobilized on behalf of one in disputes, in the establishment of a family through marriage, and in its dissolution through death or divorce. The kindred, on the other hand, is not involved in any direct way with subsistence activities.

Whether monogynous or polygynous, each household has the fundamental and corporate economic responsibility of feeding and provisioning itself. Traditional Tiruray, such as those of Figel, accomplish this through an annual work cycle of shifting cultivation, through considerable hunting, fishing, and gathering of wild resources, and through purchase of a very small amount of goods in the market.[5]

The swidden cycle of traditional Tiruray is, in its essential stages and phases, similar to that of other slash-and-burn peoples. Traditional Tiruray recognize very clearly the importance of the forest to their way of life and carefully avoid over-exploitation practices which could lead to the forest's being replaced by grassland. Also, in the traditional subsistence system, wild foods play an important role, and Figel people devote considerable time to hunting, fishing, and gathering in the rivers, streams and surrounding rain forest. They also go, by necessity, from time to time to the market at Salaman, along the coast. Traditional Tiruray do not weave nor work iron themselves, and are therefore dependent upon market sources for cloth, iron tools, and such other goods as salt and matches. Money, which plays virtually no other role in their lives, is needed for marketing. To obtain money to use for purchases in Salaman, the Figel people gather rattan from the forest, strip it, and ready it to be sold as lashing. An individual will prepare and carry to the coast only as much as is required for him to buy whatever particular item he needs. The market is not looked upon by traditional people as a significant source of foodstuff, nor as an arena for making any sort of profit. It is viewed merely as an extension of their domestic production, yielding those few needed goods which cannot be extracted from swidden, hunting, fishing, or gathering.

There are two significant leadership roles in traditional Tiruray society: the *kefeduwan* "legal authority," and the *beliyan* "shaman." Both roles are related to a cultural institution of traditional life: the *tiyawan*.

Tiyawan are formal meetings between kindreds involved in either the negotiation of an agreement (usually a marriage contract) or the non-violent settlement of a dispute.[6] These formal adjudicatory discussions are carried out in a highly metaphoric special rhetoric, and the ability to speak in them with skill and wisdom is the primary qualification of a legal leader. Sitting in a rough circle, the *kefeduwan* representing the various kindreds involved seek to find an agreement that will satisfy the rights and feelings of all participants. *Tiyawan* are in no way adversary proceedings; in the Tiruray view no side "wins." Justice "wins" in that everyone involved must be satisfied that faults are properly identified and accepted and that all rights are recognized and acknowledged. *Tiyawan* normally involve the transfer of an agreed amount of formal property items known as *tamuk*. These are goods—spears, necklaces, gongs, swords, etc.— which, in addition to their usefulness in everyday life, have great symbolic value. All *tamuk* items originate outside Tiruray society and are obtained through trade. They change ownership frequently as they are used in legal settlements, both as bride price and as fines.

Kefeduwan are, essentially, *tiyawan* specialists. The role is not tied to wealth or political power. There are no real differences in "wealth" among traditional Tiruray, nor is there any institutionalization of power. *Kefeduwan* are not "chiefs" or "headmen." The distinguishing characteristic of a *kefeduwan* is his or her ability to participate actively in the discussion at a *tiyawan*. This makes one a legal authority in traditional society. In all other ways the *kefeduwan* are like their fellow Tiruray. They carry on the same daily activities as all other people: they farm their swidden and help in their neighbors' fields, they hunt, they fish, and they gather wild foods in the forest just as do those who are not *kefeduwan*. Any person who learns to speak in the metaphorical rhetoric of *tiyawan*, who is recognized as an expert in Tiruray custom and law, and who is accepted by his companions as a trustworthy representative in formal discussions will be known as a *kefeduwan*. In Figel, some seven persons were considered to occupy this status.[7]

Kefeduwan never meet all together as a formal council of any sort, but together they may be considered to comprise the fundamental legal authority structure of the traditional tribesmen and the most revered of them stand at the pinnacle of public esteem. Tiruray exogamy rules and the propensity to marry women from far places means that throughout the Tiruray region there is a sizable network of *kefeduwan*, men and women who know each other well. The larger integration of traditional Tiruray society beyond the neighborhood work association is through this network and not through kinship (clans, etc.) or political institution (chiefs, kings, etc.).

The other principal authority role in traditional Tiruray society is that of the *beliyan*. The Tiruray conceive of the cosmos as populated by two kinds of people: those you can see, *keilawan* or "humans," and those you cannot see, *meginalew* or "spirits." Just as there are many tribes of humans, there are also many tribes of spirits, living in various regions of the cosmos and possessed of various sorts of spiritual charisma. Some classes of spirits are mean and treacherous by nature, but most—like most humans—will not bother a person who does not bother them. Thus, the Tiruray view the spirits, by and large, simply as other people, with whom one must have ongoing social relations. The problem is that the spirits cannot usually be seen by the humans, and it is therefore all too easy to offend one, even when taking the greatest care. Not seeing a spirit, one may bump into one, or throw a spear at one when hunting, or tramp on one's belongings. If offended, spirits retaliate by making the human sick, and this is seen by traditional Tiruray as the primary origin of illness.

The *beliyan* is a shaman who has received the particular charismatic ability of seeing and speaking to spirits. Like *kefeduwan*, *beliyan* may be of either sex. When asleep, his or her soul is able to leave the body, to go about, and to converse with spirits. This means that the *beliyan*, or more precisely his soul, can travel throughout the various regions of the cosmos, going beyond the sky to discuss general matters with *Tulus*, the spirit who created the universe, or seeking out offended spirits nearby home to settle disputes between them and his or her Tiruray followers. This is done in *tiyawan* between the shaman and the spirits, so that the religious leader may be understood in part as a kind of *kefeduwan*, one who specializes in formally settling legal matters with spirits rather than with humans.

There is a second aspect of the work of the Tiruray *beliyan*. In addition to his shamanic duties, he also presides over the central ritual activity of traditional Tiruray. This is the *kanduli*, a communal meal, held by neighborhoods at four different points in the agricultural year—at the very beginning of the annual cycle when the swiddens are marked off, at the first harvest of corn, at the first harvest of rice, and at the end of the rice harvest, which time is seen as ending the Tiruray year as well. At these feasts, under the direction of the shaman, each family in the neighborhood mixes some of the rice from its swidden with some of that from every other family's fields—so that when the rice is cooked and eaten, each person will eat a bit of rice from each neighbor's field he or she worked on during the cycle, and everyone that helped on a given family's field eats some of their rice. It is this cooperative work which, as I noted earlier, sociologically defines the "neighborhood," and the *kanduli* are indeed powerful and recurring symbolic dramatizations of neighborhood interdependence.

III

In contrast to the traditional neighborhood of Figel is the Tiruray community of Kabàkabà, which represents the other side of the shift from tribal to peasant life currently sweeping through Tiruray society. To understand Kabàkabà, and the very different social milieu which it represents, something of the recent history of the area must be sketched out. Traditionally, as I have noted, the Tiruray lived in relative social isolation. They protected their forested and mountainous homeland against unwanted intrusions, allowing only the entrance of certain ritually approved Maguindanaon Muslim peddlers from the surrounding Cotabato lowlands. During the present century, however, with the advent first of American rule and then Philippine independence, this self-imposed and self-enforced sequestration has largely been broken down. A large area of traditional Tiruray territory has been occupied by Christian and Muslim homesteaders from the lowlands, and with them have come far-reaching changes in the social and physical setting of Tiruray life.

Most of the forest cover of this area has been cleared, eliminating the possibility of shifting cultivation and replacing it with sedentary plow farming as the dominant agricultural regime. The population density on the land has increased dramatically, and many familiar peasant institutions of lowland Filipino life have been established: Christianity and, to a lesser extent, Islam, a variety of commercial enterprises, a network of markets, a system of schools, Western dress, roads, the municipal offices of the Philippine government, the factional intrigues of Philippine politics, and the use of English and major lowland Philippine vernaculars.

Faced with—and somewhat overwhelmed by—all these transformations in their natural and social environment, the Tiruray of the area have been forced either to adapt or leave. Many families simply packed up and moved, finding a new home deeper in the mountains where the forests still remained and where their traditional way of life could still be pursued. Others stayed and, like their surroundings, changed. Kabàkabà is a community of Tiruray who have stayed behind, who have given up many of their traditional ways, and who, in the radically new context, have learned to become Filipino peasants.

The opening up of the now heavily acculturated part of the Tiruray area—roughly its northernmost third—began soon after the beginning of

American sovereignty at the turn of the century. Irving Edwards, a Bostonian who served in the islands first as a captain in the Philippine Constabulary and later with the Department of Education, took the Tiruray as his lifetime interest, married a Tiruray woman, and for over 40 years virtually single-handedly represented American rule and influence among them. He was dedicated to breaking down what he conceived of as their "primitive isolation," to bringing them into "the modern world," and to establishing among them what he could call "law and order." To achieve these ends he pursued three main policies: attracting lowland Filipino settlers and homesteaders, building up a system of schools, and introducing Christianity.

Captain Edwards publicized the region as ideal for homesteading, and in the mid-1910s Ilocanos from northern Luzon began a migration to the Upi Valley (the heart of the acculturated Tiruray area) which has continued to this day. Beginning with a few families, by World War II hundreds of Ilocano households had been established there, and by 1967 there were over a thousand Ilocano homesteaders in the valley. Visayans—mostly Ilonggo—began coming in sizable numbers after the war, and soon rivaled the Ilocanos in number. With the encouragement of Captain Edwards, who supervised the building of a road in 1919 from Cotabato City to the valley, these settlers titled their landholdings under the homestead laws, cleared the forests, and began plowing. Those Tiruray who remained in the Upi area were encouraged to do the same. A number of Tiruray families did obtain title to valley land, but over the years almost all of them have lost their titles to the more aggressive and sophisticated homesteaders, so that by 1960 virtually all plow-farming Tiruray in the homesteaded areas were working the land of Ilocanos or Ilonggos as tenants.

The first of many government primary and elementary schools begun by Captain Edwards was established in 1916, and by the end of the 1920s some ten others dotted the hills and valleys around Upi. Three more were built in the 1930s, and another 40 since the war. A few Tiruray graduates of these schools stayed on as teachers, but, until recent years, most instruction was given by lowlander Filipinos recruited to serve "on the frontier." The school curriculum stressed fluency and literacy in English and a more Filipino, less Tiruray, life style. The most influential school was the Upi Agricultural School, begun by Captain Edwards in 1919, where from the beginning Tiruray were taught to use and care for carabao work animals and to engage in the sedentary plow agriculture of their "more modern" Ilocano and

Visayan neighbors.

At the same time that Captain Edwards was beginning an educational establishment among the Tiruray and encouraging the inflow of Christian lowland homesteaders, he sought to bring Christian missionaries to the area to work among the Tiruray. He first approached the Roman Catholic Church to send a priest, but was informed that they could not afford such a venture at that time. He asked the Methodists, and they too were sympathetic but financially unable to assign a missionary. His third try was with the Philippine Episcopal Church. In 1921, the Episcopalians sent an American missionary from Zamboanga to survey the situation and in 1926 they opened a mission with a resident priest in Nuro, the principal town of the Upi Valley. From there they began a widespread string of chapels and preaching stations in nearby Tiruray communities. Episcopal work has remained strong in and around Nuro and by 1967 six to eight priests—several of them Tiruray—were holding services in some 50 communities. Nuro, since World War II, has become the center for vigorous Roman Catholic activity among the homesteader population. Like the Episcopalians, the Catholics operate medical facilities and an academic high school in Nuro, and they have begun a number of primary schools for the Tiruray. Protestant missionary work and church building has also been very substantial.

Under American rule, Maguindanaon Muslims also began to penetrate the mountains. Taking advantage of the *pax Americana*, they started in the 1920s to settle, along with the Christian homesteaders, in what had earlier been strictly Tiruray territory. The immigration of Maguindanaon settlers grew more intense during the next decade, and with Philippine independence after the war, their noble—or *datu*—class took control of municipal political power in Upi as well as in the Cotabato lowlands. In general, the Tiruray have managed to get along fairly well with the Christian homesteaders, but age-old antagonisms between the Tiruray and the Maguindanaon have continued to fester and relations between the two have been strained at best. The Muslims look down on the Tiruray as people of low worth; the Tiruray regard the Maguindanaon as troublesome bullies. Some few Tiruray in the acculturated area have become tenants on Muslim farms, but most have preferred to work for Christian landlords, to whom they look for protection against the politically dominant Maguindanaon.[8]

Ecologically, the single most devastating change that has come with this inpouring of outsiders into the Tiruray world has been the systematic clearing of the forest cover over the occupied area. Both the Christian and the Muslim lowlanders have relentlessly cut back the trees to open their fields, and even those Tiruray who in the early days held land titles were taught by Captain Edwards to clear their property for plowing. By World War II, major portions of the Upi Valley and much of the hills and slopes northward had been deforested. This process continued in postwar years, and then—in the 1960s—was enormously increased by the introduction of intensive large-scale logging operations.

In the late 1950s, the national Department of Forestry began assigning logging franchises throughout the forestland of the municipality of Upi. Cleared land, where farming or grassland were already established, were designated as "released for alienation or disposal" and the forests were divided into "classified timberland" or "unclassified public forest." By 1966, however, *all* unreleased areas—public forest as well as timberland—had been divided into concessions for logging operations. In doing this the government took no notice whatsoever of the existence of the traditional Tiruray population residing in scattered hamlets throughout these forests.

Beginning at the fringes of the Upi Valley, easily accessible by the provincial road, the logging concessionaires began to fan into the forests and strip away the commercially highly valuable large trees, then truck them down to the Tamantaka River at the northern foot of the mountains, from where they were floated to coastal pick-up stations, sold, and loaded onto Japanese ships. When Tiruray were encountered living in a section of forest a logging company had decided to cut, they were harassed into evacuating or, if they proved reluctant, threatened with arrest as "squatters" on the company's franchised land. By the late 1960s hundreds and hundreds of Tiruray families had been displaced and forced either to retreat farther into the mountains beyond the penetration of the loggers and the "modern world" or to give up their traditional way of life and find work as tenants somewhere upon the cleared land.

All these various and complexly interrelating changes in their social and natural environment form the context within which the Tiruray who stayed experienced profound acculturation. With their forests now gone, shifting cultivation was impossible and most became plow farmers on other people's land. With so many of their traditional rituals now obsolete, most became Christians. Unable to cope with Philippine municipal law and Muslim political power, their traditional legal system withered. The once central leadership roles of the *kefeduwan* and the *beliyan* soon faded from social importance. One by one, Tiruray families in the affected area saw their swidden-based neighborhoods dissolve, and found themselves seeking new kinds of relationships with a landlord locally, and thus ultimately, with a wider world.

Tribal life continued along its old patterns far back in the mountains, but those Tiruray who chose to stay in the region of rapid change—by 1967 probably some 15,000 out of a total population of just over 26,000—had become Filipino peasants, living in communities such as Kabàkabà.

IV

In 1967, there were some 69 persons in 12 families ("pots") living in the community of Kabàkabà, and viewing it as their *inged*, the word which in discussing Figel I glossed as "neighborhood." It is an *inged* to them in the sense that they live near each other and will occasionally help each other with farm work, in the sense that they daily associate more with each other than with people who live elsewhere, and in the sense that they all work a tract of land owned by the same person. But Kabàkabà is not a neighborhood in the traditional Tiruray sense of being a cooperation group for shifting cultivation. On the whole, each family here works its own assigned part of the total land—which belongs to someone living elsewhere—and is living and working where it is because that landlord has given it tenancy status. Some of the Kabàkabà families are related, but they are not there primarily because of these relationships but rather because it is in Kabàkabà that they were offered a piece of land on which to live and farm.

The shift of the meaning and use of the term *inged* manifests a basic shift which has occurred in the orientation of these Tiruray toward the land and toward other people. In Figel, among traditional Tiruray, the critical social relationship with regard to subsistence and settlement was that of neighbor and neighbor. There land was an essentially free good, and could be thought of as a given. In Kabàkabà, and throughout the acculturated, peasantized area, land is a very scarce commodity and is allocated at the will of those who own it. Thus the critical social relationship has become that of tenant and landlord. One's neighbors—the other tenant families on one's landlord's property—are the given factor.

The land on which the Kabàkabà neighborhood stands belongs to

89

Hamilton Edwards, the older son of Captain Edwards and his Tiruray wife. Hammy—as he is known to all in the area—manages the Tiruray Cooperative Association in Nuro and lives in Mirab, a small village with a Tiruray and a Muslim section, located seven kilometers north of Nuro on the road to Cotabato City. Kabàkabà is located some three kilometers off that road to the east of Mirab, to which it is linked by a foot and carabao trail.

Hammy's Kabàkabà land covers a little over 26.5 hectares, and is bounded on all sides by land owned by other people. The terrain is similar in contour to that of the Figel area—the hills a little less steep—but is entirely deforested. Most land which is not the site of a house is in cultivation; what little remains is covered with grasses and weeds.

Just as Figel's history was typical of how a traditional neighborhood comes into being, so too the history of Kabàkabà's formation is typical of the way in which peasant Tiruray communities come into being.

In 1947, Cora Edwards, Hammy's sister, purchased the piece of land now owned by Hammy. It had been cleared and farmed before the war, but was unworked grassland when bought in 1947. Angì came in 1948 to be Cora's tenant and began to work part of the land. He is distantly related to Cora through her grandmother, but this relationship played no role in his becoming her tenant; he was given a place to work because he needed land and Cora needed tenants. In 1953, Entuh—unrelated to either Angì or Cora, but hearing that she was a fair and sympathetic landlord—moved from a nearby farm to Kabàkabà as her tenant. Entuh's brother and his family came at the same time and worked for Cora for two years, then moved to a farm along the coast.

In 1955 Hammy purchased the land from his sister agreeing to keep Angì and Entuh. He immediately installed several additional and unrelated tenant families, who stayed for awhile then drifted away to other places. In 1956, Tandang married a daughter of Entuh's sister and Entuh persuaded Hammy to give him part of the Kabàkabà land to work. Kantér came in 1961, and with him his two sons, Butê and Sasù; all three brought their families and settled in as Hammy's tenants. Kantér is a distant cousin of Angì's wife, but this did not influence his coming. He and his sons were simply looking for good land and a good landlord.

Bekey, a brother of Hammy's mother, who had been doing wage labor in Cotabato City, approached Hammy in 1963, and, expressing a desire to return to farming, was given a piece of the Kabàkabà land. Hammy asked his

90

uncle to serve as a sort of unofficial supervisor of his various tenants there.

Early in 1965, a man named Endah transferred to Hammy's land from a nearby farm where he had found the landlord difficult to work for. With him came his brother-in-law, Atoh. They erected, and two years later still shared, a single house, though Endah affirmed that he would "soon" build one of his own when he could afford it. Later that same year, Tayetéy married a daughter of Kantér and was given a piece of Kabàkabà land to farm for Hammy. A few weeks later, his father, Dalalagan, asked to be Hammy's tenant, was accepted, and transferred his family to Kabàkabà. They moved into Tayetéy's house, although they maintain separate kitchens. Dalalagan too plans to build his own house "shortly."

Finally, in 1966, Lumbayaw—a bachelor and half-brother of Kantér—moved in with Kantér and began helping him with his farming. A year later Hammy gave him tenant status and some land to work of his own. While Lumbayaw continues to live in his brother's house, he thereafter did his own cooking.

Thus was completed the roster of family heads which in 1967 constituted the Kabàkabà neighborhood. The total population of the community includes them and their nuclear families plus some seven additional persons. Bekey has taken into his "pot" a divorced niece of his wife, along with her two children and three younger siblings. Tandang's younger brother lives with him and helps him in the fields, and similarly, a niece and nephew of Kantér live and work with his family.

The freedom with which traditional Tiruray arrange themselves into various settlements within a neighborhood is not available in tenant communities such as Kabàkabà. Houses are assigned sites by the landlord in a scatter over his land, and the neighborhood-settlement distinction simply disappears. So too does the sharing typical among households of a traditional settlement—rooted as it was in forest subsistence practices.

The 12 families of Kabàkabà occupied in 1967 only nine houses—although, as mentioned above, the norm of a single family per household was still recognized. They had all built houses which were essentially similar in construction to the houses of Figel, but with several features modified in imitation of lowlander houses in the Upi Valley area. The traditional ramp window-doors of the Tiruray house, for example, have been replaced with more Western style swinging doors and windows, and the notched log ladders by pole step ladders .

91

None of the Kabàkabà men have more than a single wife. Polygamy—never very common even in traditional areas—has virtually disappeared in the acculturated region under fierce Christian opposition.

Whereas a Figel swidden is highly generalized, producing scores of different cultigens, the fields of Kabàkabà are specialized in four crops: rice, corn, tomatoes, and onions. The last three of these are grown almost entirely as cash crops to be sold in the Upi market. Typically, a Kabàkabà farmer grows one crop of dry upland rice each year. If, as is commonly the case, he is using not only Hammy's land but one of his carabaos as well, he must divide his yield evenly with Hammy. If he owns his own work animal, he gives the landlord only 20 percent. The tenant's share of the rice crop is entirely for his own family consumption. In addition to rice, Kabàkabà people crop corn several times each year, and keep continuous patches going of tomatoes and onions.[9] After giving Hammy his share of these crops—the basis is the same as for rice—and after keeping a small amount for their food, they sell the rest in the market for cash. With the income, they then purchase additional rice and other food for their table. Thus, whereas Figel crops are almost all eaten by those who grow them, most of the production from Kabàkabà is intended for sale. Clearly, while market relations are only of minor significance to traditional Tiruray, to the people of Kabàkabà markets have become of central importance.

While Figel swidden cultivation is importantly supplemented by hunting, fishing, and gathering, these activities play almost no role at all in the acculturated Tiruray region. The forests in the traditional interior abound with game and the Tran Grande River is rich in aquatic resources; neither condition obtains in the peasant area. The forests are almost entirely gone, cleared for plow farming or obliterated by logging. A few small gallery thickets, which contain some birdlife and an occasional monkey, remain here and there along rivers and streams, but wild chickens, pigs, and deer—the game most prized by forest hunters—have long ago disappeared from the fields. Similarly, with the forests gone, the possibilities for gathering wild resources for food, building materials, and the like have largely disappeared.

The rivers of the acculturated region are seriously depleted of wild aquatic life and, moreover, their banks are privately owned property, no longer freely accessible. Neither of the small creeks that run through Kabàkabà contain fish of significant size or in significant number and there is no effort whatsoever to exploit them for food. The nearest river of any size, which

92

might serve as a source for fish or crustaceans, runs some six kilometers away to the southwest. The Kabàkabà Tiruray say they would like to go there to fish, but it is far and, besides, they would be accused of trespassing. Furthermore, with the larger population now along its banks, it has been pretty well "fished out."

In short, the subsistence economy of Kabàkabà is radically altered from that of traditional Tiruray society. Kabàkabà people do not and cannot subsist almost entirely on their own domestic production, and the essentially non-Tiruray marketplace is no longer viewed as a foreign, minor, and peripheral extension of that production. Just as fully as the Ilocano or Maguindanaon homesteaders in the Upi Valley, the Tiruray there have become full participants in the rural Filipino market system.[10]

Earlier I discussed the *kefeduwan* (legal) and the *beliyan* (religious) as the central authority roles in traditional Tiruray society. In the areas where acculturation is well advanced, both of these roles are in marked decline. They continue to exist, with little real authority and in greatly truncated form, but those playing the central leadership role in peasant Tiruray society are unquestionably the landlords—persons who, with few exceptions, are not themselves Tiruray.

Landlords take a strong proprietory and paternalistic position with regard to any disputes involving their tenants. When a difficulty emerges among one's tenants, they bring it to him or her for settlement. Similarly, the landlord represents the interests of his tenants in conflicts of any sort with people of other communities or with the municipal government. Kabàkabà people try especially hard to keep out of scrapes with the Upi police or any other representatives of the local Muslim political structure, but they rely on their landlord to intervene or negotiate for them when they do get involved.

Thus, in the matter of disputes, the traditional institution of the *tiyawan* has faded from significance in the socially more diverse and complex acculturated area. With it has disappeared the old importance of the role of the *kefeduwan*. Even the entirely intra-Tiruray affair of marriage-making has changed significantly in such a way as to diminish the effective place of the *kefeduwan*. Instead of two kindreds through their *kefeduwan* negotiating in *tiyawan* a complex brideprice of traditional ceremonial goods, the practice has become almost universal in the peasantized region for the father of the bride simply to ask for a cash payment from the father of the man. Certain highly respected elder persons are still referred to by folks as *kefeduwan*, and

93

their wisdom occasionally consulted, but little functional role remains for them. Under the new conditions, the traditional Tiruray legal system has simply ceased to exist.

In much the same way, the role of the shaman, the *beliyan*, has faded from importance. The communal feasts and the planting and harvesting rituals—where the shaman was prominent and central—were all associated with swidden cultivation and have no place in plow-farming practices. Most of the Tiruray in the acculturated region have become Christian. With few exceptions, to be sure, the conversions have been nominal and institutional. The old animistic world view has continued to exist under a thin veneer of Christian belief and terminology, but, nonetheless, the old leadership and ritual expression has been replaced with the Christian institutions characteristic of the wider Filipino nation.

Thus, the two main social authority roles of Tiruray society are, in the region of marked change, virtually gone. In their place are a new set of elite positions which derive their character from participation not in Tiruray traditional life, but in the Filipino mainstream. As of 1967, some 48 Tiruray had become schoolteachers, three were ordained priests, two were lawyers working with the national government, two were nurses, and one had become a government agriculturist.

V

Change is characteristic of human society and Tiruray life prior to this century doubtless adapted and evolved in various ways. But the forces which came to play upon it in the decades I have described in this paper brought about not only more rapid and disorienting change but a fundamental shift in structure.

In the period before the 20th century—the period which I have referred to as traditional—Tiruray society was self-contained and integral; in Kroeber's terms, it was "tribal." Its subsistence system of swiddens, hunting, fishing, and gathering provisioned Tiruray society with only the slightest influx of outside goods. Its religion was its own. Its leadership was entirely Tiruray and followed entirely Tiruray patterns. In this sense, life is still tribal in isolated traditional communities such as Figel.

But in Kabàkabà, Tiruray society has come to have a very different

94

relationship to the larger Philippine world. There, Tiruray subsistence is embedded in and dependent upon a system of markets which stretches nationwide and a local class of non-Tiruray landlords. Their religion, like that of so many other people throughout the Philippines, is Christianity. They vote in the elections of Philippine municipal, provincial, and national government, and are followers of the national political parties. They send their children to public schools. They have learned to speak the national language. Tiruray society there is no longer an entity apart in mountainous seclusion; it is—as Ilocano or Ilonggo society has been for several centuries—one of the many subsectors of a larger Philippine society. Tiruray society in Kabàkabà is "peasant." Its people are no longer Tiruray and Tiruray alone—they have become Filipinos.

Notes

[1] Kroeber (1948: 284).

[2] See, for example, Dalton (1972).

[3] See Schlegel (1972), which is chapter 2 of this book.

[4] Traditional Tiruray residence is predominantly patrilocal, although there are instances of matrilocal residence, especially when the man's kindred had not been able to complete the brideprice for his wife. Neolocal residence also occurs, when there is felt to be an important economic advantage to be had elsewhere than the man's or woman's parental neighborhood. The kinship is bilateral. For a fuller account of Tiruray kinship terminology and behavior, see Schlegel (1970: 16-22).

[5]For a detailed description of the Tiruray subsistence system and the transformation it is undergoing, see Schlegel (1977; 1979).

[6]For a full account of the Tiruray legal system, see Schlegel (1970b).

[7]Grace Wood Moore's interpretation of *kefeduwan* as headmen or chiefs with dependent followings over which they have political power is, in my opinion, incorrect and misleading. See Wood (1957) and Moore (1972).

[8]Relations between the Tiruray and the Maguindanaon Muslims have, in recent decades, frequently degenerated into open warfare. The armed conflict between Muslims and the Philippine government began a whole new and terrible phase in 1971, following a flurry of Tiruray-Maguindanaon fighting.

[9]Tomatoes and onions, with corn, are the main cash crops of Kabàkabà—a sort of neighborhood specialization. Other communities grow various other marketable crops such as cowpeas, mongo beans, or pechay.

[10]A study of the diet in these two communities, with data on all food eaten—both kind and amount—by two typical and randomly selected adult males revealed dramatically this change. For example, the Figel individual's diet for the year contained 104 different kinds of food which he had grown or obtained from wild sources and only nine which he bought at market—of which six were snack foods consumed at the market itself. The Kabàkabà individual, in contrast, grew or gathered 26 kinds and purchased 33. See Schlegel and Guthrie (1973), which is chapter 8 of this book.

Chapter 7

TIRURAY TRADITIONAL AND PEASANT SUBSISTENCE

A Comparison

My 1979 book Tiruray Subsistence: The Transformation from Shifting Cultivation to Plow Farming *set out to describe in some detail and with quantified data both the traditional subsistence system (swidden, hunting, fishing, and gathering), as it was experienced in Figel, and the peasantized subsistence system (sedentary plow farming under tenancy), as it was lived in Kabàkabà. In doing this, I was also able to make some systematic comparisons of the two systems with regard to relative efficiency, productivity, and resulting diet. This essay is a summary article setting forth the essential contrasts and comparisons. It was first published in a book edited by Harold Olafson,* Contributions to the Study of Philippine Shifting Cultivation, *published in 1981 by the Forest Research Institute of the University of the Philippines, Los Baños.*

Many observers from differing perspectives have viewed shifting culti-vation (swidden) systems in the humid tropics in a negative way. In 1957, the Food and Agriculture Organization (FAO) staff wrote a report which stressed the low carrying capacity of most forms of shifting cultivation and the harmful effects on the environment which result from exceeding this capacity. Appealing for research and technical effort to overcome its serious problems, they called tropical shifting cultivation

> . . . the greatest obstacle not only to the immediate   increase of agricultural production, but also to the conservation of the produc-tion potential for the future in the form of soils and forests.[1]

In the eyes of a multitude of forestry operators, agronomists, and government officials, shifting cultivation in most tropical nations has been regarded as wasteful of potential, destructive of the environment, technologically backward, and typical of a more "primitive" level of society than that of settled agriculturists.

Social scientists, at least in recent years, have tended to be more generous in their evaluation of shifting cultivation, recognizing numerous positive aspects and stressing that under traditional circumstances many forms represent a highly stable adaptation to the tropical environment, which is essentially conservative of both the fertility of the soil and the integrity of the forest.[2] Nevertheless, much of the social science literature continues to refer shifting cultivation systems to a level somewhat below that of settled agriculture, and to regard swidden cultivators as rather more "backwards," plow farmers as more "developed." Characteristic, for example, is this quote from a cultural geographer otherwise fully sympathetic to shifting cultivation as an adaptation:

> . . . shifting cultivation, in broad terms, was the elementary and pioneering cropping system used by the early agricultural occupants of many forested regions all over the world. . . . The substitution of a better and more advanced cropping system has been slow, gradual and related to the rest of group culture. . . . Where group cultures have not advanced shifting cultivation remains the standard practice.[3]

"Better and more advanced" in what way? The assumption that sedentary plow agriculture is a "higher" form than shifting field cultivation need not derive from an ethnocentric bias. The usual basis for the assumption is that, compared to shifting cultivation (with its hand tools and dibble sticks), settled permanent field agriculture (with its work animals and plows) is technologically more complex and sophisticated and thus, by its very nature, a more productive and less prodigal use of the land.

Assumptions of this sort are all too often merely challenged by counter assumptions. The purpose of this paper is to question the notion that sedentary plow cropping necessarily marks a productive "upgrading" of shifting field slash-and-burn cropping by presenting neither a logical nor an ecological argument but rather some data, drawn from my research among the Tiruray.[4]

The Tiruray

The Tiruray have lived in their forested mountains, with swidden and foraging subsistence system, since time immemorial. Even their myths of origin tell of no different location or way of life. And they lived there, practicing their shifting cultivation system, without evident damage to the environment. Since the beginning of the present century, Tiruray forests—especially in the Upi Valley and northwards—have been cleared away and permanently destroyed, but this is not the work of traditional Tiruray social and subsistence patterns but of a whole range of severely acculturating forces.

The story of cultural contact and associated ecological change began with late 19th century Spanish military and missionary efforts in the Cotabato area, touching the northern fringes of Tiruray society. American occupation, to which the Spanish gave way early in this century, introduced very profound influences on and acculturation among the Tiruray. The decades under American rule, interrupted by World War II and ending in 1946, when Philippine independence was recognized, were a time of vigorous efforts to break down Tiruray isolation and to introduce "modern" ways and institutions.

The area directly affected was roughly the northern third of the Tiruray homeland. Here a system of public primary and elementary schools were established, many along the road which was built to connect the lowlands to the Upi Valley, others on a network of trails reaching well into the interior. At the southern Upi end of the road was established an agricultural school, where stress was placed on the technology, the skills, and the ideals of sedentary plow farming as an advance over the "primitive" swidden-keeping traditional in the area. The Tiruray in the American-administered region (effective administration dropped off sharply as one went beyond the roads and the valley into the southern interior) were taught to title formally and thus to "own" land, a concept entirely novel to them. They were led to clear away the forests so the land could be properly cultivated. They were instructed in the care and use of the carabao as draft animals. All of this represented the technical side of American presence, but stress was also placed on the Tiruray's conversion to Christianity from "paganism," on the introduction of Western institutions and ideas of "law and order" to supplant the traditional legal system, on use of English, and, by the mid 1910s, on an ever-increasing immigration to the area of Christian homesteaders from Luzon and the Visayas and of Muslim homesteaders from the Cotabato lowlands.

The rapid and profound acculturation which characterized the American period was well advanced in the region when the Republic of the Philippines assumed sovereignty, and thereafter its main characteristics were preserved and, to an extent, extended. In particular, the ecological changes were intensified when, in the 1950s, logging franchises were awarded and timber-cutting activities began to push far into the still forested and traditional interior south of the Upi Valley.

The effect of all these major changes on Tiruray society was to divide it, in a sense, into two. Many families in the acculturating area, having lost control of their social and physical environment, moved away from all the change and sought to continue their accustomed life style in the remote forests with communities of still traditional people. At the time of my research (in the late 1960s), I estimated that somewhat less than half of the Tiruray, perhaps some 10,000 persons, were still living in the forests according to the old way of life. The remainder, in the northern area, had become a Tiruray version of Philippine peasantry. They had taken up plow farming, had been drawn deeply into the cash-and-credit market economy typical of Philippine peasant society, had begun sending their children to school, had adopted Christianity, and had learned to settle their disputes in Philippine municipal courts or through the intervention of their usually non-Tiruray landlords. Between the two extremes of society—the "traditional" and the "peasant" sectors—there is no clearly marked cultural fault line but rather a loosely defined zone of transition in which is found people with greater or lesser contact with and involvement in the new institutions, practices, and ideas.

The two neighborhoods where I did my research—one "traditional" and one "peasant"—are representative of these two sectors of Tiruray society. Figel, located deep in the interior, some three kilometers inland and 20 kilometers up the course of the Tran Grande River from its mouth, is the community where subsistence patterns were studied as typical of the traditional Tiruray. Figel neighborhood comprised some 126 persons, in 31 nuclear families and 29 households, living in seven hamlets. All the people of Figel are related to each other by some consanguineal or affinal tie, though this fact does not reflect any Tiruray rule of custom, but rather the historical development of the community through voluntary association for work cooperation along lines of kin closeness.

Figel is elevated about 120 meters above sea level in a major riverine valley, surrounded by dense forest. Humidity is constantly high (mean near 75 percent), temperatures show very little seasonal variation (most daily readings fall between 22° and 37° C), and rainfall is relatively heavy and well distributed throughout the year (peaking in July and August). The surrounding jungle supports a wide, dense, and highly varied assemblage of wild animals and birds, and is itself a typical greatly diversified tropical rain forest.

Kabàkabà, located just north of the Upi Valley, in the heart of the acculturated area, is the neighborhood whose subsistence activities were studied as typical of the peasantized Tiruray. As with the other peasant Tiruray neighborhoods, it is smaller than its traditional counterparts, and was comprised of 69 persons in 12 family-households. Kabàkabà is a neighborhood to its members in the sense that they live near each other, help each other occasionally with farm work, and associate with each other more intensely than with people living elsewhere. But it is, of course, not a neighborhood in the traditional sense of people who associate together to cooperate in shifting cultivation.[5] Here each family lives and works where it does because their landlord, who lives elsewhere, has given them tenancy status and assigned them a part of his or her land. Some of the Kabàkabà families are related, but they are not there primarily because of those relationships but because it is there that they were offered a piece of land to work.

Kabàkabà stands on a slight slope some 500 to 580 meters above sea level, and, except for some very small thickets along the Kabàkabà Creek, is completely cleared of trees. Most of the area is in cultivation; the rest is covered with grasses and weeds. Two small creeks run through Kabàkabà, and the nearest sizable river is some five kilometers away. The neighborhood land is a three-kilometer hike from the main provincial road, where the residence of the landlord is located. Humidity, temperature, and rainfall are not significantly different from those in Figel (some 50 kilometers to the south). Since the rain forest is gone, gone too from the Kabàkabà environment is the abundance of plant and animal resources available to Figel people.

The Figel Traditional Subsistence System

The traditional Tiruray subsistence system, as represented by Figel, consists of shifting cultivation, hunting, fishing, gathering of wild resources, and marketing. These will be briefly described in this section, and the comparable aspects of the peasant system at Kabàkabà in the next section.

The cycle of shifting cultivation activities carried out by Figel people is broadly similar to many other "slash-and-burn" regimes found elsewhere in the humid tropics. The first stage in the process of replacing temporarily the native forest vegetation with humanly selected cultivates is site selection. From the end of the previous year's harvesting work until approximately mid-December, the men of the community range the surrounding forests primarily to hunt but also to keep their eyes open for sites for their next swiddens. [6] Each person looks for a place for his family's new swidden according to certain well-defined criteria: vegetation type (virgin forest is preferred), soil type, land topography, distance from the residential settlement, etc. [7] Traditional Tiruray have no sense of private or corporate land ownership; all sites are occupied by right of usufruct only for as long as the crops introduced continue to bear. Selected sites are discussed informally among the Figel men, and then, in late December, are ritually marked. [8]

The next main stage of the shifting cultivation cycle is cutting away the natural vegetation and consists of two main activities. First, through January, the lower underbrush growth is slashed. This is done cooperatively, the Figel neighborhood men working together on each of their swidden sites in turn until all have been slashed. Next, by similar cooperative effort, the large forest trees on the sites are felled. This generally occurs during February and March, and involves labor which is both quite heavy and dangerous. Once all the sites are cleared, they are allowed to dry for a number of weeks, then are burned—again by the men—in late March and early April.

Planting of new vegetation, its care, and its harvesting make up the next stage of the cycle and involve the neighborhood's women as well as its men. Corn is planted by the women in the swiddens first—usually it is April by this time—in rows a meter or two apart. [9] Rice is planted next, after the corn has begun to sprout. [10] The Figel swiddens are planted in turn, the men dibbling and the women laying the seed and cooking food for the planting party. As the grains grow, each man plants a wide variety of fruits, vegetables, spices and the like in his swidden amidst and around the rice and corn. Finally a

102

second corn crop is planted, again by the women, after the main rice crop has been harvested (July through September). Occasionally the field is divided at this time between corn and a cash crop such as tobacco. Care of the planted swidden occupies the women many hours in weeding and the men major portions of time in fencing, building scarecrows and guarding against wild pigs, monkeys and rice birds. Harvesting corn is done by women on their own swiddens, but harvesting, hauling, threshing, and drying rice require the efforts of both men and women and are, again, community cooperative efforts on the neighborhood's fields one after the other.

After the second corn crop is harvested, a variety of residual productive plants continue to be harvested for some time. There is, however, no further working of the site; it is allowed to lie fallow so that the process of natural reforestation may take place. New swiddens, the following year, are cut in another place from primary or secondary forest, with no effort to return to any specific site previously cut by the same individual. Shifting of the fields is thus random and not rotational in character.

These different activities—selecting, cutting, burning, cropping and fallowing—make up the normal shifting-cultivation cycle of traditional Tiruray.[11] They form, however, only one part of Figel's total subsistence activities. The rain forest all around contains plentiful wild game which is hunted and many wild plants which are gathered. Similarly, the Tran Grande River abounds in fish, eels, crustaceans, and the like. The Figel people are shifting cultivators, to be sure, but they are also hunters, fishers, and gatherers and these foraging activities produce a significant portion of their subsistence base.[12]

All adult males hunt regularly, and in certain seasons—especially June to December, when their major swidden labor is finished for the year—hunting and fishing are their main activities. The most highly prized game are wild deer and pig, though monkey and a great variety of fowl are also taken. Many different methods, traps, snares, and weapons are employed, mostly by single individuals, although in some instances several men will go hunting together, and certain hunting techniques are specifically group activities. Fishing contrasts with hunting in that it is done by both men and women, though by the latter to a much lesser extent. Again, a large variety of techniques, traps, and devices are employed and a considerable number of different aquatic resources are taken from the river and they form, with the meat from hunting, a significant portion of the traditional Tiruray diet.[13] Finally, with

103

regard to resources taken from wild sources, it would be difficult to overstate the importance to the food base of wild flora gathered from the forest. The forest contains a variety of nourishing edibles: starches, vegetables, seeds, nuts, and fruits, as well as other goods needed for daily life from firewood to medicines.

The last element in the traditional subsistence system is marketing. Although the great majority of the goods needed and used by Figel people are either grown, hunted, or gathered, certain items come from outside the indigenous Tiruray world and are purchased at a coastal market. Traditional Tiruray do not weave or smith, so clothing and iron tools must be purchased, as well as salt, cooking pots, bedding, ceremonial exchange items, and the like.[14] Marketing thus plays a role, although a very small role, in the total subsistence activities. Figel people use the market at Salaman, Lebak, one of the several weekly markets found in peasant towns of the province. Their commitment to the market, however, is completely peripheral. They typically buy only such goods as they cannot produce or procure domestically, using cash they receive on the same market visit in exchange for forest products, especially stripped rattan. Figel people are, in fact, quite unaware of the market as a place for maximizing economic advantages. Their focus is entirely on meeting one's family's specific immediate needs, and therefore the Salaman market is viewed by Figel Tiruray solely as a minor adjunct to their domestic subsistence base, a source of a few special goods.

The Kabàkabà Peasant Subsistence System

The peasant Tiruray subsistence system, as exemplified by Kabàkabà, consists of sedentary plow agriculture in place of traditional shifting cultivation, virtually no hunting, fishing or gathering, and a greatly expanded interaction with and dependence upon the market.

A Figel shifting cultivator is, in a real sense, his own person, but a Kabàkabà plow farmer is not; he works as a share-crop tenant for a landlord. In the usual arrangement, the landlord provides the land and the working animal, in return for which he receives half of each crop grown by his tenant.[15] The landlord of Kabàkabà is considered to be fair, even generous, by his tenants in the administration of this relationship, and such mutual respect is quite common throughout the area.

104

The four main crops grown in Kabàkabà—rice, corn, onions, and tomatoes—are not integrated into a single cycle of activities as was the case in Figel, but are grown separately by every family on discrete plots, with each plant following its own timetable.[16] Each family normally grows a single rice crop each year, but may plant as many as three corn crops. Also, different families plant and harvest corn at different times throughout the year. A typical year's grain cropping for a given family might be as follows:

January	Begins plowing a rice field.
February	Harvests corn planted in the previous year's rice plot. Prepares and plants the field again in corn.
March	Finishes preparation of the rice field and plants it.
April	Begins another corn field.
July	Harvests corn planted in February.
August	Harvests the rice field.
September	Replants the rice field in corn.
October	Harvests the corn planted in April.
November to December	Goes to harvest rice on Upi Valley homesteaders' paddies, on a share basis.

Tomatoes and onions are, like corn, grown steadily throughout the year, without any seasonal rhythms. The work of growing and of selling these crops falls on the women. In a typical year, a family may harvest as many as four crops of tomatoes and five of onions.

Thus the Kabàkabà men are kept busy preparing fields by repeated plowing and harrowing, planting grains, plowing and cultivating corn fields, caring for the carabaos and bulls, and dragging sacks of grain to their landlord's house and to market. The women are occupied with weeding in the rice and corn fields, with care of the onion and tomato plots, with harvesting on all the various family fields, and with selling their vegetable produce in the market.

In Kabàkabà, exploitation of wild resources is virtually nonexistent. The tiny thickets along the creek and the surrounding cultivated fields allow some limited shooting of certain birds. Occasionally a monkey may appear and raiḍ a corn field, but the area has long ago been cleared of all wild pigs, deer, and chickens. Similarly, the creeks and the Mateber River, some five kilometers away, contain very little food resources, being either too small or long ago "fished out" due to the larger adjacent population. Thus, Kabàkabà people do almost no hunting or fishing. They buy their fish and meat in the local Nuro market. And, in like manner, with the forests gone so too are the main sources for any significant gathering, so virtually all of a family's needs must be bought in the market. The contrast between the subsistence activities of Figel and Kabàkabà is nowhere more striking than in the almost total elimination of the hunting, fishing, and gathering factors.

On the other hand, market relations assume vastly greater significance in Kabàkabà. In their peasantized subsistence system, the marketplace has become a central economic institution. Kabàkabà people use the market in Nuro, some seven kilometers away in the Upi Valley—a weekly peasant market dominated, like the Salaman market, by Muslim and Christian vendors and patrons. There they both buy and sell many more things than the Figel people do in Salaman. Farming needs such as work tools, rope, sharpening stones, rubber and rattan, and a whole range of household needs such as kerosene, kitchenware, flashlights and batteries, soap, starch, medicines, and the like—all must be purchased. Paper and pencils and other school needs are bought for the children, along with candy and comic books. Moreover, in marked contrast to Figel people, the Kabàkabà families obtain much of the food they eat at the Nuro market. Sugar, coffee, tea, oil, lard, bread, vegetables (other than onions and tomatoes), as well as meat and dried fish, garlic, pepper and other spices—all come from the market. Even the starch staples must be purchased for daily eating as most of what is grown is sold. Cash to buy these items is thus a major need for Kabàkabà people, not the peripheral sort of thing it was to the Figel Tiruray, and the most common way of obtaining the needed cash is from sale of their share of their farm produce. In short, the market has become a major and crucial feature of the peasant Tiruray subsistence system. By no means have the Kabàkabà people entered the market arena on favorable terms. Like many peasant farmers elsewhere in the world, they are subject to the exploitation of countless middlemen and to a temporal cycle of selling cheaply at harvest time and buying dearly between harvests. But whatever the terms, the market and money have become central institutions in their lives.

Comparisons and Conclusions

In this final section, I will present several sets of figures in terms of which these two subsistence systems may be compared. But, first, I would say a word about Tiruray feelings and perceptions. The shift from the traditional way of life in the forest to that in an acculturated community such as Kabàkabà has not only involved a marked change in subsistence activities, but it has also meant a radical reworking of many aspects of Tiruray existence: diet, dress, and demeanor, as well as political, legal, and religious relations. The Tiruray involved in this shift have not found it congenial; rather, they have resisted becoming Filipino peasants. Where possible, many have tried to avoid the changes by moving away from them to a place still isolated in the forest. But others have been caught in the changing social and physical environment and have had to change with it, whether they cared to or not.

Why this resistance to change? The reasons are surely complex, and involve, at the very least, a natural and quite human dislike of seeing a long-accustomed and happy way of life altered to something new. But the Tiruray also state quite openly a very pragmatic basis for their opposition to peasant-ization. They say that, as they perceive the situation, they are being forced to work much harder than the traditional Tiruray and for less return. The data from my research suggest that they are quite right in this perception.

In the course of my fieldwork, my field assistants and I took careful measurements of many aspects of the subsistence systems in both Figel and Kabàkabà. Among these we recorded the amount of corn and rice seed planted in all the various fields of the two communities over a year's time (Figel in 1966, Kabàkabà in 1967). We also recorded the yields from each of these plantings. Putting these yield figures together with field sizes, we can compare the yields between the two systems in the customary local units of cavans per hectare. Taking rice first, the swiddens of Figel produced an average of 51.9 cavans per hectare (which is 2038 lbs/acre).[17] In contrast, the Kabàkabà plowed fields yielded an average of 38.2 cavans per hectare of rice (1499 lbs/acre)—a decrease in productivity per hectare between the two rice systems of some 26 percent.

A similar situation is found when corn yields are compared. Figel swiddens produced an average of 19.6 cavans per hectare (979 lbs/acre) in the first corn planting, and 21.2 cavans per hectare (1059 lbs/acre) in the second corn crops. Taking the two together, the average yield for corn from Figel swiddens was some 20.3 cavans per hectare (1014 lbs/acre) in the year we recorded. This compares with an average yield of corn crops on Kabàkabà plowed fields of 18.7 cavans per hectare (934 lbs/acre)—again a decrease in productivity of almost 10 percent.

There is a problem with the customary cavans per hectare yield figures when one compares swiddens with plowed fields. The latter are typically completely cleared and fully planted, whereas the swiddens are covered with varying amounts of fallen tree trunks, stumps and other debris from the slashing and burning activities—so that a hectare of swidden is really less than a hectare of usable, plantable plowland. And one swidden is not the same in this regard as another. Thus, swiddens do not compare well with each other or with plowed fields in terms of yields given in produce per hectare. To counter this difficulty, I also put the yield figures for both Figel and Kabàkabà together with the amounts of seed planted, thus giving a "seed-yield ratio" for each swidden and each plowed field. Looked at in these terms, the decline between the two systems is even more pronounced. In rice, the Figel swiddens averaged a seed-yield ratio of 1:40, whereas the Kabàkabà fields averaged a seed-yield ratio of 1:28, a decrease of some 30 percent. The corn seed-yield ratios are 1:124 for Figel and 1:95 for Kabàkabà, a decline of 23 percent.

These yield comparisons become even more meaningful when joined to labor input figures. My research team kept records of average labor costs of the various activities involved in the shifting cultivation cycle in Figel and in the plow agriculture system in Kabàkabà. These records show that the labor invested by a typical Figel family on a one-hectare swidden through an entire annual cycle amounts to some 2500-2600 hours of work. But the comparable round of rice, corn, and cash crop plow cultivation for a year on a hectare of land costs a Kabàkabà family almost twice that amount of labor, some 4970-5000 hours.

In sum, the two systems of cultivation differ greatly in both yields produced and labor expended, and the shifting cultivation form requires much less labor and yields much greater results. I did not keep comparable quantitative records on the exploitation of wild animal and plant resources, but clearly such figures would only exaggerate further the differences noted in agricultural yields. Hunting, fishing, and gathering are of great importance in the traditional forests and of virtually no significance in the cleared peasant area. The labor hours which exploitation of wild resources cost traditional people are balanced by the time required of peasant Tiruray for their greatly expanded market activities.

These data clearly render plausible—in hard economic terms—the general Tiruray reluctance to shift from their traditional ways to the peasant life of a plow-farming tenant. And they surely suggest that settled permanent field agriculture, however more complex technologically, cannot be considered *a priori* to be necessarily a more productive regime than shifting cultivation.

Notes

[1]FAO Staff (1957:9)

[2]See, for example, Conklin (1957), Spencer (1966).

[3]Spencer (1966: 4, 5).

[4]For a full and detailed report on Tiruray subsistence activities, both traditional and peasant, containing the complete data underlying this essay, see Schlegel (1977). For a somewhat abridged version, with most of the descriptive detail but less of the quantitative data, see Schlegel (1979).

[5]The word *inged*, which I gloss as "neighborhood," is specifically used in Kabàkabà, but with awareness of its shifting meaning.

[6]Although I give the approximate timing of activities here in terms of calendar months, the traditional Tiruray do not base their timing decisions on the Western calendar but on a system of star sightings and an indigenously conceived zodiac. See Schlegel (1987), which is chapter 4 of this book.

[7]Actually, not every family cuts a swidden every year. In 1966, the year

I kept records in Figel, some 17 swiddens were established by the 29 households. The following year 25 swiddens were cut, and this was considered by the Figel people to be a more typical year in this regard.

[8]Traditional Tiruray neighborhoods celebrate a corporate ritual feast four times during the cultivation cycle: before marking new sites, following the first corn harvest, at the beginning of the rice harvest, and upon completion of the rice harvest. These rituals give expression to the corporate interdependence of the neighborhood families with each other and with the various spirits associated with food production. A variety of lesser individual ritual acts occur at different points in the cycle. These ritual performances are almost entirely gone in Kabàkabà.

[9]Seventeen different varieties of corn are distinguished, with maturation periods ranging from two to four months. Twelve varieties are soft and sweet, known as "Tiruray corn," and five varieties are the harder so-called "Cebu corn."

[10]The Tiruray distinguish some 137 different varieties of upland, dry rice: 25 of these are glutinous varieties, used mainly in ritual contexts, and the other 112 are non-glutinous. Some of each are planted in every swidden, usually in approximately the ratio of 1:10.

[11]In addition to this normal cycle, two alternate successions are practiced, though only infrequently. Additional grain crops may be introduced to a swidden beyond the normal one rice and two corn crops. Or, a field in an early stage of fallow may be slashed and burned. It is recognized that both these practices greatly increase the possibility of a terminal succession of the plot to grassland, rather than to re-establishment of the forest, and they are therefore strongly discouraged.

[12]Identification of all wild flora and fauna regularly exploited, as well as all domesticated plants grown on swiddens, is given in Schlegel (1977; 1979).

[13]A record of all food consumed by representative Figel and Kabàkabà families over an entire year, along with a nutritional analysis of the two diets,

is presented and discussed in Schlegel and Guthrie (1973), which is Chapter 8 of this book.

[14]Prior to the establishment of markets in the early part of the present century, Tiruray obtained such goods through a system of ritually established trade-pacts with Maguindanaon Muslim peddlers; see Schlegel (1972), which is chapter 2 of this book. Also (1977; 1979).

[15]Other arrangements pertain when the tenant owns his own working animal (the division then giving 80 percent to the tenant) and when the tenant uses a working animal owned by some third person (40 percent for the tenant, 40 percent for the owner of the animal, 20 percent to the landowner). These sharing schemes apply to rice, corn, and entire fields of cash crops. Vegetables grown in small doorstep gardens need not be shared with the landlord, but he has full rights to the entire produce of any permanent crops, such as coconut or fruit trees.

[16]The reduction of the highly diversified swidden produce—on the average some 30-60 plant types in a single field—to a mere four crops is one of the most striking of the many contrasts between the two systems. Not every peasant Tiruray family specializes in onions and tomatoes, as do the Kabàkabà families, but the growing of only one or two cash crops besides corn is the common practice. Others commonly grown include peanuts, beans of various sorts, eggplants, pechay, and mustard. These, like corn, are grown specifically to raise cash in and for the market. In Figel, where the forest is still intact, families could raise cash for the market by preparing forest products, such as rattan lashing, for sale. The peasant shift to cash-crop growing may thus be seen as a quite direct adaptation to the loss of the forest.

[17]The specific data from which the averages given in this essay are derived may be found in Schlegel (1977).

Chapter 8

DIET AND THE TIRURAY SHIFT
FROM SWIDDEN TO PLOW FARMING

Early in the time that I was doing my fieldwork in Figel and Kabàkabà, I met Prof. Helen Guthrie, a nutritional scientist from Pennsylvania State University. We discussed the way in which the diets had altered so radically from the one community and way of life to the other and we concluded that we had a rare opportunity to collaborate on a significant and relatively unusual comparative study. Armed with a balance scale and other appropriate tools for observing, measuring and recording just what people were eating in the two communities, I set forth to gather a year's data from each. This information was in due course analyzed by Prof. Guthrie and our joint work resulted in the present essay. It first appeared in 1973 in the journal Ecology of Food and Nutrition *(vol. 2, pp. 181-191), and has subsequently been reprinted in a 1980 book* Food, Ecology and Culture *by J. R. K. Robson.*

During 1966 and 1967, one of us (S.A.S.) who is an anthropologist, conducted field research on the subsistence activities of two Tiruray communities, each representing a contrasting pole in the ongoing transformation of Tiruray society. The first community was Figel, a neighborhood of traditional Tiruray living along the banks of the Tran Grande River, deep in the forested mountains. There, the old way of life was still being maintained and the traditional economy of swidden farming, hunting, fishing, and gathering from the forest was intact. The other contrasting community was Kabàkabà, a neighborhood in the heavily acculturated northern grasslands. In Kabàkabà, the forests had disappeared and with them, of course, not only swidden farming but almost all opportunity to hunt, fish, or gather. The Tiruray there were plow-farming peasants.

112

Methodology

Systematic data were collected by one of us (S.A.S.) on the social organization, the farming practices, the hunting, fishing, and gathering activities, and the market relations obtaining in both communities. As a part of this research, qualitative and quantitative dietary data were recorded from mid-August 1966 to mid-August 1967 of the food consumed by one typical and randomly selected adult male from each community. At the time of the field work, Silu, from traditional Figel, was 35 years old, a man of medium frame, with a weight of 59.1 kg., and 1.7 m. tall. Bekey, of peasant Kabàkabà, was a 54-year-old man also of medium frame; he weighed 64.1 kg., and had a height of 1.7 m. Both of these men were about 5 cm. taller in stature than the average Filipino man of their age,[1] and each weighed somewhat more. While it was not possible to have the subjects given a physical examination to assess health status, observations over the period of this study and the previous year indicated that both men were robust, in good health and able to carry out a full range of activities associated with hunting and farming. At no time during this period were they ill or unable to work nor was there any observable change in their weight over the period of observation.

The record of food eaten by Silu over the year was kept meal-by-meal. One of the research group was always present in Figel. The same procedure was followed in recording Bekey's meals for the first month and a half, after which Bekey (who, unlike Silu, is literate) kept his own data, with an observer present approximately one-third of the time. The average size of portions was determined by use of a small balance. In the case of foods eaten frequently, a series of weighings was averaged. In the case of foods seldom eaten over the year, all readings were averaged. In both cases, weights over 5 gms. were rounded off to the nearest 5 gms. Every effort was made to record the total food intake for both men. While it is conceivable that some food obtained by gleaning was not recorded, it is the opinion of the investigators that the recorded food patterns corresponded so closely to those of the total community and utilized available food resources that any foods overlooked would represent a very small portion of the total intake. The fact that Silu frequently reported that he had nibbled berries or other fruit while hunting enhances our confidence that these men were fully cooperative in helping the investigator to obtain a complete record.

The data from this research were then tabulated and coded by a

113

nutritionist (H.A.G.). The nutrient content of the diet was calculated by computer using data from tables of food composition prepared for use with Philippine foods.[2] A comparison of the nutritional value of the diet of a traditional Tiruray and that of a peasant Tiruray and an evaluation of their nutrient intake in relation to recommended dietary standards for use in the Philippines, form the basis of this paper.

Results and Discussion

In the traditional Tiruray neighborhood of Figel, there were 126 persons in 31 families scattered over seven settlements. In the acculturated peasant community of Kabàkabà there were 69 persons in 12 families living in a single settlement as tenants of an absentee landlord.

Tiruray divide food conceptually into four categories: starch staples including rice, corn, yams, and taro; viands or side dishes which include meats and vegetables; spices such as salt and garlic; and snacks including fruits, coffee and rice cakes. The foods eaten by Silu and Bekey are listed in Tables I, II, and III.

The food record of Silu showed that during the year he ate some 42 different types of domesticated food including six starch staples, 19 viands, eight spices and nine kinds of snack food. All were grown on his swidden and garden. In addition, wild food derived from hunting, fishing and gathering provided one starch, 52 viands, one spice and eight different snack foods to give both variety and substance to his diet.

Bekey, the Kabàkabà man whose diet was recorded, is typical of the peasant Tiruray. Like his neighbors, he grew one rice crop per year. His share of this crop was consumed entirely by his own family. In addition, he cropped corn several times a year, and grew tomatoes and onions the year round. After giving the landlord his share of these latter crops, and keeping a small amount for food, he sold the balance for cash in the market. With the income, Bekey purchased additional rice and other foods for his table. A few starches and vegetables were raised in a garden by the house, but Bekey's dependence upon the market as a source of his food was in marked contrast to Silu's virtual independence of the market. While Silu had grown or gathered 104 different types of food, and had purchased only nine, Bekey grew or gathered 26 kinds, and bought 33. The loss of the forest is of major

114

significance: Bekey did virtually no hunting or fishing, and very little gathering. Only four items of food in his diet came from wild sources, in contrast to the 62 kinds of wild food exploited by Silu.

Bekey grew three starch staples (rice, corn, and bananas) and purchased four kinds (rice, sweet potatoes, manioc, and taro). He utilized four wild viands, grew 13 types and bought 13. Five kinds of spices were grown and seven were purchased. One type of snack food was grown and nine were bought. Wild sources contributed no staples, spices, or snacks of any sort to Bekey's diet.

Most Tiruray who are familiar with both the traditional and the peasant way of life are quick to assert that the traditional diet is far superior to the peasant diet. In part this is because of certain sentimentality toward the "old way," but primarily it is because of the far greater variety of foods available to those who are able to exploit the forest and the rivers. Nutritional analysis, however, does not support the popular view. (See Table IV.)

In the following discussion of the nutritive intake of Silu and Bekey, the recommended dietary allowances for Filipinos are used as a reference point recognizing that these are more applicable to groups than individuals and that failure to achieve these levels of intake does not necessarily imply dietary deficiencies. Only by a biochemical and physical examination of nutritional status is it possible to judge nutritional status.

Silu, who depended to a larger extent on wild food and had very little access to processed food, consumed a diet which provided less than half the energy recommended for a moderately active adult male living in the Philippines.[3] The distribution of calories from protein, fat, and carbohydrate was 13, 13, and 74 percent respectively. These values represent only half of the 25 percent from fat and considerably more than the 50 to 60 percent from carbohydrates usually recommended. While the percentage of calories from protein falls within an accepted level, the fact that the diet provided only half the recommended energy level suggests that much of the protein would be diverted for use as a source of energy rather than for its unique role in the maintenance of tissue. Since over one-third of the protein came from wild food, primarily animals, the *quality* of the protein was assumed to be high. Processed foods contributed only insignificant amounts of protein. While no values are available for the NDpCal% of the wild animal protein consumed, it is to be expected that the values would not differ materially from those of the protein from domestic animals. The values for the latter range from

NDpCal% = 5-11.

The fat was contributed mainly from animal sources. If fatty acid patterns of wild animals can be assumed to resemble those of domestic animals, then much of the fat was composed of saturated fatty acids. In western societies, there is concern over the adverse effects of these in the etiology of atherosclerosis. However, this is greatest when associated with a high fat and high calorie intake, obesity, and the stresses of modern life. None of these conditions are present in the case of Silu.

In contrast, Bekey who had an energy intake only slightly below recommended levels, obtained 10 percent of his calories from protein, 30 percent from fat, and 60 percent from carbohydrate. This distribution is similar to that found among people in modern societies. When comparing this diet to that of Silu, we find that it has a much higher fat content and a slightly higher protein and carbohydrate content. In this case the protein was obtained primarily from domestic and processed foods, with insignificant amounts coming from wild sources. The total protein intake of 57 g, derived largely from cereals such as rice with reported NDpCal% values of 1.8 to 5.8,[4] is assumed to be of lower quality than the animal protein in Silu's diet. It approximated the recommended level of 63 grams for Filipinos. This recommendation is based on the fact that a significant portion of the protein commonly found in the Philippine diet is cereal protein and is higher than the recommendation would be for higher quality protein. The fat content of Bekey's diet was derived primarily from animal sources. In this case, the saturated fat in a diet more adequate in calories may have a greater atherogenic potential. However, the fact that the carbohydrate was primarily complex cereal starches rather than simple sugars should reduce this possibility.[5]

As is true in many tropical countries,[6] the calcium content of the diet was quite low. For Bekey, who used canned milk occasionally, the calcium intake was close to the recommended levels of 500 mg. Silu, however, obtained most of his calcium from wild plants and achieved an intake of only 60 percent of the recommended level. While we do not have information on the oxalic acid content of these green leafy vegetables, there is a high probability that certain of them at least will be similar to spinach, chard and rhubarb with sufficient oxalic acid to reduce the availability of the calcium in these foods.

The relatively low iron requirements of adult males were met by the diets of both men. Bekey, with a large intake of rice and beans, had an intake well above the recommended levels. Should these men have suffered from

116

intestinal parasites reportedly affecting 80 percent of the population, however, it is entirely possible that the iron requirement would have been higher. These diets would not meet the higher iron requirements of adult women.

While the vitamin content of the diets of the two men fell below recommended levels, they were not grossly inadequate. Thiamin requirements were satisfied primarily through the use of rice and beans. The rice was, of course, not enriched but it was also not milled at all. Wild and processed foods contributed only minor amounts. The inadequate riboflavin intake in Bekey's diet reflects the less extensive use of meat.

The intake of ascorbic acid, which is solely provided from plant materials, is acceptable for both men with practically all being provided by domesticated foods. Some plants, such as papaya, provided much Vitamin C (123 mg/per portion) and were consumed sufficiently often to make a significant impact on total intake. Wild plants were not major suppliers of ascorbic acid. Some, such as the wild aquatic morning glory, *urai*, and jute, which are relatively rich sources, were eaten in such small amounts so infrequently that their contribution over a period of a week or a year was minor. Green leafy vegetables, such as *pechay*, *taro*, and *lindeg*, were among the richest providers of this vitamin.

Vitamin A came almost exclusively from plants, green leafy vegetables being a major source. For both groups, wild foods, especially *urai*, wild aquatic morning glory, jute, and *taro*, provided about one-fifth of the Vitamin A value. For Silu, with an extremely low fat and a marginal Vitamin A intake, there is reason to question the efficiency of absorption of the precursor of this fat-soluble vitamin.

The extent over a period of 52 weeks to which the diet of these two men met the recommended dietary allowances[7] is given in Table V.

In interpreting these data, it is important to recognize that these recommended allowances represent levels of intake that will promote a high level of health in essentially all Filipinos. Failure to meet these levels is not necessarily an indication of malnutrition. In fact, there is considerable evidence that people with chronically low intakes undergo a series of physiological adaptations which enable them to function adequately at the lower intake.[8] From the data it is evident that the diet of Silu fell below the recommended levels in over 40 weeks for all nutrients except iron and Vitamin C. These nutrients were provided in less than recommended amounts in over half the weeks of the study. Similarly Bekey had a diet which failed to meet the recommended allowance for all nutrients except iron, Vitamin A, and Vitamin C in over 40 weeks of the 52-week study. The latter were adequate in about one-third of weeks and iron every week.

When the dietary intake is evaluated on the basis of the number of nutrients provided in inadequate amounts in each week of the study, it again becomes evident that, while both diets were below suggested standards, Bekey's diet was slightly better than Silu's (See Table VI).

An analysis of the source of the various nutrients showed that domestic foods provided at least 90 percent of the intake of calories, fat, carbohydrates, thiamin and ascorbic acid, 80 percent of the iron, and 50-70 percent of the protein, riboflavin, and niacin intake for both men. For Silu who engaged in significant hunting, fishing and gathering, wild foods provided a higher proportion of all nutrients except fat, carbohydrate, thiamine, and ascorbic acid than they did for Bekey. This reflects the fact that the wild foods that provided seven percent of his energy intake were generally animal or green leafy vegetables. Both of these are considered to be protective foods, in that their contribution to the intake of several nutrients exceeds that of their contribution to energy. Processed foods, which contributed only four percent of the calories in Silu's diet, made a larger contribution only for calcium and protein, a function of the occasional use of canned milk. For Bekey, the contribution of wild foods was insignificant except for Vitamin A, for which they contributed one-fourth of the intake. Processed foods, however, provided about one-fourth of the calcium, protein, and niacin, but less than one-tenth of the intake of other nutrients.

The range of the intake from week to week was quite wide. An attempt to identify a seasonal basis to the fluctuation revealed no consistent pattern for either man. For Silu, high intakes were from three to eight times greater than the low weekly intake for all nutrients except Vitamin A and thiamine. For both of these nutrients comparable values were 13 and ten. For Bekey, the range from high to low was smaller, being less than three-fold for all nutrients except fat, Vitamin A, riboflavin, and thiamin. The high weekly intake for these four nutrients was five times the low intake. This suggests that the nutrient intake of the traditional Tiruray, who augment their swidden farming with considerable exploitation of wild resources, is much more erratic than that of the peasant Tiruray, who deal with a market on a regular basis. Such variations in intake do underline the need for caution in generalizing from short-term food intake records in a traditional society.

118

Conclusions

Clearly the shift from swidden to plow farming among the Tiruray has involved major changes in diet and nutritional sources. These forms of cultivation may be said generally to occur in quite different ecological settings: swidden in a dense forest abounding in wild life, and plow farming on cleared fields. Thus the transformation of the economic base of society from one to the other will necessarily show concomitant changes in the subsistence practices and resources beyond a mere alteration of agricultural method. Without the forest environment, the possibility of hunting, fishing, and gathering wild resources drops off markedly. And, on the other hand, dependence on a market and on the acquisition of purchased foods increase markedly. These various shifts are reflected quite clearly in the data of this study,

Two further conclusions seem to emerge from the Tiruray data: First the Tiruray presumption that, because of far greater variety, the diet of the traditional people (Silu) is considerably better than that of the people who have adopted the peasant culture (Bekey) is not substantiated by the data in this study. They may for sentimental and nostalgic reasons value the former more highly, but the data indicate unambiguously that the subsistence patterns of Kabàkabà result in more consistent diets of higher nutritional value.

Since both Bekey, whose nutrient intake falls slightly below recommended levels in a number of nutrients, and Silu, whose intake is seriously below these standards, are vigorous and healthy men with no overt evidence of nutrient inadequacy fully able to live active and strenuous lives, it appears that they have adapted to a lower level of nutrient intake than that recommended for men in the Philippines or that the recommendations have been set at an unnecessarily high level. It is also possible that with higher nutrient intakes these men would have experienced a higher level of health and vitality with greater resistance to disease and increased life expectancy.

119

Table I

Plant Foods of the Tiruray

Tiruray name	English name	Sources: Wild (W). Domesticated (D) or Purchased (P)		Use	Average size of single portion	Portions throughout year	
		Figel (Traditional)	Kabakaba (Peasant)			Silu (Traditional)	Bekey (Peasant)
afus	a bamboo	W	W	young shoots are eaten	200 g	2	8
agum	urai	W	W	young leaves are eaten	30 g	22	34
babasal (fruit)	squash	D	D	fruit is eaten	240 g	10	87
babasal (leaves)	squash	D	D	young leaves are eaten	70 g	—	3
badak	jackfruit	D	D	fruit is eaten	225 g	2	30
bahar	fishtail palm	W	W	palm heart is eaten	210 g	22	—
bana	long beans, anapai, cowpeas	D	P	pods and seeds are eaten	80 g	17	39
baris	a small palm tree	W	W	palm heart is eaten	200 g	7	—
bawang	garlic	D	P	used for flavoring only	trace	12	15
bayabanu	soursop	D	D	fruit is eaten	80 g	12	—
bayabas	guava	D	D	fruit is eaten	50 g	9	—
bayinggusan	lemon grass	D	D	used for flavoring only	trace	41	—
belatung	mongo bean	D	P	beans (not pods) are eaten	100 g	22	122
belatung kayew	pigeon pea	D	D	beans (not pods) are eaten	100 g	1	—
bisuwilas	common bean (white and red)						
bongo (flesh)	coconut	D	D	beans are eaten	100 g	4	—
		D	D	soft white flesh from			
bongo (milk)	coconut milk	D	D	young nuts is eaten; flesh is grated and squeezed with water to yield an oily white milk which is used as a broth to cook vegetables	45 g	26	28
bongo (oil)	coconut oil	D	D	the milk (see previous entry) is boiled until it becomes oil and is used as a cooking oil	120 g	81	547
					trace	26	14

120

burungkut	pomelo	D	D	similar to, and is eaten like, an orange	25 g	10	—
didif	a fungus	W	W	flesh is boiled and eaten	20 g	11	—
fagew	a fern	W	W	fronds are eaten	15 g	4	—
farey	rice	D	D/P	grain is boiled and eaten	425 g	321	730
feriya	snake gourd, ampalaya	D	D	fruit and leaves are eaten	10 g	—	4
feriya uwak	wild ampalaya	W	W	fruit and leaves are eaten	10 g	2	—
fusow	a plant similar to taro	W	W	young leaves are eaten	10 g	3	—
giya	ginger	D	P	used for flavoring only	trace	3	14
kafaya	papaya	D	D	if mature, fruit is eaten; if young, is cooked and eaten as a vegetable	150 g	17	43
kafé	coffee	D	P	bean is boiled and drunk	200 ml	68	376
kalamunding	calamansi	D	D	juice is used as a spice	trace	8	—
kalamunggay	a tree	D	D	the young leaves are eaten	15 g	4	—
kamais,	corn	D	D	kernels are eaten as grits or "on the cob"	250 g	320	68
kamangkis	tomato	D	D	fruit is eaten with other vegetables	5 g	12	646
kangkung	wild aquatic morning glory	W	W	young leaves are eaten	70 g	8	54
kelambug	a tree	W	W	fruit (very sour and green in color) is eaten	10 g	1	—
kelawag	tumeric	W	D	used for flavoring only	trace	2	1
kelubih	a small palm	W	W	the bud is eaten	25 g	5	—
kerur	jute	W	W	the young leaves are eaten	15 g	7	—
kuwey	okra	D	D	fruit is eaten	60 g	—	4
labu	common gourd	D	D	flesh is eaten	230 g	—	13
lansuna	onion, leek	D	D	stalk is eaten	5 g	39	641
lekef	a legume, similar to mongo bean	W	W	pods and seeds are eaten	100 g	1	—
lengkang (tops)	taro	P	P	young leaves are eaten	50 g	9	20
lengkang (tubers)	taro	P	P	tubers are eaten	70 g	6	2
lengoh	sesame	D	D	seeds are toasted, powdered and eaten with rice	20 g	3	—
lindeg	a herbaceous vine	D	D	the leaves are eaten	50 g	4	—

TABLE I—Continued

Tiruray name	English name	Sources: Wild (W), Domesticated (D) or Purchased (P)		Use	Average size of single portion	Portions throughout year	
		Figel (Traditional)	Kabakaba (Peasant)			Silu (Traditional)	Bekey (Peasant)
luwaf	sugar cane	D	D	peeled and chewed for the juice.	40 g	113	—
mani	peanut	D	D	nuts are shelled and eaten	60 g	1	—
mangga	mango	D	D	fruit is eaten	50 g	5	—
mangkalen	a tree	W	W	brown fruit (somewhat similar to an onion) is eaten	30 g	1	—
nongo	a rattan	W	W	the heart is eaten	30 g	15	15
referas	a mushroom	W	W	flesh is boiled and eaten	50 g	4	—
sabi	pechay, mustard	D	P	the leaves are eaten	70 g	—	31
saging (blossom)	banana	D	D	the blossom is eaten	40 g	3	32
saging (fruit)	banana	D	D	the fruit is eaten	90 g	141	148
saging (stalk)	banana	D	D	the heart of the stalk is eaten	40 g	1	—
salikuwa	songe gourd, patola	D	D	the fruit and leaves are eaten	80 g	9	22
segutung	eggplant	D	D	the fruit is eaten	85 g	127	115
tandag	chili pepper	D	P	the fruit and leaves are eaten	40 g	—	4
tegef	a tree	W	W	fruit (very similar to jackfruit) is eaten	50 g	1	—
timun	cucumber	D	D	fruit is eaten	40 g	11	—
tutang	a tree	W	W	green colored fruit is eaten	35 g	1	—
ubi (tops)	sweet potato	D	P	leaves are eaten	70 g	30	19
ubi (tubers)	sweet potato	D	P	tubers are eaten	100 g	159	107
ubi kafuk	manioc	D	P	tubers are eaten	100 g	93	92
ubi tugi	tugi yam	W	W	tubers are eaten	60 g	1	—
ufi	a tree	W	W	fruit (similar to jackfruit) is eaten	50 g	1	—

Table II
Animal Foods of the Tiruray

Tiruray name	English name	Sources: Wild (W), Domesticated (D) or Purchased (P) Figel (Traditional)	Kabakaba (Peasant)	Use	Average size of single portion	Portions throughout year Silu (Traditional)	Bekey (Peasant)
babuy	domestic pig	D	D	flesh is eaten	80 g	1	58
babuy talun	wild pig	W		flesh is eaten	80 g	29	—
banla	a fish	W		flesh (lean) is eaten	15 g	1	—
bekesan	python	W		flesh is eaten	40 g	1	—
begiyang	goby fish	W		flesh (fatty) is eaten	30 g	12	—
belanak	mullet	W		flesh (fatty) is eaten	50 g	11	—
beleg	eel	W		flesh is eaten	50 g	123	—
belulu	sleeper fish	W		flesh (lean) is eaten	30 g	75	—
busék	a bird	W		flesh is eaten	25 g	1	—
fait	barb (fish)	W		flesh (fatty) is eaten	20 g	66	—
fak	frog	W		legs are eaten	20 g	1	—
figek	mountain bass	W		flesh (very fatty) is eaten	30 g	6	—
ibi	sailtail lizard	W		flesh is eaten	25 g	1	—
kabeg	giant fruit bat	W		flesh is eaten	20 g	1	—
kadurug	flathead goby fish	W		flesh (fatty) is eaten	25 g	2	—
katifa	freshwater catfish		P	flesh (fatty) is eaten	30 g	2	62
kelimbungan	small fruit bat	W		flesh is eaten	25 g	3	—
kelungkung	owl	W		flesh is eaten	20 g	1	—
kumang	crab	W		flesh is eaten	15 g	4	—
kurong	shrimp	W		flesh is eaten	20 g	119	—
lebuted	beetle larvae	W		larvae are boiled and eaten	15 g	2	—
lefingon	goby (fish)	W		flesh (lean) is eaten	15 g	16	—
lemeto	goby (fish)	W		flesh (lean) is eaten	15 g	2	—
lemugon	a fish	W		flesh (fatty) is eaten	30 g	1	—
manuk (eggs)	chicken (eggs)	D	D	eggs are boiled or fried and eaten	1 egg	18	7

123

TABLE II—*Continued*

Tiruray name	English name	Sources: Wild (W), Domesticated (D) or Purchased (P)		Use	Average size of single portion	Portions throughout year	
		Figel (Traditional)	Kabakaba (Peasant)			Silu (Traditional)	Bekey (Peasant)
manuk (flesh)	chicken	D	D	flesh and viscera are eaten boiled or fried	60 g	27	42
manuk talun	wild chicken	W	W	flesh and viscera are eaten boiled or fried	40 g	21	—
muted	sleeper (fish)	W	W	flesh (fatty) is eaten	50 g	75	—
odon (honey)	honeybee	W	W	honey is eaten	30 g	2	—
ramagan	spotted pomadasid (fish)	W	W	flesh (fatty) is eaten	30 g	1	—
ruwan	murrel (fish)	W	W	flesh (lean) is eaten	50 g	4	—
seladeng	deer	W	W	flesh is eaten	80 g	3	—
sulit	a bird	W	W	flesh is eaten	5 g	1	—
suwara	water monitor (lizard)	W	W	flesh is eaten (mostly the tail)	60 g	4	—
suwil	a fish	W	W	flesh (lean) is eaten	20 g	11	—
temaing (honey)	honeybee	W	W	honey is eaten	20 g	1	—
télék	a bird	W	W	flesh is eaten	60 g	1	—
tilafiya	leather jacket (fish)	W	P	flesh (fatty) is eaten	50 g	32	32
tingo buwaya	a fish	W	W	flesh (lean) is eaten	15 g	1	—
tukob	a fish	W	W	flesh (lean) is eaten	20 g	18	—
ubal	monkey	W	W	flesh is eaten	60 g	12	—
uber	a fish	W	W	flesh (lean) is eaten	50 g	4	—
unafan	a fish	W	W	flesh (fatty) is eaten	40 g	14	—

124

Table III

Processed Foods Consumed by the Tiruray

Tiruray name	English name	Sources: Wild (W), Domesticated (D) or Purchased (P)		Use	Average size of single portion	Portions throughout year	
		Figel (Traditional)	Kabakaba (Peasant)			Silu (Traditional)	Bekey (Peasant)
asukar	sugar	P	P		10 g	19	367
bagoong	bagoong	P	P	very salty sauce of tiny fishes	10 g	—	23
binageré	vinegar	P	P		5 g	—	5
efan	bread	P	P		20 g	3	10
enor	cooking oil (canned)	P	P		60 g	—	18
fangus	dried fish	P	P		25 g	8	401
faniyalam	faniyalam	P	P	a kind of rice cake made of rice flour mixed with sugar and fried in coconut oil	60 g	—	1
gatas	milk	P	P	used in tea or coffee	30 g	4	1
korenbif	corned beef (canned)	P	P		20 g	6	4
miki; bihon	rice noodles	P	P		70 g	—	27
sa	tea	P	P		250 g	2	1
saldinas	sardines (canned)	P	P		15 g	2	62
saldinas	squid (canned)	P	P		15 g	—	1
serbésa	beer	P	P		350 g	—	1
suman	suman	P	P	a glutinous rice cake mixed with sugar and salt	90 g	—	3
timus	salt	P	P		5 g	648	788
tuba	tuba	P	P	a palm wine	1500 g	1	1
udang	dried shrimp	P	P		10 g	—	5

125

Table IV
Number of Nutrients in Which Diets
Failed to Meet Recommended Levels

Number of nutrients	Number of weeks (Traditional)	(Peasant)
4	2	4
5	3	3
6	7	11
7	2	17
8	21	17
9	17	0

Table V
Number of Weeks in Which Diets Failed to Meet
Recommended Dietary Standards

	Silu (Traditional)	Bekey (Peasant)
Energy Intake	52	42
Nutrients		
Protein	52	46
Calcium	52	49
Iron	29	0
Vitamin A	44	34
Thiamine	40	49
Riboflavin	47	52
Vitamin C	32	29

Notes

[1]Matawaran, Gersavasio and de Gala (1966).

[2]Food and Nutrition Research Center (1964).

[3]Intengan (1970).   [4]FAO (1970).

[5]Yudkin (1967).   [6]FAO (1962).

[7]Intengan (1970).   [8]FAO (1962).

126

Chapter 9

REPERCUSSIONS OF NAIVE SCHOLARSHIP

The Background of Local Furor

This little essay came about because of a minor controversy which was entirely local to the Tiruray region and was certainly no more than a small tempest in a tiny teapot. But it did raise some interesting issues about how one comes to ethnographic "knowledge" and about the use of proper informants, and I wanted to comment on these points. The article appeared in the Philippine Sociological Review *in 1967 (Vol. 15, Nos. 3-4, pp. 108-113). I am more than a little embarrassed and chagrined by that essay, because in a footnote I foolishly, and I think irresponsibly, named the author of the magazine article whom I was criticizing so harshly. His intentions were, as I did say in the article, the very best and in fact he went on to do graduate studies and has become a highly professional and respected social scientist. I wish I could rewrite 1967 history and delete that footnote! I have done the best I know how to do so now, by leaving it out of this version of the essay, and by adding my belated apologies to him. That said, I think the essay—suitably amended—is still fun and enlightening. It tells of one of the consequences of the rapid social change which the Tiruray have experienced, change which has left acculturated Tiruray generally knowing very little about their ancestors' traditional way of life.*

The Tiruray have never enjoyed a very "good press." To be sure, not much about the Tiruray has been printed at all; but what has been published would, in most cases, strike a literate Tiruray as both inaccurate and unfair.

In an article entitled "Around Mindanao" in the March 16, 1901 issue of *Outlook Magazine*, Phelps Whitmarsh, for example, ignoring or perhaps ignorant of a half-decade of drought and disease, noted that the Tiruray near Cotabato City had long been in a state of famine. Stating that it was clearly the direct result of the withdrawal of the Spanish Jesuit mission at Taman-taka, he summed up the Tiruray as

. . . a lazy, worthless lot apparently degenerates. They live together indiscriminately, fathers sometimes taking their own daughters to wife, and are without doubt the lowest of the Mindanao peoples.

Although he did not share Whitmarsh's colorful fantasy that the Tiruray were given to incest (the one offense, in fact, in Tiruray native law which carries an obligatory death penalty), a lieutenant of the Tenth U. S. Infantry, G. S. Turner, ended a summary of Tiruray customs prepared for the 1903 Census by informing his readers that

> ... in general they are ignorant, shiftless savages, ruled by superstition and fear, with little moral or legal restraint upon their desires or passions.[1]

I have never heard of any Tiruray reaction to these surely quite offensive statements; it is unlikely that many Tiruray, if any, ever saw them. Only a handful could read in 1901 and 1903, and they read the Spanish they had learned from the Jesuits and were, in any case, unlikely to see either the *Outlook Magazine* or the *Census of the Philippine Islan*ds.

Today, however, a great many Tiruray read English and Tagalog and, like so many of their fellow Filipinos, enjoy the various popular weekly magazines. Thus, when the *Weekly Graphic* recently carried a short half-page piece entitled "The Tirurays of Cotabato," authored by a history professor at a nearby college, it was seen and read by many Tiruray. While the article was emphatically sympathetic—expressing concern that the Tiruray "are a fast-vanishing tribe unless the government does something to save them from extinction"—it nevertheless incited a roar of protest and indignation among virtually all who read or heard of its contents. For several weeks, wherever Tiruray professionals were gathered, extant copies of that issue of the *Graphic* were sure to appear and to be passed back and forth. The alleged injustices of the article in question were the subject of almost continuous and frequently heated discussion, and such Tiruray eminences as the public relations officer of the Tiruray Welfare Association and a local Tiruray parish priest were among those aroused to address letters of adamant protest and correction to the editors.

All of this excitement resulted from a friendly sketch of Tiruray customs which was, by count, only 48 sentences long. Yet, if one goes through the article and numbers the sentences (and some have done just that), then considers their content one by one (they did that, too), one can understand all the furor and the resentment.

Sentences 1-3 locate the Tiruray as concentrated around Upi, Cotabato, and set forth the tribe as numbering some 5,000, as rapidly vanishing, and as doomed to extinction if without that government intervention. Now it is true that many of the old traditional customs of the Tiruray are vanishing as the society becomes increasingly peasantized, but it is also true that the number of Tiruray people is well in excess of 26,000, a fact as easily obtained as a copy of the 1960 Census, and that the birth rate is, in fact, rising.

Sentence 4 of the article asserts that the Tiruray are culturally similar to "the Negritos, the Manobos, the Bagobos, the Bilaans, and the Maguindanaos," groups which are hardly culturally similar to each other. The fifth sentence describes many Tiruray as "still nomadic"; no Tiruray was ever nomadic. Sentence 6 describes their diet as consisting of root crops and vegetables, but the following sentence states that as a result of contact with other tribes, "such as the Maguindanaos who have learned to go to school already," some Tiruray plant rice. Well, not only do all of them plant rice, but they have been doing so for a long, long time and have been doing so with consummate sophistication. Data from an isolated "oldway" Tiruray community, far up the Tran Grande River and quite out of contact with Maguindanaon teachers, show that the people of that community know and maintain over 130 different varieties of upland rice, and that several members of the community realized 1966 yields in excess of 50 cavans per hectare. Regarding the allegation that the Tirurays are already learning to go to school, schools for the Tiruray had been established since 1910. The Upi community itself is an offshoot of the foundation of an agricultural school for the Tiruray. Today there are no less than 48 Tiruray government teachers, besides a number of lawyers, nurses, clergymen, and agriculturists.

Sentences 8-12 make up the second paragraph of the article and deal with the Tiruray personality (they are peaceful when not angry, certainly a fact) and Tiruray religion. Most are said to worship "trees, rocks, flowers, rivers, and wild animals," none of which any Tiruray has ever "worshipped"; but some, it is reported, have been converted to Anglicanism, "the only missionary group that has penetrated the Tiruray area"—an observation that not only omits from mention the work of the Christian Missionary Alliance and of three Roman Catholic schools established specifically for Tiruray students, but even excludes the considerable mission work among the Tiruray in Salangsang, Lebak, of the United Church of Christ in the Philippines and the intensive work in the interior by the Christian Missionary Alliance.

The remaining 36 sentences are as packed with virtually unrelieved misinformation as were the first 12. Traditional Tiruray wear their hair long, but it does *not* "cascade up to the ankle of the feet" (sentence 15). Marriages are *not* arranged at birth (sentence 21). When they are arranged, the girl's side does *not* approach the boy's side (sentence 21)—it is invariably the reverse. Early marriages are *not* predicated on a desire for more children to help with the work (sentence 23). Final marriage negotiations are *not* instigated by the girl's parents (sentence 24), but by the boy's. Rice is *never* used as part of a brideprice (sentence 26). Much of the brideprice *does* go to the girl's parents (sentence 27). *Kanduli* is a religious agricultural or healing ritual and does *not* occur at marriage negotiations (sentence 29). These negotiations are *never* the expense of the girl's side (sentence 29). They do *not* take place the night before the wedding (sentence 30). The bride and groom are *not* informed that they are to be married on the morning of the wedding (sentence 33), but on the evening before. The wedding ceremony does *not* last one whole week (sentence 35). The expenses of the ceremony are *never* shared by both sides (sentence 36). During the marriage festivities, the bride and the groom are *not* kept in separate houses, and there is *no* sense of guarding the girl from any "envious spirits" (sentence 37). The *kefeduwan* is by *no* stretch of analysis or imagination anything like a Tiruray "high priest" (sentence 38)—he is a strictly secular legal authority. He does *not* have the couple sit "facing the sun" (sentence 39); they are seated facing east, regardless of the time of day, and weddings are *not* always "solemnized" in the morning, let alone at the rising of the sun (sentence 40). The sun is *not* the "god of new life" (sentence 40). The *kefeduwan* gives the couple advice, but he does *not* chant any prayers (sentence 41).

The article has only 48 sentences, of which 39 could be said to contain substantive assertions, and of those 39, 31 are simply and flatly wrong.

Now why? The author of that article certainly had no desire to get his facts awry and no intention to popularize a false picture of the Tiruray—yet he certainly did both, and it is for this reason that so many Tiruray readers of the *Graphic* became so upset about what had been written about their people. How did it happen? The explanation lies in the naïveté of the author's method of data collection.

The Tiruray, today, are not everywhere alike. In common with so many ethnic minority groups around the world, the Tiruray are undergoing rapid change in their physical and social environment and in their way of life. The Tiruray around Upi have known more than half a century of intense contact with lowland Filipino homesteaders and with American military, educational, and missionary enterprises. Over the years they have experienced varying degrees of acculturation. They have become plow farmers. They have been drawn into the cash, credit, and market economy typical of other Filipino peasants in different areas. They have adopted Western clothing. They have come to esteem formal education. They have learned to speak the local form of Tagalog. These "modernized" Tiruray have turned from their older religious ways and leaders to adopt Christianity and to follow clergy who are either American missionaries, Filipinos from Luzon or the Visayas, or, in a few cases, profoundly Westernized Tirurays. They attempt, at present, no leading role in local or national politics, but they are an important part of the constituency of those Maguindanaon or homesteader leaders who do.

In striking contrast are the diminishing but still large number of Tiruray who live either so deep in the mountains or so far up the Tran Grande River that they have remained beyond the effective range of contact, or who have retreated over the years farther and farther into the hinterlands, preferring to relinquish their traditional homes rather than their traditional way of life. Among these "remote" people, Tiruray society and culture remain quite intact. The people follow strong leaders of the old type, both legal and religious. They draw their subsistence from the rivers and the forests—fishing, hunting, trapping, gathering, and engaging in a sophisticated and highly conservative annual cycle of swidden cultivation. They wear their own style of clothing and their hair long; they speak only Tiruray; they take great pride and satisfaction in their way of life.

Between the two extremes summarized above, one does not find a marked cultural fault line, but a wide area of greater or lesser contact with and of greater and lesser involvement in non-Tiruray institutions and patterns of interaction. During the more than half-decade that I have been traveling about through a great variety of Tiruray settlements and through areas where scattered Tiruray families live amidst other sorts of settlers, I have been forcibly struck by the fact that the transformation of Tiruray society is an ongoing process along a sort of continuum of increasing structural realignment stretching from the still isolated people I have termed "remote," through various gradations of exposure to outside influences and changing circumstances, to the Upi valley area and those Tiruray who live such a thoroughly different sort of life than did their ancestors.

Roads are rapidly being completed into the most isolated areas of Tiruray occupation. Schools and chapels are being erected along the roads and deep into the interior. Homesteaders from Luzon, the Visayas, and other parts of Mindanao are penetrating ever deeper into the mountains. Although the government is trying to impose a log ban, there are still scores of illegal loggers doing great ecological damage. Such trends as these are intricately interrelated with each other and with other political, social, and economic factors which have emerged in the last half-century since American hegemony over both mountains and lowlands first forcibly broke the isolation of the Tiruray in their cordilleran redoubt and opened the area to outside interests and influences. I believe it is doubtful that in another 20 years it will be possible to locate a single Tiruray community where isolation and ecological conditions remain to permit the traditional Tiruray way of life. A once viable mountain society, now caught up in the waves and currents of what we speak of as history and judge to be progress, is rapidly becoming fragmented into an array of relatively individuated peasant families. Gone with the forests are the rich rewards of hunting and gathering, as well as the swidden mode of cultivation. The legal system which, with remarkable juristic elegance, knit together those forest farmers, and a religious system which projected their legal-moral notions to a superhuman plane of social relations, are both vanishing entirely, and with them the influential legal and religious leaders so crucial to the fabric of the old Tiruray culture. The region where the Tiruray live, the world in which they live, is becoming ever less *Tiruray* and ever more *Filipino*.

Now, if the older Tiruray forms of leadership are disappearing along with the older Tiruray social context in which they functioned so effectively, new manifestations of a Tiruray elite are appearing which are appropriate to the wider Filipino world. These include the teachers, the managers of cooperatives and credit-unions, the lawyers, the more prominent landlords, the nurses, the agriculturists, the clergymen, and even a Manila college professor, all Tiruray; but fully integrated into and committed to the larger arena of Philippine social, intellectual, and economic affairs. I mentioned earlier that the old-style Tiruray tribesman takes great pride in his way of life, in being Tiruray. Most acculturated Tiruray have no interest whatsoever in actually

132

living "like Tiruray." They consider life in the mountains and forests harsh and primitive, and they want to live "like Filipinos," and the more comfortably, the better. But many, especially among the new professional and semi-professional elite, are nonetheless proud of their ethnic identity and heritage, proud of "being Tiruray."[2] They send their children to college to equip them for a more comfortable life in a wider world, but they speak with distinct and honest satisfaction of the rugged and noble ways of the "old folks." Most are unclear regarding the precise details of the old way of life, and they have lost track of the intricacies of the ancient customs, but they know in a general way the form of traditional Tiruray culture and they feel that it is one in which they can take filial satisfaction. It was the way of the old folks, and it was good.

All of these, of course, are the background of the big furor caused by the small article. The "Tirurays of Cotabato," whom the author of that article was intending to portray, are the traditional Tiruray, the remote and isolated people, the old folks. His informants were several Tiruray students of his college, children of some of the most profoundly acculturated people of that ethnic group, who, being yet another generation removed, know even less than their parents about the details of customs and rituals they have never seen. And his readers were the new Tiruray elite, who may not be able to say with scholarly rigor what the customs all *were*, but certainly can recognize what they *were not*, and who took as a sort of personal affront this widely distributed and nationally read popular presentation of misinformation about their cultural heritage.

As I have suggested, the explanation of how this happened lies in the way the article's author went about collecting his data. His work was not based on field research, but neither was it based on malice or dishonesty. He did not set out to blacken the Tiruray nor to misrepresent them. He had no intention of promulgating merely colorful rumors, and above all he did not make up his article out of whole cloth. He based every word he wrote on exactly what a group of Tiruray informants told him about their customs. But in using the informants that he used—in assuming, without a modicum of further investigation, that a Tiruray is a Tiruray—he was naive. And the result of that naïveté was, nationally in the Philippines, a half-page of condensed ethnographic error, and, locally in the Upi area, a public relations disaster.

Notes

[1]Turner (1903: 549-552).

[2]Many poorer Tiruray farmers and migrants to urban areas, have less educational and economic defenses against the widespread lowlander equation of Tiruray = "native" = backwoods hick. For this reason, they are apt to take far less satisfaction in being Tiruray than to those who are in more elite situations. Thus, whereas the Tiruray attorney may proudly take a leading role in the Tiruray Welfare Association, the Tiruray dock-worker in Cotabato City is more likely to speak only Tagalog to his friends and to become Roman Catholic, both as being "less Tiruray."

Chapter 10

THE MANY SOCIAL WORLDS OF SOUTHEAST ASIA

This essay and the next are not specifically focused upon the Tiruray, but rather draw from Tiruray material to make some larger point. The present essay was written sometime in the early '80s, at the request of Dr. David Steinberg, the distinguished Philippine historian who is presently president of Long Island University. He and a number of others from various social science fields were putting together a book on Southeast Asia intended for the general reader, and he asked if I would write about the great social variety in the region as it is seen by an anthropologist. The book was to be published by the Asia Society. The articles were all written, and I think were all very helpful, but, alas, the Asia Society turned out unable to fund the book. I have used the present article in xerox form for years with university students being introduced to Southeast Asia. It is nice to have it finally available for a wider readership.

One of the first encounters I ever had with this fascinating part of the world was reading a travel pamphlet entitled *The Southeast Asian World*. But I learned from many years of working and traveling in the region that there is not just one "world" in Southeast Asia but many. Peter Gosling has called the Southeast Asians the "most diverse population in the world in terms of number of different languages and cultures found within the region." There are many important similarities, too, but the social and cultural variety is spectacular. There are people living in such diverse environments as isolated tropical rain forests and crowded modern cities. Some live in inland villages, some in coastal towns, some scattered in mountains, some packed into valleys, some on boats, some in great luxury, some in slums. There are stridently egalitarian societies and others which are rigidly hierarchical. And Southeast Asians live according to very different creeds: most Filipinos are Catholic; most Indonesians are Muslims; most Thais are Buddhists. The history of the region is complex and it has left a complex social heritage. This essay will tell a little about representative peoples who inhabit some of the many social worlds of contemporary Southeast Asia.

I

All societies change over time, and are influenced by their neighbors as they undergo historical interaction. But, still, it is possible to think of the small, black ("Negrito") Semang people of Malaysia as living representatives of roughly the sort of social world which characterized all of Southeast Asia long ago before agriculture began to develop or make its way into the region. In those days, most of Southeast Asia was covered with dense forest, and although little such tropical forest remains now in most of the area, the Semang live in one place where it does: in the river valleys cutting down the central mountain range of the Malay Peninsula, near the Thai-Malaysian border. They number somewhere around 2,000 persons. The climate in their forests and mangroves is, like so much of Southeast Asia, tropical and rainy; the days and nights are humid. But the forests are rich in game to be hunted and wild foods to be gathered, and the streams are bountiful with fish and crustaceans to enrich the diet.

The Semang are nomadic gatherers and hunters. Each small band of a dozen or so persons has a particular place which it considers home base, but spends most of the year wandering around the forest, looking for food. They stop wherever they are at night. Each family of husband, wife, and small children builds a temporary lean-to shelter, making a circular pattern open to a common center. Older unmarried boys build their own little lean-tos near their parents; older unmarried girls sleep with their parents, on the other side of the hearth. They use these small shelters for a night or perhaps two, then abandon them and move on in their constant quest for food.

The women do the gathering of foods and other useful items from the forest. The Semang, like all people who make their life in the forest depths, know it intimately and are familiar with all that live there. They gather leaves, roots, fruit, fungi, nuts, and the like, as well as insects and larvae to eat, and other forest goods as charms or medicines. Wild bamboo is particularly helpful, and is put to use in making everything from baskets to tools to musical instruments. Except for certain trees which are especially valued, nobody "owns" anything in the forest; its abundance is free to all for the taking. While the women gather, the men hunt for birds and small animals. Their main weapon is a six- to eight-foot long bamboo blowgun, through which they propel poison-tipped darts made from the center rib of a palm leaf. They also set a variety of traps and snares. When the band comes upon streams or rivers, both men and women fish—using hook and line, spears, small fishtraps, and occasionally poisons.

Although most of what they need they get from the forest, the Semang trade with neighboring peoples for a few items such as metal tools, cloth, and tobacco, in return for which they give forest products, especially rattan and commercially valuable tree saps and resins.

Semang family life is very informal. Most families are monogamous, although a few men have wives and children in more than one band. Divorce is easy and occurs often. Premarital sex is allowed, and a compatible young couple marry simply by going off into the woods together for a few days. The boy gives some gifts to the girl's father, and later, should the marriage break up, these bride gifts are returned. Any young people may marry so long as they are not members of the same immediate family or, usually, part of the same band. Men and women are considered quite equal in status, and help each other with their various tasks. The women do most of the cooking and making of clothes, but both men and women care for the young. The oldest male with leadership qualities is generally the informal headman of each band, but this position carries no special privileges or legal authority. In general, as among most people of the world, the aged are well respected.

The Semang social world is not only inhabited by themselves, but by myriad spirits and gods, with whom they daily interact. Spirits dwell in the trees of the forest and the waters of springs and rivers, in caves, on the mountains, in flowers and fruit. There are also certain gods, who look over the lives of the Semang and who punish them for offenses against the moral rules. People who offend the gods or spirits can propitiate them by a form of blood sacrifice in which they mix some of their blood with water and throw it up into the air.

Each band has one or more men who are priests and mediums, who receive their special powers to deal with the higher beings from tigers, and who are believed to become tigers themselves after death. These religious leaders use a special language in communicating with the spirits or in rituals of healing. They also heal in more mundane fashion using medicinal herbs from the forest.

The Semang in their wooded home are hardly typical of Southeast Asian people. There are not many of them and there are not many other peoples in the region living a similar nomadic gatherer-hunter existence deep in a forest. With each passing year, the forested area is diminished and the folk who are so marvelously adapted to life within it diminish as well. But those that survive represent the very oldest of the many Southeast Asian worlds.

II

Nomadic forest people similar to the Semang constituted Southeast Asia's only way of life until some unknown time long ago, well before the Christian era began in the West, when cultivation of domesticated plants first appeared in the region. We do not know whether cropping was developed locally in Southeast Asia or was introduced by immigrants from somewhere else, but the earliest form seems to have occurred in the wooded hills. This was the so-called "swidden" system of cutting, burning, and cultivating small plots in the forest, growing food on them for a period of a year or two, then starting again on a new site, abandoning the old one to fallow and become reestablished as forest.

Like the hunter-gatherers, there are not a great many swidden cultivators left in Southeast Asia today, but there are some where the mountain forests are still intact—and they represent another of the distinctive social worlds of the area. The Tiruray people of southeastern Mindanao Island in the Philippines are a typical example.

There are about 30,000 Tiruray. About half of them have been heavily influenced by outside forces and have adapted a peasant lowlander style of living; the other half still follow the old traditional ways. Every new year each family selects, partly by ritual means and partly by the wisdom of long experience, a new swidden site in the forest within an hour's hike from its home settlement. The men of the neighborhood together slash the under-growth, working each of the neighborhood sites in order, then return to each site one after another to fell the large trees. The swiddens are allowed to dry for a few weeks then burned off. The whole neighborhood joins together—men, women, and older children—to plant the fields in sequence, first in corn and then in dry, upland rice, the two principal Tiruray staples. The growing plants are weeded and guarded from monkeys and wild pigs by each family, which also plants many other vegetables, fruits, and spices in the swidden in and around the rice and corn. The various crops are harvested as they mature, but the Tiruray do not recut or reburn their plots, as they know this would inhibit the swidden from returning to forest. They work each plot for a year, and prepare a new one the next year.

The Tiruray, like the Semang, have an intimate knowledge of the forest in which they live, and, along with their swidden cultivation, are expert at gathering a wide variety of wild foods and other useful goods from their environment. Tiruray men also are adept at hunting for small game and exploiting the rivers for fish, shell-fish, eels, and crustaceans. Unlike the Semang, however, the Tiruray are not nomadic. Traditional people live in small settlements of a few houses each, scattered through the forest. The houses are on stilts, quite small, generally about three-by-five meters, made of bamboo and wood tied together with rattan, and roofed with grass. Each household usually consists of a single nuclear family, though in rare instances men have two or more wives and families in their home, each with her own separate cooking area. Children marry at puberty or shortly after, the marriages arranged by their elders and sanctioned with an elaborate brideprice of such items as necklaces, swords, spears, gongs, and brass boxes. These are obtained by trade with the lowlanders and are given by the boy's family to the girl's family. The families of several nearby settlements constitute a "neighborhood" by their helping of each other in swidden activities.

Tiruray culture is completely egalitarian. No one is considered to be "over" anyone else and all people live in much the same way. There are two part-time "leadership" positions which may be held by either men or women. Legal leaders have no political power over their followers but exercise authority to settle grievances and to establish and disestablish marriages. They are very important to Tiruray life, as without their settlements people are likely to feud and shed blood over any offense, major or minor. The other type of leader is the religious shaman, who has the special ability to see and talk to the spirits. Each neighborhood has one or more of both sorts of leader.

For the Tiruray, as for the Semang, the world is filled with spirits who live in the forest, the swamps, the rivers, the caves, and the mountains. The spirits are people, like the humans, who differ mainly in that they are invisible to humans other than the shamans. Some spirits, like some humans, are by nature cruel, but most co-exist peaceably with the Tiruray, not bothering them if they are not bothered. Should a human inadvertently offend a spirit, the spirit makes him or her sick—this is the origin of illness for the Tiruray— and the shaman has to search out that spirit in a dream and settle the grievance, much as the legal leader settles grievances among the humans. At four times during each year, Tiruray neighborhoods hold ritual feasts to celebrate their interdependence, and at these offerings of food are always made to the spirits. The soul of a person who dies goes to live in a special place in the spirit world, where life is peaceful and happy, and from which the soul has no desire to leave.

The Tiruray lived this traditional life in their forested hills for untold centuries, keeping others such as the lowland Muslims out, until early in the 20th century when the American occupation of their area of the Philippines broke their accustomed isolation. Since then they have lost control of the forest, and logging companies have cut much of it down. At first the Tiruray would retreat farther into the interior to avoid the deforestation, the Christian missionaries, the Muslim immigrants, the schools—all the elements which were impinging on their world. But finally many of them simply gave in to the changes and changed themselves into plow farmers on open fields. About half have given up the old ways, have become Christians, have adopted Western clothing and the Filipino national language, have begun sending their children to schools. The time is coming when the Tiruray will be pretty much like other rural Filipino peasants. Like the social world of the Semang, that of the Tiruray and other traditional swidden cultivators is slowly but inexorably passing from the Southeast Asian scene.

III

Going back once again in history, two new elements entered and greatly altered the Southeast Asian cultural scene. The first was the development of wet-rice paddy agriculture and the second was the coming of strong Indianizing influences from abroad. With wet rice came the possibility of far larger population densities, the gathering of people into rural villages, the development of private ownership of property, and the beginnings of a more hierarchical social order. This lay the basis for the rapid developments in culture and political institutions which came with the spread, to some parts of Southeast Asia, of important aspects of the Hindu-Brahman world of India. Where there had been only small wet rice villages before, in the millennium after Christ great Hinduized kingdoms and empires arose both on the mainland and in parts of what is today Indonesia. The result was the emergence of a very different sort of social world than had previously been known in the region. A representative of that Hindu world today is the

140

beautiful and fabled island of Bali.

Bali is a small island, which lies just east of Java in Indonesia and is the part of that nation which most fascinates foreigners. Its two million or so people are not as tightly packed together as those on Java, but still average about 350 per square kilometer. Bali is mountainous, its center dominated by a cluster of active volcanoes, and high ridges run to the sea, marking off numerous well watered and fertile valleys. Its history is largely unrecorded, but the broad outlines are known. From the eighth to the 11th century A.D., Bali was influenced directly from India, and from the 11th century to the 15th century it was influenced from Hinduized Java. In the 15th century, Java was converted to Islam in a series of armed struggles, and many Javanese nobles, scholars, and princes fled to Bali where they soon took on Balinese identity and formed an aristocratic upper layer of society. Bali never became Muslim. Rather, isolated from Islam and then from colonial influence until the present century, when Dutch authority was established, its synthesis of Hinduism and local custom remained intact. The Dutch did not encourage change in either the economy or the religious life. The Indonesian Republic, established in 1950, increased tourism and pushed public education, but the long established, deeply aesthetic, world of Bali has maintained its beauty and integrity.

Balinese live in villages made up of hamlets containing from ten to several hundred nuclear families. These hamlets, administered by elected elders and by regular meetings of all male household heads, have several governmental duties. They maintain local security, legitimize marriages and divorces, settle disputes, keep up public roads and buildings, raise certain taxes, assign house lots, and put on elaborate cremation rituals for their members. They can even expel a person whose behavior has become intolerable.

The hamlets, however, do not regulate rice land ownership and management. This is done by a different kind of organization, the irrigation society. The Balinese rice farmers may well belong to several irrigation societies, as each society oversees all the farm land irrigated by canals from a single dam, and a person typically works a number of small plots scattered about the countryside. The irrigation group is led in much the same way as hamlets, by elected elders and total group meetings. It has many duties which require hard effort on the part of the members: maintaining the irrigation systems and their associated temples, carrying out temple rituals related to agriculture, apportioning the water, scheduling the paddy work, fining those who abuse their membership. Growing wet rice is hard work, and like rice paddy farmers throughout Southeast Asia, the Balinese devote much of their time and daily effort to this enterprise.

From the Indian influences have come two important aspects of Balinese life, though both have been extensively reformulated and domesticated: their system of social statuses and their religion. The so-called Balinese "caste system" differs in so many ways from the Indian prototype that it would probably be better termed a "title system." It is similar to Indian caste in that one's social status is inherited from one's father, in that mobility between levels is not supposed ever to occur, and in that marriages are quite rigidly regulated in terms of status. But unlike the Indian system of caste, the Balinese are not divided up into a ranked hierarchy of occupational and religiously functional corporate groups, and there is not an elaborate ethic of ritual avoidance between statuses. In Bali prestige is distributed among individuals through the inheritance from father to son of explicit titles which attach to one's name. The four main groups of the Indian system are present: the Brahamana at the very top followed in descending order by the Satria, the Vesia, and the Sudra. The top three divisions are the nobility and make up only about ten percent of the population; the other 90 percent being Sudra commoners. But the nobles are broken down into strictly ranked titles, and these are really what count in assigning status—not the four gross divisions. People generally marry within their title group, and the gentry carefully keep long genealogies to establish their claim to noble birth.

Religion permeates every aspect of Balinese life. The Balinese are famous for being Hindu, but their Hinduism is thoroughly mixed together with the spirits, magic, and charms of the old pre-Hindu religious cosmos. It is thus not Indian religion; it is Balinese religion thoroughly at home on the island. The gods and the deified ancestors live high on the volcanoes, above the humans who occupy the middle world between mountains and ocean. In the sea live the demons and hostile giants. The life force of the Balinese people is seen as weakened by evil magic, the work of witches and devils, but it is strengthened and nurtured by good magic, by ritual offerings and temple performances which lure the gods to come down and be with the people. By meticulously, faithfully tending the temples daily and by offerings and sacred dance at temple festivals, the humans seek to attract the gods and ancestors to stay among them.

Temples are everywhere in Bali—in villages, but also in rice fields, on the beaches, in every houseyard, on lonely hill tops. Each hamlet has three principal temples honoring the foundation of the hamlet, the souls of the local dead, and the fertility of the nearby fields, and there are many others wherever one turns. Each has an outer courtyard where preparations are made for feasts and dances, connected by an ornate carved gate to an inner courtyard where the altars and shrines stand ready to house the gods when they visit earth. There are one or more multi-tiered wooden pagodas, symbolizing the cosmic mountain of Hindu lore, the ultimate seat of the gods, and many other simpler shrines and offering sheds. The keeper of each temple is a commoner hereditary priest. He maintains the cleanliness of the temple, leads its rituals, and officiates at feasts. The Balinese are not particularly sophisticated about doctrine, but they put great stress on ceremonial detail, and they enthusiastically throw themselves into their ritual duties, making beautiful food and flower arrangements as offerings, dancing with long practiced elegance and precision, even, on occasion, falling into a trance.

Temple ritual stresses equality and community solidarity, and within the temple all social status differences are irrelevant. It is just the opposite with the elaborate ceremonies which involve the uppermost Brahamana rank priests. Not all members of that "caste" become actual priests. The training and purification process is long and hard. But those who do are closely linked to high noble families and are supported by commoner followers for whom they bless the holy water used in all Balinese rituals. The Brahamanas are the people, in this social world, of greatest purity and holiness.

Bali is a land of aesthetic charm and loveliness unrivaled on earth. This has made it a powerful draw for tourists; I once arrived at a temple ritual to find 26 other tour buses parked outside. But if the curious from the outside world do not inundate and spoil it, it will go on much as it has in the past —a very special Southeast Asian social world where all of life is a kind of cosmic theater and every act is filled with faith and beauty.

IV

In the 14th century, when Hinduized kingdoms were flourishing in Java and Bali, on the mainland of Southeast Asia another cultural force from India was making itself felt. At roughly this period, Burma, Thailand, Laos and Cambodia were adopting Theravada Buddhism and its pervasive world view. Thus was created in Southeast Asia another different social world, of which life in a Burmese village may be taken as an example. There are some 30 million people in Burma, much less closely packed together than in Bali, and four-fifths of these live in rural villages where Theravada Buddhist life goes on much as it has for so many centuries.

At the heart of this life is the idea that human existence is the scene of constant flux and suffering. The great absolute of reality is the Law of Karma: there is a cosmic balance in which every evil action increases one's sufferings in the next life, and every good act decreases that suffering. After many rebirths and many lives of diligent effort, one can hope to achieve Nirvana through wisdom, concentration, and morality, and thus to transcend mundane reality. To this end the Burmese villager "makes merit" by avoiding the vices such as anger, by keeping the key precepts of the faith such as not taking life, and by performing merit-giving acts, such as giving food to a monk or becoming a monk himself for a period of time.

The many monks, with their shaved heads and yellow robes, are perhaps the most characteristic sight in a Burmese village. Although women are barred by their sex from the monasteries, men and boys enter and leave at will, and a few actually stay for life. Most boys put on the yellow robe, at least briefly, when they are adolescents, and go through an elaborate initiation which can involve their entire village in the feasting, dancing, and other festivities. Life in a Theravada Buddhist monastery is simple and one must follow strict rules of celibacy and avoidance of hot food after noon. Monks beg for their food in the village, they meditate and chant, and they operate monastic schools where village youngsters are taught basic literacy. Led by an abbot, the monks set examples for the laity of piety and simplicity of life, but they are not ministers to the temple congregations; every Burmese man and woman, monk or layman, is on his or her own spiritual course.

The laity are, of course, less concerned with daily religion than the monks, but every house has a special shelf set aside for a statue of the Buddha. Here the family can chant from time to time to honor Buddha and to help focus their minds on his truths. On "duty days" they go to the temple where— each person in his or her own section, determined by one's birthday—they bow, offer flowers, make a libation, chant and meditate on life's sufferings. This done, they often hold a picnic on the temple grounds.

There are many temples in rural Burma, as the people are enthusiastic builders of pagodas. Some are small, some large; some falling apart, some covered with layer upon layer of gold leaf. Generally, the Burmese pagoda is shaped like a bell with a large base and a tapering spire, over which is erected a metal umbrella, covered with gold leaf and hung with bells.

Buddhism deals with ultimates in life, but to cope with everyday crises Burmese villagers propitiate spirits. These spirits, as elsewhere in Southeast Asia, are encountered everywhere and are understood to explain some illnesses and accidents as well as the fertility of land and women. Woven into the fabric of village Buddhism, the spirits are seen as the immediate cause of much that happens, although, of course, the ultimate cause is Karma. To placate the spirits, Burmese build many little shrines near their houses, fields, and paths, and make myriad offerings and rituals. One's life is also subject to fate, to the impact of fixed cosmic elements such as the heavenly bodies, the cardinal directions, the component elements of the body, and so forth. Therefore, in early childhood everyone has a horoscope drawn incorporating these influences, and this is consulted throughout life.

There is not much manifestation of caste among the Burmese, beyond the distinction between royalty and non-royalty, a matter that has little effect on rural life. Social life is, however, strongly ascriptive and people remain generally in their roles and statuses given by birth and family. This is especially true of the sexes. The distinction between masculinity and femininity is fundamental in Burmese thought. Rice, the main staple, and all the divinities associated with the earth are nurturing by nature and thus taken to be feminine; the essence of masculinity is potency to fertilize the earth and the women. Men are thus viewed as by nature in a higher spiritual state than women.

While men and women work together in the rice fields, the men generally take on the physically demanding labor of plowing and preparing the paddies, while women plant, weed, and harvest the grain. It is the women, too, who take to the market and sell the lighter foodstuffs grown by the family in their gardens. Heavier goods such as rice are sold through middlemen. These had largely been Chinese and Indians in rural Burma until the Ne Win government took power in 1962 and nationalized all trade. Today most middlemen roles are played by military persons representing national trade corporations. Like peasants everywhere in Southeast Asia today, Burmese villagers aspire to a higher standard of living and a better life. To be wealthy—except for monks—is a good thing, and to enjoy the comforts of wealth is seen as a consequence of previous good Karma, even though this may not jibe with the official secular socialism of the state.

Some villagers are local shopkeepers, but most are farmers, who get the use of their land from kinfolk. Until recently there had been widespread sharecrop tenancy in rural Burma, but that was abolished in the late 1950s and early 1960s by government-sponsored land reform. Villagers live in households of either one nuclear family or, occasionally, of a man, his wife and unmarried children, one married child and his wife and children. Within any one village almost everyone is related somehow, either by blood or marriage, and the social rules allow a person to marry anyone who has never lived in the same household. Marriages and divorces are made quite easily, but premarital sex is seen as an offense against the spirits.

The state defines the village as a unit of administration, but the Burmese people think of each village as the territory of a certain guardian spirit who enforces local customary law. Villages are also popularly defined in terms of the congregations of particular local temple monasteries. Each village has its headman, who is typically caught between pressures down from the government he represents, and those up from the villagers whom he also represents. Village headmen are formally elected, but often in practice sons follow fathers in a sort of hereditary line. The local scene may well also include certain strongmen and charismatic leaders, who serve as patrons of their followers, and who may well try to bolster their position by running for public office. In the minds of the people, of course, legitimate power is vested in those who "have merit," determined by their previous Karma.

The formal national government of Burma often seems remote from the village, even though it is tied to it by important daily relationships. Again, Buddhism has been a powerful unifying force. U Nu, the first post-colonial prime minister, was a devout Buddhist and identified his government with the faith, thus legitimizing socialism for many villagers. The subsequent Ne Win government based its legitimacy on secular ideas, and these have resonated far less with rural people.

Buddhism goes very deep in Burma and has stood up well under modernizing influences. As modern medical practices and western technology become more and more widespread, they may erode some of the spirit beliefs of the rural Burmese, but it seems unlikely that the basic Theravada Buddhist underpinnings will be soon affected. Belief in Karma, devotion to the precepts of the Buddha, and charity to the monks remain fundamentals of this social world.

146

V

From the 13th to the 15th century the Islamic faith began to spread into the Malay areas of Southeast Asia. Muslim teachers and missionaries accompanied, and often were, the traders who plied the port cities of the region. The Islam to which they called people was a tolerant and flexible sufistic form which was prepared to absorb and incorporate into the religion of Mohammed many of the older Hindu and animistic beliefs and institutions. As Muslim merchants married into local ruling families, little by little, sultanates began to emerge along the coasts and eventually Islam penetrated farther inland. By the 15th century, the Muslim religion had come to dominate the Malay Peninsula through Sumatra and Java and coastal Borneo to as far east as the southern Philippines. The spread of Islam in the archipelago, like the spread of Buddhism earlier on the mainland, gave rise to new social and cultural realities, new ways of understanding and relating to life. Of these, our example is a fishing village in Malaysia.

In the many fishing villages of one or two thousand people that dot the east coast of the Malay Peninsula, the vast majority of the male villagers fish for a living, although most families also augment their income with some coconut trees and some families grow rice as well. Most of the people are Malays, but there are always a few Indian and Chinese shopkeepers.

The typical village fronts on a wide, sandy beach where boats are landed, where fish are first offered for sale, where nets are mended, and where on occasion teams of men fish with large hand-pulled nets. The nearby waters are warm and quite shallow and teem with a huge variety of fish. Although large, expensive trawlers from other places—some from as far away as Japan—often intrude themselves, almost all of the local activity is inshore fishing, done within a short distance from shore. In recent years, some ice has been available, but the facilities for preserving a fresh catch for any length of time are lacking, so little fishing is done for long-range export. Most of what is caught locally is sold locally or eaten fresh, and the rest is dried and salted for sale in the village market or farther inland.

The boats are individually owned, and each family which possibly can afford it owns a boat. They are small, generally under 10 meters in length and quite narrow in beam, powered by an inboard motor, and often brightly painted and decorated.

Most of the villagers' time is spent on fishing in one way or another, either catching fish or marketing them. Groups of five or six boats, each with a crew of about four men, go out early in the morning, well before daylight, under the leadership of a master fisherman who is often, but not always, the main owner of the tackle being used by the group. It is his job to find and spot the fish, to organize the drop and the handling of the net, and to oversee the division of the crew's shares of money received for their catch when it is sold on the beach. The master fisherman receives the largest share of any of the crewmen, and everyone hopes to fish with an especially skillful master fisherman so that all their shares will reflect a large catch. Also receiving large shares are the boat captains and owners, and the various owners of the equipment. Crew membership is by voluntary association, and often changes, although certain very successful crews may stay together for some time.

Many kinds of nets, often home-made from cotton twine but occasionally purchased, are used. The most important kinds are seines, lift nets, and gill nets. Most are too expensive for a single owner, so are owned and kept in repair by several families. Other needed fishing items of all sorts, some from outside the village, must be bought in the market. These include such things as construction materials, barbed hooks, nylon drop lines, net weights and floats, knives, and the like.

The fish are first sold on the village beach, when the boats return in late morning. Some fish are bought by wholesalers for resale inland; others are bought by small- scale dealers who will retail them in the village and at the market. This sort of middleman role in fish dealing involves little equipment or capital and is often engaged in by temporarily unemployed persons to provide a little income. The buyers and the boat captains negotiate a price after much congenial bargaining, and the various dealers divide up the day's catch. Most sales are on credit and accounts are settled weekly, after the fish have been resold for cash.

Just in from the beach, before one reaches the people's houses, are usually many rows of coconut trees and the village market. Like Malay markets everywhere in the region, its stalls form a rectangle, roofed over with galvanized iron, within which are many tables in rows on the mud floor. Vendors rent the stalls and tables to sell all manner of fish, meat, rice, vegetables, fruit, tools, and other items both perishable and unperishable. Most of the market vendors are women, wives of the local fishermen. Cloth goods, bakery products, and a variety of hardware are also sold in shops near the market, the largest of which are run by Indians and Chinese, whose business networks reaching far beyond the coastal village give them an important edge over the Malay shopkeepers.

Beyond the market and the coconut fields, are the houses of the village. Most houses are simple, functional, and inexpensive, with split bamboo walls and floors and thatched grass roofs. Mats for sleeping, sitting, and praying make up most of the sparse furnishings, along with such necessities as water containers and cooking utensils. Fishing gear is repaired and stored within the house, and the family's clothing is stacked near the walls or hung from pegs.

Most households contain a single nuclear family though some house multiple families, each with its own kitchen. Being Muslim, the men may have up to four wives, but few have more than one at a time. Following Islamic custom, marriages are arranged for the young girls soon after puberty, generally to a man she had not known before. These marriages seldom last long, generally ending in divorce, which is easily accomplished in the Muslim manner by the husband's declaring thrice that he divorces his wife. Divorce in these villages is not thought to be a dreadful thing and is very common.

Muslim women in the Malay world are much freer in their activities than is common, for instance, in the Middle East. Malay women are not veiled and they mix freely with men, not only in the market but in the various aspects of village life. Like most Southeast Asian women, they receive all cash earned by their husbands, strictly control the household and all family funds, and are very influential in domestic life. Women have their own place in the mosque during Friday services.

Islam is a powerful force bonding villagers together into a social unit, and linking them with other sections of national, and indeed of international, life. Religious chants are heard over people's transistor radios, along with popular secular entertainment, and loudspeakers broadcast the calls to prayer and sermons from the mosque throughout the community. People are on the whole quite faithful in observance of Islam's "five pillars": they pray five times daily, recite the traditional affirmation of Allah and the prophet Mohammed, fast during the month of Ramadan, pay the required religious taxes, and, when able to afford it, make the pilgrimage to Mecca. No one goes out to fish on Fridays, the weekly holy day of Islam, when the principal mosque service takes place. The leader of the mosque, the Imam, and the several other Muslim religious teachers chant the Koran and hold instruction in the evenings to teach the children to do the same. Through the evenings

149

of the fasting month, men gather at the village prayer houses and the mosque to recite the holy book in its entirety. They often stay around the prayer houses other evenings before and after the evening prayers to chat and gossip, just as during the day—when not on boats or asleep—they hang around the village coffee shops. For prayer, the men commonly wear a modest sarong and a distinctive Muslim cap.

In the rural Malay version of Islam, the Muslim elements are well mixed in with familiar Southeast Asian animistic features. Along with the Imam, the local representative of orthodoxy, the villagers turn to spirit-mediums for certain spiritual and therapeutic needs. The Imam typically denounces the spirit medium as a consort with evil powers, but the medium and his followers see him as a good Muslim, augmenting the work of the orthodox leaders. The villagers believe in a multitude of good and harmful spirits, and see no conflict between these beliefs and formal Islam.

Fishermen living in settled villages are in many ways like farmers in settled villages; both are deeply involved with markets and tied politically as well as economically and religiously to larger social units. But they are different in some very fundamental ways. The yields of agricultural workers, and their risks, are seasonal. Most grow rice, a staple crop which can be stored. Men work side by side with women and with older children. Investment is mostly in land which is permanent property. Fishermen's yields are daily and so is their risk; their yields are not a staple, but must be sold to buy the staples; their work world is male only; and their investment is in boats and gear which deteriorate and must eventually be replaced. The work life of a fisherman is much more physically dangerous, his basic equipment much more expensive. His fundamental knowledge is of the nature of the sea and the winds, not the soil and the rains. Out in his boat hauling nets, at home with his wife mending nets, at the beach selling fish, or on his mat in prayer—his life is lived out in another of the many different social worlds of Southeast Asia.

VI

The sweep of Islam through the Indonesian archipelago carried it, by the beginning of the 14th century, to the southern Philippines. The Muslim faith became well established in the Sulu Archipelago and parts of Mindanao, and it was working its way north to the large island of Luzon when, in 1564, a

Spanish expedition under Miguel Lopez Legaspi first claimed the Philippines as a Spanish colony. In 1571 the Muslim outpost at Manila was conquered and made the Spanish capital. The Cross of Catholicism and the Crescent of Islam were in confrontation in Southeast Asia, just as they had long been in western Europe and northern Africa. An imaginary line between the Muslim south in Mindanao and Sulu and the Catholic Philippines to the north, became one of the world's many great cultural fault lines, and antagonism between the two areas and faiths continues in the Philippines to the present day.

In the north, in the Visayan Islands and Luzon, Catholic Spain took deep hold and administered the Philippines until the turn of the present century, when the United States took over as colonial authority. The Philippines became independent in 1946. The decades of United States occupation left many important legacies, but the long centuries of Spanish rule had made of the Philippines a predominantly hispanized, Catholic nation—a blend of the ancient and traditional with yet another of the world's great religious traditions. This last of the social worlds of Southeast Asia which I will discuss in this essay is illustrated by the Ilocanos, the third largest ethnic group in the Philippines. Some three million people speak the Ilocano language, and many are great travelers who have emigrated to distant places like Hawaii and California. But the Ilocano homeland is the narrow strip of lowlands between the mountains and the sea on the west coast of northern Luzon.

The territorial organization of the Ilocos reflects the Spanish system. The two provinces of Ilocos Norte and Ilocos Sur are divided into municipalities of some 15 or so thousand people, of which about a third live in the town itself. There, commonly facing a central plaza, is found the Catholic parish church, the elementary school, often the local market, and the municipal town hall. The other people live in small settlements of one to 20 families, every three to five of these *sitios* being clustered to form a *barrio*. Often the barrio has a small chapel, where Mass is celebrated once a year, at the time of the barrio fiesta, by the priest from the town parish church.

Ilocano homes are built up on stilts and usually are made of bamboo and thatch, like the Malay houses described in the last section, but they generally have several rooms, including a living room as well as a bedroom and kitchen. On the living room walls are a great number of certificates, diplomas, photos, movie star pictures, and a mirror. There are several small chests, a wardrobe, a few simple chairs and a table. The bedroom seldom has beds, which are a prestige item in the Ilocos, but always has a religious shrine where holy pictures, rosaries, and small statues serve as charms, and where at weddings and funerals plates of food are placed to honor the home's ancestral spirits. An important part of the Ilocano house is the porch, where visitors are often entertained, where people can sit in the evening, and even sleep in very hot weather. At night all the windows are closed up tight to discourage the evil spirits outside, and a white cross is painted in several places on the exterior of the house to guard against flying witches.

Again, the nuclear family is the basic social-economic unit, and at marriage every couple is usually given a separate house. Ilocanos are monogamous and divorce is forbidden by law, but it is very common for the more well-to-do men to have a mistress in another house in a different location. Marriages are arranged by parents, a family usually seeking a wife for their son from the relatives of the mother, or, at least, from the mother's barrio. The man's family gives some of its land, if it has land, to the couple, and so most newly married people settle in the barrio of the husband's father. The use of kinship terms in addressing barrio-mates is very common, both to actual kin and to non-kin according to the person's estimated relative age. Thus one greets a woman slightly over one's own age with the term for "older sister," a man one's father's age as "uncle," and so forth.

Custom requires that at both weddings and baptisms one or more couples "stand up" as sponsors. These people become godparents of the marrying couple or the child, but more importantly they become *compadres* and *comadres* of the parents, a role that is very important in Ilocano life. *Compadres* are like ritual kinsmen, and are expected to do favors and to offer help to each other through life. The *compadre* relationship, along with actual blood and marriage relationships, provide people with a stock of social and political alliances which are central to Ilocano activities. It is through such alliances—some between equals in status, others between patrons and clients—that many aspects of Ilocano life, from barrio fiestas to provincial politics, are organized and carried out.

The Ilocos area is famous as a tobacco-growing region, but the majority of Ilocanos are wet rice farmers, like so many Southeast Asian people, and they have the same important relations with local and regional markets. There are not many huge land holdings in the two provinces; most people are either rather small scale landowners or sharecrop tenants on a neighbor's land. As in most areas of the rural Philippine lowlands, there are two relatively distinct

152

social classes: those folks known as "big people" who own land and the "little people" who do not. The landowners typically have a long-standing and close paternalistic relationship with their tenants, not only providing them with land to work in return for a share of the harvests, but helping them when they are in financial need, seeing that they get medical care when necessary, providing a white dress for a tenant girl's first communion, and the like. In return, the tenants support their landlords not only in daily work in the fields, but in a wide variety of social and political activities.

Starting in the mid-17th century, Spain entrusted the Christian conversion of the Ilocanos to the Augustinian friars, and construction of the massively buttressed stone churches typical of the area began. The early missionaries saw themselves as soldiers of Christ, waging war against the devil. There were no temples in the Philippines as there had been in Mexico, but the Spanish friars cut down all the sacred groves of trees and preached vehemently against all "pagan" practices. In spite of these efforts, the Catholicism which developed over the centuries among Ilocanos, as among other Filipinos, was an intimate mixture of the Spanish imported faith and local spirit belief and magic. The people took very enthusiastically to the sacrament of Baptism, which they believed would cure illnesses, and to the Mass, for its pageantry, incense, colorful vestments, and ritual. In general, Catholic practices were more fully grasped than Catholic doctrines, and both in popular practice took on a distinctive Filipino flavor. The veneration of the saints fit beautifully with older respect paid to spirits, and the preaching of religious miracles evoked traditional beliefs about magic. Preconquest lore regarding spirits, both ancestral and environmental, malignant beings, witches, and magical healing all lived on as vital elements in the folk Catholicism of the people.

VII

In this essay I have passed in review some of the many social worlds of contemporary Southeast Asia—some, but not all. There are others. The sea nomads, the Badjaw, who spend their lives on tiny boats going from place to place and living both on and from the sea, form a still different setting for Southeast Asian life. So do the overseas Chinese, who inhabit every large city in the region, keeping often to their own ways but playing a tremendously important role in the economics of their various countries. And, I have said nothing of the many Westerners who live generally quite luxurious lives in the larger urban areas, and who are a major part of the connection between Southeast Asia and its worldwide economic context.

But most of the region south of China and east of India is neither urban nor boat-dwelling, but rural. Most people live in the sort of social worlds I have tried to portray. They are worlds which have been long established and reach back far into historical time, some even to prehistoric ages. They are worlds which came into being through many influences, domestic and foreign, and their futures today still depend on many factors, often outside their control. Formal Western colonialism is no longer part of the scene. But political influences, technology, and ideas from both the East and the West continue to intrude and to mix with internal forces of change. The future of such people as the Semang and the Tiruray is inevitably bound up with the future of the larger societies and nations of which they are part, and indeed the futures of all the many social worlds of Southeast Asia will be shaped in the days to come, as they have been in the past, partly by their own history, their own customs, and their own genius, and partly by forces that are nationwide, regionwide, and worldwide.

Chapter 11

THE ANTHROPOLOGIST AS OUTSIDER

This essay was originally written in 1979 as my Professorial Inaugural Lecture at the University of California, Santa Cruz. A few years after becoming a full professor, one is asked to give a formal lecture to a general audience on some aspect of one's research, and I thought it appropriate to speak about my own humanistic approach to anthropology and about the theoretical stance called "social constructionist," which has informed my work from its earliest days. An edited version of the lecture was subsequently published by the Philippine Quarterly of Culture and Society *(vol. 12, no. 1, pp. 57-66), and that is what is presented here. Like the previous essay in this volume, this one is not entirely about the Tiruray, but it draws heavily on Tiruray material.*

I

My purpose is to say something about what it is to be a cultural anthropologist. But I want to begin not with the usual materials of classical cultural anthropology: the ways and beliefs of some exotic people in some remote island or jungle. I will give you a bit of that shortly. I want to start by saying a few words about two slim French novels, *Nausea* by Jean-Paul Sartre and *The Stranger* by Albert Camus. Each in its own way fascinates me because I find in their rather anguished central figures a sort of kinsmen—kinsmen in my efforts both to be an anthropologist and to live a meaningful life in my world of daily existence.

First, then, a brief look at Sartre's *Nausea*. The book presents itself as being the journal of an historian named Roquentin. He lives a life of quiet blandness. He resides alone in a hotel in Le Havre. He works. He has quiet conversations in the library. He has a strangely impersonal sexual liaison. He says of himself, "I live alone, entirely alone; I never speak to anyone, never; I receive nothing, I give nothing."[1]

But Roquentin's placid existence is interrupted by several disturbing occurrences. At one time, he becomes suddenly disquieted when, standing on a beach, he skips a stone into the sea. Another time, in a busy cafe, he is abruptly afraid to look at a glass of beer, which turns for him into looking into

155

deep waters, into fear itself. Again, in the cafe, he suffers nausea at the ordinary sight of a person's suspenders. Then someone plays the American record, "Some of These Days," and just as suddenly Roquentin senses order and logic coming out of chaos.

His journal is an effort to chronicle these disturbing events and his thoughts about them. What the reader gets so clearly is Roquentin's encounter with meaninglessness. Or, better, with the precariousness, the fragility, of meaningfulness in daily experiences. He has his ordinary life, with all its unspoken, taken-for-granted assumptions of meaning, purpose, point. But his nausea is to see past these meanings, to see that they are not so firm, not so utterly real, not truly an indelible part of the world.

As the journal goes on, we see the breaking down of his firm sense of values, his structures of meaning. His memory had seemed to give events order and coherence, but he had become too exhausted for memory and was living in an increasingly unordered, incoherent present. He sees a chair but cannot identify it: "Things are divorced from their names," he says. "They are there, grotesque, headstrong, gigantic and it seems ridiculous to call them seats or to say anything at all about them: I am in the midst of things, nameless things." [2] Again, in a park, he looks at the roots of a large tree and once more firm reality dissolves, frightening him. He cries out, "Never, until these last few days, had I understood the meaning of 'existence.' I was like the others . . . I said, like them, 'The ocean *is* green, that white speck up there *is* a seagull. . . .' " [3]

He feels insignificant, absurd. Meaning, he glimpses, comes not from reality but from him; meaning and order are not intrinsic in the world. We humans make meaning. We make order. Roquentin had encountered both in the song, "Some of These Days," where note followed note in melodious coherence created by the songwriter. Life itself, the world, may lack intrinsic meaning and order but a person can give order, can create meaningfulness. Why should he not create something—a novel perhaps—which, like the song, would be a bearer of order and meaning? The novel ends with his decision to leave Le Havre and seek a more creative life.

Roquentin's experience is one which many, perhaps all of us, can identify with. We may well have had some similar experience when the fragility of life's meanings presses itself into our consciousness. I remember an incident which happened to me many years ago when I was an undergraduate. I had to get up one Saturday morning to spend the weekend studying for a biology exam. I had not been working too hard in biology that term, so I knew I had to study hard that weekend. I woke up Saturday morning, and the sun was pouring into my room. I remember I opened my eyes, and I lay there, and I thought something like this, "I'm going to get up, and I'm going to study biology all weekend, and I'm going to study very hard, and I'm going to pass the test with an A, and then I'm going to study a lot of other things and pass a lot of other tests, and then I'm going to get a degree, and then I'm going to go to work, and I'm going to do a lot of useless things for a lot of useless years, and then I'm going to die." And I just could not see why I should get up that morning. I lay there thinking to myself that it is all so terribly meaningless. I was like Roquentin when he skipped the stone, when he was afraid of his beer, when he could not make sense of the roots of a chestnut tree. For at least a fleeting moment, meaning was gone. (What happened? I got out of bed, got "reality" back, took the test, and went on with life.)

Let me leave the Sartre story there and say a few words about Camus' *The Stranger*. "Mother died today," it begins. "Or, maybe, yesterday; I can't be sure."[4] Meursault, the Algerian French central character of the novel, is also keeping a journal, and this tone of utter indifference remains throughout the book. Meursault, one quickly learns, feels very little; he is profoundly uninterested in the events of his life. He reports on his mother's funeral in a manner devoid of feeling; it had simply not affected him beyond leaving him rather tired out from the long vigil. The day after, he takes a swim, meets a girl, goes to see a film comedy with her, then takes her to his room and sleeps with her. But this account of these events is like that of his mother's funeral: the events happened, he was there, but he felt next to nothing. It is all without significance to him. He is indifferent.

Then one day, the hero—should we call these men heroes?—meets a pimp who is engaged in a petty feud with an Arab, and becomes fatefully involved. Meursault spends a day on the beach, runs into the Arab, begins to quarrel with him, and ends up shooting him in self-defense. Lacking witnesses, Meursault is arrested and charged with murder. Now he becomes, with his great indifference, his own worst enemy. The legal authorities are shocked at his attitude. He does not protest his innocence or express grief about the tragic death. He is simply indifferent. He remains unaffected when asked about his mother's recent funeral and even disclaims feeling love for her: "I could truthfully say I'd been quite fond of Mother—but really that didn't mean much."[5] His interrogator, hoping a religious note will soften

Meursault, holds a crucifix before him and calls on him to repent. But it means nothing to Meursault. Finally, he is tried, convicted, and condemned to the guillotine. The prosecutor's final words to the jury: "I would have you note that on the next day after his mother's funeral that man was visiting the swimming pool, starting a liaison with a girl, and going to see a comic film. That is all I wish to say."[6]

A priest visits him before his execution, again calling on him to repent, and Meursault at last cries out in anguish, saying of the priest:

> None of his certainties was worth one strand of a woman's hair. . . . Nothing, nothing had the least importance . . . all alike would be condemned to die one day. . . . And what difference could it make if, after being charged with murder, he were executed because he didn't weep at his mother's funeral, since it all came to the same thing in the end?

And, then, as he goes to sleep the night before he is to be beheaded: "I laid my heart open to the benign indifference of the universe. To feel it so like myself. . . ." He had lived his life with a sense of complete indifference, a sense of unreality and meaninglessness. As for Roquentin, so for Meursault: the world is unreal. His approaching death had brought him to awareness of the lack of intrinsic meaning in reality, just as had his counterpart's nausea done for him.

Colin Wilson, the psychologist-philosopher *cum* literary critic, one of the restless intellects of our time, once called these two characters, Roquentin and Meursault, "outsiders."[7] They were outsiders because they came to stand apart from the general taken-for-granted everyday reality of French or Algerian French culture, and to see into its true status as humanly constructed structures of meaning. The outsider is one who comes to realize that most unsettling of existential insights: that there is no ultimately real world for human beings; there are only the various "worlds" which are culturally given and humanly constructed, worlds whose values and meanings and order depend on the precarious consensus of those who inhabit them and construe them as "reality."

Most people, of course, do not have this awareness. They simply take their own culturally given reality for granted. Anthropologists, philosophers, and existentialist novelists may recognize their worlds of reality as culturally and socially delineated, but most people, in most of the world, for most of human history have not. Roquentin and Meursault are "outsiders" because they have lost the innocence of the typical "insiders," who naively take *their* worlds as *the* world, and who question neither the universal verity of their values nor the cosmic grounding of their meanings.

II

Now, I said in opening this paper that I find in these two characters from French existentialist fiction a kind of kinship. I do, because the cultural anthropologist's craft makes of him or her just such an "outsider." At the heart of the enterprise of cultural anthropology has always been the world-wide fact of cultural difference. People live in societies and social worlds which are wonderfully different, and a large part of studying human experience consists of looking at particular human experiences as they are lived out in particular social and cultural realities. The Indonesians have a lovely saying about cultural differences: "other fields, other grasshoppers." So, whether the anthropologist focuses on the economic aspects of a society's life, or on their legal aspects, or on their language, central to the inquiry is to be found a fundamental awareness of cultural difference.

Typically—though not necessarily and not always—cultural anthropologists study the social and cultural ways of people other than themselves. Ever since the days of Boas, Malinowski, and Radcliffe-Brown, it has been the common rule that a novice cultural anthropologist is not considered fully trained without a year or two of field research, of intense life with and among some people of other cultural ways. More and more, in recent years, American graduate students in America have been doing their fieldwork here in the United States, exploring the cultural worlds of big business, or New England fishermen, or some California counter-culture commune. But, as I said, typically the pre-doctoral fieldwork is done abroad somewhere in a Latin-American village, or a Southeast Asian rain forest, or an African city.

When I, for example, was doing my pre-doctoral field research. I went to live for two years among the Tiruray—a warm and generous people—who live in the mountains of southwestern Mindanao in the southern Philippines. They number about 25,000 persons, scattered through the forest in small communities of ten to 20 families, and make their living by slash-and-burn cultivation and by hunting, fishing, and gathering the rich stock of wild resources in the nearby rivers and forests. I lived with the Tiruray for two years, deep in the tropical rain forest, a long many hours' hike from the nearest road. I learned to speak their language, to know and respect their customs, to understand their world, and to live their life. It was, in many ways, a strange and wonderful experience—as anthropological fieldwork usually is.

From beginning to end, I was clearly an outsider among the Tiruray. I was a different color; I wore different clothes when I got dressed up; I spoke *their* language with *my* accent; I stood about a foot taller than a man should grow; and so forth. One sometimes hears of visitors to an alien people "going native" and totally blending in with the local scene. I doubt, myself, whether this is ever really possible, but it certainly was not possible for me. For starters, I was too white and too tall, and far and away too clumsy in climbing hills and in squatting on bamboo floors. There was no way I was going to be able to "blend in" with the Tiruray. I was an outsider, and neither the Tiruray nor I ever forgot it. East was East and West was West, and while it was true that the twain met, they certainly never merged.

But I was an outsider in another and far more profound way. For the Tiruray lived in a "Tiruray world," a "Tiruray reality," and I did not. Let me give two examples, one from the Tiruray understanding of human nature, and one from Tiruray spiritual beliefs.

My first book based on those two years of research was about the Tiruray legal system and how it is grounded in their view of morality. Their moral system, in turn, grows out of their understanding of human nature.[8] So, first let me describe a bit of the Tiruray understanding of human nature, as an example of a piece of their reality, their phenomenal world. The best way to do this—actually about the only way to do this—is to lay out for you some Tiruray words and concepts.

The Tiruray believe that at the core of every human being is his or her *fedew*. This word actually glosses as "gall bladder" but it means for them much what English speakers mean by "heart." If I wanted to say I was "broken-hearted" in Tiruray, I would use an expression involving the gall bladder. It is your gall bladder which is "stout" and which is "weary" and so on. Now the *fedew* can be two ways basically—it actually can be dozens of ways but they break down into two fundamental states—"good" and "bad." Good is *fiyo fedew;* bad is *tété fedew.* Your *fedew* is good if it is just the way it ought to be, if everything is going right: your food tastes good, your spouse is faithful, your hunting is going well, it is not raining on you. Everything is

160

going just the way it should—you have *fiyo fedew*. Its counterpart is *tété fedew*, "bad hearted" (bad gall-bladdered!), which is when something is going wrong, and it can occur in two importantly different ways. You can have something go wrong in the world that you cannot control—you are caught in the rain and you do not have a leafy umbrella, you are wet and cold and *tété fedew*. Or you are tired to the bone, because you have worked all day and you are just plain weary. Or your child dies. There is nothing you can really do about that—nobody did it to you—but you are *tété fedew*, grieved, sad. This is one way in which your *fedew* (your gall-bladder, your "heart") can be bad. The other way is when your heart is bad because someone caused it: someone stole your husband, or ran off with your spouse, or killed your child, or stole your spear. Here it is not just that the world is unpleasant, but someone has done you in—and you are *tété fedew*.

The Tiruray believe that human nature is such that when this latter situation occurs, a person may very well explode into violence. This is an amazing belief to outsiders, because the Tiruray are in some ways so gentle and kindly, but they feel it is intrinsic to human nature that a person whose *fedew* is wounded will want to kill the assailant. People are indeed gentle and kindly because they are taking such care not to give anyone a bad *fedew*. For "people are people"—hurt, they erupt into physical violence.

There is another concept, *adat*. *Adat* is an Arabic word in origin, but it is very common in Southeast Asia and means "custom." If I enter someone's house, I first wipe the mud from my feet, because that is the custom, the *adat*. But for the Tiruray, *adat* has a meaning which is not always recognized elsewhere in Southeast Asia; for Tiruray *adat* means "respect." I wipe my feet before entering your house not merely because it is custom but also because it is respect for you. Indeed it is custom because it is respectful. *Adat* rules are rules of respect. People will say of other people that they have "good *adat*," meaning they are respectful of others, or that they have "bad *adat*" if they are not. And behind this judgment for the Tiruray is always an assessment of whether they are helping other people have a good *fedew*. And it is very important, because if a person is given a bad *fedew*, he or she may very well blow up, pull a knife, and go after the offender.

This leads to other related terms. *Salà* is responsibility for causing someone a hurt *fedew*. *Benal* is one's understandable desire for physical vengeance when offended. *Bonò* is setting out, spear or sword in hand, to satisfy *benal*. And so forth. Tiruray legal institutions are too complex to

161

describe here, but they are rooted in this view of human nature, a whole system of rules and regulations, of customs and understandings, directed at avoiding killing by channeling *benal* away from physical revenge and into the legal arena. And the basic rule of Tiruray morality underlying their legal system is what I've termed "the *fedew* rule": *never* do *anything* to give *anyone* a bad *fedew*. The Tiruray, like people everywhere, do not always live up to their moral imperatives, but that is their basic moral norm and they work hard in their lives at following it (and thus avoiding the unpleasant consequences of not doing so). What this means in practice is that the Tiruray try to be very sensitive to other people's wants. Given human nature, as they construe it, nothing else makes social or moral sense. It was a heady experience for me, an outsider, to live among people with such a scheme of proper behavior. I never before in my life had lived among people who had such sensitive feelers out, who put such great effort into care for the happiness of their fellows. It was truly memorable to live among people who did that.

Now, as I said, these understandings about human nature are part of the Tiruray view of the character of the world. They make up part of what a social theorist might call their "reality constructs." What I want to stress though is that to the Tiruray these do not constitute "a view of human nature." They are not understood as a "theory." They quite literally spell out what the world is like. For the Tiruray, the world is this way, and must properly be lived in this manner. For them, what I have been describing is not a reality construct; it is reality, or, at least, a part of it.

My second example of Tiruray reality concerns the spirits with whom human beings share the cosmos. Spirits, to the Tiruray, are "people you cannot see." Some are tiny and some are giants, but in general they are like people in most ways, except that they are invisible to all but shamans. Indeed, the charisma which identifies an individual as a Tiruray shaman is precisely that he or she can see spirits. Some spirits, especially those who live in the western reaches of the cosmos, are by nature cruel, but most spirits, again like humans ("people you can see"), are neither good nor bad. The same moral rules apply. Treat them right and they will be kind in return; anger them and they will retaliate by making you sick.

Let me describe a few of these spirits in the midst of whom the Tiruray dwell. One class of spirits are the *etew rasak* or "swamp spirits." The Tiruray can always tell you, among other descriptive characteristics, the size, color, and color of clothing of any spirit, and the *etew rasak* are short, black, and wear black clothes. They reside in swampy places, are the spirit protectors of wild pigs and tend to be mischievous in their dealings with humans, lusting after them sexually, and occasionally attempting to seduce individuals who are in the forest alone. The *etew rasak* has the ability to change his or her appearance to that of an attractive human, so that any casual sex in a swamp area is very risky, as intercourse with such a spirit is generally fatal to the human being. Thus, the Tiruray are always wary and particularly warn their adolescents to strictly avoid any situation where an incident of this sort might occur.

Another class of spirits are the *menowo tuduk*, the "mountain spirits." Human-sized, white, and wearing white clothes, they are found on mountain tops and have more spiritual charisma than the *etew rasak*. The *menowo tuduk* are serious and sober in their relations to humans, and often serve as messengers to deliver instructions to the Tiruray shamans from *Tulus*, the great creator spirit. *Tulus* lives "beyond the sky to the East" and sends messages to the *menowo tuduk* through still another class of awesome spirits, the *telaki*, who serve as *Tulus'* "angels." Shamans often build their houses on mountain tops, where they are close at hand to the *menowo tuduk*, should they have a message for them from *Tulus*.

There are many, many other types of spirits of various sizes, colors, and personal characteristics living in the rivers, caves, forests, and fields, interacting in their various ways with each other and with the Tiruray in daily life. Again I want to make the point that these are not a set of "religious beliefs" to the Tiruray; they are an intrinsic part of the way the world is, an element of sheer actuality. The spirits, which most Tiruray never actually see, are as real and unquestioned a part of the real world to them as the North Pole or the rings of Saturn, which most of us never see, are to "modern" people. In fact, the spirits are perhaps more real, because the Tiruray deal every day with spirits, and we do not deal very often with either the North Pole or the rings of Saturn.

The point is, of course, general. Every society has its own view of reality, given in its cultural heritage. And most people never do what we are doing now: stand back and see these views of reality as "views"—as social and cultural reality constructions. As I said earlier, most people, in most of the world, through most of human history, have simply taken their version as sheer, simple, unproblematic reality—as the way the world is.

From my perspective as an anthropologist, I see *their*—the Tiruray—world view, and *their*—the Tiruray—morality, and *their*—the Tiruray—religious belief system. I see these not as the way the world is, but as the Tiruray construction of how the world is. For the anthropologist outsider, as for our fictional outsiders, Roquentin and Meursault (and as for me that morning in college), the fact is that the world is not intrinsically any of these ways. Every society "knows" its own way, its own world. In normal, everyday life ordinary people do not see this. The outsider sees it, and to see it, to record it, and to interpret it is the classic work of a cultural anthropologist.

III

Now, all of this has profound implications for the anthropologist as a person, because, inevitably, we see our own world as a cultural construction, too. The so-called "modern" world in which we live is no different from the Tiruray world in this respect. Where the modern world is different, and this is what makes it so theoretically interesting, is that it is thoroughly pluralistic. The United States is a tremendous mixture of people of varied social, religious, ethnic, class and age affinities, amidst conditions of continual interaction and great mobility. In this sense we have an almost unprecedented social pluralism.

But, more importantly for our discussion, the modern world is pluralistic in consciousness. The impressive consensus of an isolated people like the Tiruray, for example, about the nature of reality, is not present in modern America or Europe, where there is found a huge assembly of differing world views and conflicting moralities, representing various social traditions and countless cultural innovations. It would be a sensible question here to ask someone to describe his or her personal ethics, but such a query would be utterly unintelligible to a Tiruray. One's notions about proper behavior are not a philosophical system to Tiruray. They are a direct expression of the way reality *is* in its normative aspects. And they certainly are not understood as some sort of personal, individual commitment; they are part of the shared social affirmation of that reality. We, in contrast, live amidst great cognitive complexity, and indeed, from a sociological point of view, this cognitive pluralism may be seen as one of the critical features which define "modernity."[9]

Does this mean the cultural anthropologist is "worldless"? No, not necessarily. But it does mean two things. First of all, it means he or she is not

164

innocent. The anthropologist is a form of the classic outsider, a bit like our existentialist protagonists, Roquentin and Meursault. He or she sees the true precariousness of "meaning in the world." And it means that there is a difference between one's objective task as a scholar and one's existential task as a human being in the world.

The objective task for me is to be an anthropologist: to see, to record, and to interpret meaning systems in the cultures of this world, and to think, teach, and write about the human experience in the light of what the data show. But my existential task is to be a person: to grasp meaning, to lead a life which is personally meaningful, to seize—from all possible concerns—those on which my life is to be built. This is really the task of all "modern" people as I have defined modernity, but it is made a close part of one's professional life in my field of studies. For the cultural anthropologist, the objective and the existential tasks draw very near to each other.

Or, at least, they can; they do for me. Studying "other worlds" can open up wonderful new horizons for meaning. I will never be the same since I studied the Tiruray, for they showed me that openness and kindness are real and deep possibilities in daily life—human beings can live that way. And, in the years since I lived in that rain forest, I have tried to grasp openness and kindness the way the Tiruray do, as a key to meaning in human existence.

We are all potentially "outsiders." We outsiders can see an essential meaninglessness in this world, in its nausea and in its strangeness, as it was glimpsed by Roquentin and Meursault, or we can see that life is various, diffuse, and open, but united for each of us by a quest for meaning. And we can live in that quest.

Notes

[1]Sartre (1964:6).
[2]Sartre (1964:125).

³Sartre (1964:127).

⁴Camus (1946:1).

⁵Camus (1946:80).

⁶Camus (1946:118).

⁷Wilson (1956).

⁸Schlegel (1970).

⁹My understanding of "modernity" is indebted to the theoretical work of Peter Berger, as is indeed much of the general stance toward social and cultural reality underlying this address; see particularly Berger and Luckmann (1966) and Berger (1977). Of course, as cognitive pluralism is more and more recognized, it has become the foundation of what many call "post-modernism."

Figel settlement.

Balaud and other legal authorities conducting a legal discussion.

Tiruray woman grinding dried corn in a home-made grinder.

Silù of Figel, preparing to hunt with his bow and arrows.

Chapter 12

THE CUSTOMS OF THE TIRURAY PEOPLE

By José Tenorio (Sigayan)
(Translated and annotated by Stuart A. Schlegel)

This piece is rather different from the rest in this volume, and it needs a bit more introduction. I did not write it, but merely translated and annotated it. The essay—actually a short book—was written by Sigayan as Costumbres de los Indios Tirurayes. *It was a product of the Spanish Jesuit mission in Tamantaka, near Cotabato City.*

Since their first unsuccessful campaign under Figueroa against the Maguindanaon in 1578, Spanish relations with the Muslims of Cotabato had consisted of centuries of ephemeral treaties and mutual hostilities. The Jesuits had a small mission of two padres in Cotabato in 1748, but they had to evacuate after a mere six months. Only in the middle of the 19th century, when the Spanish brought steam-powered gunboats to bear, were conditions in Cotabato sufficiently stable for the Jesuits to return. In 1859 they were invited to resume missionary work in Mindanao, and in 1862 a mission was opened in Tamantaka concerned both with conversion of the Muslim Maguindanaon of the lowlands and the animist Tiruray of the mountains.

One of the Jesuits at Tamantaka, Padre Guerrico Bennasar, took the work among the Tiruray as his own. A French visitor to the mission in 1866 wrote:

> *We were welcomed at Tamantaka by Father Guerrico, a Jesuit. He had established near the fort a mission for the Tiruray, a tribe of the hinterland with a primitive culture. . . . The father taught them Christian doctrine, and how to read and write and even to sing. . . . Father Guerrico knows Tiruray thoroughly, and has written a grammar and a dictionary of the language. The education of his beloved Tiruray is the one obsession of his life.[1]*

Sigayan—or José Tenorio, as he was named at baptism—was a member of the first Tiruray family to accept baptism at the Tamantaka mission. This occurred in 1863, a year after the padres had arrived. Some nine years later,

171

in 1872, he wrote, at Padre Bennasar's request, the little volume which is here translated.

Costumbres *was written by Sigayan in his native Tiruray language, and sets forth what is, to the best of my knowledge, the earliest "ethnography" of his own tribal customs to be written by a Filipino. In 1892, Padre Bennasar published Sigayan's treatise at the Tipografia "Amigos del Pais" in Manila, in a diglot edition, accompanying the Tiruray text with a rather free translation into Spanish and several footnotes.*

I made this translation of Sigayan's remarkable volume in 1969, and it was published in 1970 in Philippine Studies *(vol. 18, no. 2, pp. 364-428). I based the translation upon the Tiruray text, not the Spanish text which is from time to time more a paraphrase or expansion than a translation. My translation adheres very closely to the Tiruray, and, in consequence, a certain price has been paid in prose style. I have added footnotes wherever it has seemed useful, for textual considerations or for elaboration of context.*

Three Tiruray men were of invaluable assistance to me in the preparation of this translation: Mamerto Martin, Aliman Francisco, and the late Ansu Tenorio. Without their aid, I would certainly have floundered. Funds for the project were provided by generous grants from the Foreign Area Fellowship Program and the Department of Anthropology of the University of Chicago.

I. Concerning Tiruray Houses and Food

1. The Tiruray people—if you wish to know where they come from—live in the area between Tamontaka[2] and the land of the Dulangan,[3] which I will not mention again, for the Dulangan are a different tribe. I refer only to the Tiruray people. Their land reaches beyond the smaller branch of the Tran River to the sea coast and as far as the *memilagé*.[4]

2. I must explain to you that the Tiruray do not stay permanently in a single place, nor do they group their houses together to form a village where they could stay permanently. You will never find any such thing as that among them. They are scattered all over their homeland area. It is like a village to them, wherever a father, mother and children, along with their close relatives, have their own piece of land which they name after some nearby water.[5]

3. Now, I will inform you that the largest number of houses they will build close together is ten houses, five, two, or perhaps three houses close together. That is frankly how they are. They most of all prefer a single house all by itself. That one house would already be a village to them!

4. Their houses are poor—in fact laughable. Just consider their posts. There is lots of timber in their place in the mountains, yet with all that wood they get posts that are only the size of a man's arm. They do not get bigger ones—the size of a man's thigh—for their posts. Only a few have good-sized posts for their houses. It is as though their houses were little field huts. Why, in fact, that is all they are: little field huts! No, not even field huts! They are the nests of doves![6] Consider the way they stick the posts into the ground. It is not firmly, but as though they do not have bones to really dig in the ground.[7] So they stick their posts a few inches into the soil. Thus, if there is a wind they must put supports on the house or it will fall down. Consider the beams of their houses, which are all of soft wood—for that is what they get for beams. Anyone going up into one of their houses would think that it is about to fall down.[8] The flooring of the house is made of tree bark; very few use bamboo. There is no wall. Some few people put walls of bark, but others merely hang several fronds of rattan. It is just luck that they survive with such a house—one with no walls and the wind free to pass through![9] The roof too is of rattan fronds; very few make use of grass thatch[10] roofing.

5. Now, with regard to cooking, this is done in the house on a stove near the doorway. Their gangway is a log, cut with notches for steps, although there are a few who make ladders with rungs.

6. For cooking, they use only a covered earthen pot,[11] nothing else. They have neither frying pans nor kettles.[12] Their ladle—a coconut shell! They have neither spoons nor forks, and most people eat off leaves, for few have plates. They use coconut shells for bowls.

7. These people are poor; they have no personal property. Each woman has just one sarong,[13] and the only clothes she has is what you see her wearing. So too with the men; all that they own are the clothes actually on their bodies. There are only a few among them who possess extra clothing. This is because

they do not know how to weave. The Tiruray are not like the Maguindanaon, whose women can weave. The Tiruray are ignorant! There are a few among them who know the art of weaving—but not many.

8. Now, with regard to food, the Tiruray eat rice, yams,[14] taro, corn, bananas, and a wide variety of other plants as well as the fruit of trees.

II. Concerning Their Beliefs, Their Religion, and Beliyan[15]

9. Now, when these people, who live in the forests—they are like monkeys, if you ask me when they themselves pray, they are not like the Maguindanaon who have their *pandita*[16] and who have forms for their prayers. The Tiruray people can (from their ignorance) adjust in everything they do, except praying to Tulus.[17] But, still, they too know that—according to them—they have a single Tulus, whose place they say is only in heaven. They do not realize that God's habitation is everywhere around here.[18] Now, these people also pray to Tulus, and they have among them their *beliyan*. If you were to ask what a *beliyan* is, they would say it is like the Maguindanaon *pandita*. But there is a difference, because the Maguindanaon have their scriptures; the Tiruray have none. (The Tiruray have never known anything about writing.) The one called a *beliyan* by the Tiruray is shameful and laughable. They say he has dreams; he sees Tulus and he talks to Tulus.

10. Now, in such a case, what the *beliyan* does is go around calling the people to assemble. He makes a *tenines*[19] in a place where the people can gather together. Here is what they do there: the *beliyan* tells the people that he has seen Tulus and that, whenever he ate, Tulus ate with him from a single dish. And all the Tiruray around believe him.

11. Here are some other things that the *beliyan* does. He dances, with a wooden kris in his right hand and with small jingle bells and a decorated wooden shield.[20] When he is finished dancing he has the men dance—and the women—for that, they say, is their only worship of Tulus and their manner of praying.

174

12. Then, the *beliyan* tells the people that they will actually go to the place of Tulus for, according to him, that is what Tulus has said. Therefore some of the Tiruray who are listening believe and, believing it to be true, are happy.

13. Now, here are the other things they do. The *beliyan* cooks food for Tulus, who, according to their belief, will eat it. And they set out a betel quid, which they say Tulus will also chew. They bring it to the *fesayawan*[21] and place it in a *rangà.*[22]

14. Playing the *togò*[23] is another activity of the *beliyan*; he has the people play the *togò*. If it is played, he says, Tulus can hear it. If they play on two gongs,[24] according to him, Tulus will answer.[25]

III. Concerning Their Divinities and Supernatural Beings

15. Now I will tell you what these Tiruray say. It is that they are all able to go to heaven. They also know that there is a *narakà*[26] but they claim that none of the Tiruray go there, not even one. The Tiruray say that the Maguindanaon are the ones that go to *narakà* because their god is a different one.

16. They know about the existence of Damangias,[27] but they say that he is far removed from them. Who is it that they call Damangias? He is a fellow who, in the old days, would test the righteous people. There are, as well, those whom they call *saitan*. It is they who are said to cause sickness.

17. Now, aside from Tulus, they say there is a man named Lagey Lengkuwos. He used to live on earth, when there were as yet no *beliyan*. He was always going to visit heaven and coming back again. Lagey Lengkuwos is said to have had a wife, whose name was Metiyatil Kenogon. Even though they never drew close together, still they had a child, whose name was Matelegu Ferendam. The child was male.

175

18. Now, in other stories about them, it was not Metiyatil who gave birth, but rather her necklace, which was known as Tafay Lalawan[28] and which was a family treasure of great sentimental value. They were suddenly astonished to hear a child crying for its mother.

19. They claim it is Lagey Lengkuwos who will escort the Tiruray *beliyan* to heaven. They will be able to see him because he will have his body. He is not really a god, but they say he is a spirit. According to them, there once were lots of *beliyan*, both men and young women: Endilayag Belalà, Endilayag Kerakam, Lagey Bidek Keroon, Lagey Fegefaden, Lagey Lindib Lugatu, Lagey Titay Beliyan, Omolegu Ferendam, and yet many others. I cannot mention them all, for there are so many. But I will mention the names of the women: Kenogon Enggulon, Bonggo Solò Delemon, Kenogon Sembuyaya, Kenogon Dayafan, Bonggo Matir Atir, Kenogon Enggerayur—there are so many of them that I cannot mention them all.[29]

20. All these various individuals are said to come to earth to visit the *beliyan* of the Tiruray, who are able to see them all and talk with them. Now what do you think of all the stories of the Tiruray people? Do you ridicule them? Might they possibly be true?

IV. Concerning a Variety of Superstitions and Charms

21. I have still more to tell you concerning the foolish ways of the Tiruray, about their silly beliefs. (There is no way to escape Damangias!)[30] They have charms, which they call *lambus*[31] or *agimat*,[32] which they tie around their waist or arm, or hang around their neck. Some people wear them hanging from their ears, passing below their jaw. Others wear them wound all around their body; others on their back; others wear them in their rings. When a tree seems strange to them, they will go and get a piece, and they say it has some significance. It is the same with stones, various kinds of grasses, soil, rice, water, resin, oil, large sea shells and small ones, and flintstone. They get charcoal or ashes. Similarly, they get the *lateng*[33] tree, and they collect attractive grasses, the *begongoh*[34] tree, cats, fish, chickens, birds, snakes, the

moon, the stars, various bugs and the sap of trees.

22. Now about all these Tiruray charms[35] I have been mentioning, I will just be very brief. The significance for them, they say, is that they are all "shields for the body." What are they calling "shields for the body"? The various things I mentioned—their charms—which they say keep sickness out of the body. That is why they get all those grasses.

23. Now, with regard to water, the use of that is *kebel.* What is *kebel?* Your skin gets thick and hard, and even if you have someone slash you with a bolo, the skin will not be penetrated. Another of their charms that I mentioned gives a cloak of invisibility. How is that? If you wish it so, your companion cannot see you. You put the leaf of a certain tree in your waist, so that you will not be visible.

24. Another charm is their *falusud.* What is this that they call *falusud?* It changes a man's mind; if he did not previously like a certain woman, he will become attracted to her. Similarly a man can beguile the mind of a woman whom he loves but who does not care for him.

25. I will now discuss what they get from the moon; it is the *faramanis.* What is it that they call the *faramanis?* It is a special beauty—a handsomeness of men and a beauty of women which others, looking at them, see as like the beauty of the full moon.

26. How do they capture the beauty of the moon and stars? They utter a prayer. In addition, they put a little oil into a bowl and then put an egg in that. According to them, they must do this when the moon is full; all who have done it will then get their beauty. This procedure must be done at night when the moon is full and bright and when the sky is cloudless. If the moon should become covered with a cloud during the recitation of the prayer, they cannot receive the full beauty. Now, what good is it to catch the moonlight? These people are laughable! They maintain that it makes both men and women beautiful, and they say that, with their beauty so increased, they will love each other.

27. Now, another one of their charms is a grass, which they use for

filiyos. What is *filiyos?* It is a charm which prevents us from being hit when someone stabs at us. Or, if someone shoots, it will miss. They say that even if someone should knife us in the belly it would miss its mark—and the blade would be deflected to one side or the other of our body.

28. Another of these charms is what they mean by *fekimoy.* What is it that they call *fekimoy?* They use the word in this way: should someone attempt to stab us, he cannot slash us as he is paralyzed in striking position. What I mean is that he cannot move, he cannot budge his arm and he cannot speak.

29. Another one of the charms they use is *felungkang.*[36] What is it that they call *felungkang?* Here is the meaning. Even though someone may be extremely angry at you, if you have the *felungkang* his anger may not be turned on you. Even though he is very angry, the anger will be removed from him.

30. Another charm is the *falimu.* What is the *falimu?* The meaning of that to them is that no person that sees you is ever unkind to you; everyone is always kind to you (if you have this charm).

31. Now, another of their charms is *falulud tamuk.* What is it that they call *falulud tamuk?* They say that if we have the *falulud* we will collect all sorts of property and all sorts of *tamuk.*[37] All such things will come to us. They will be easy to find. Even if we do not find them, and even if we do not have means to get them, still they will come to us.

32. Another of their charms is the *ungit*[38] of the dog. What is the *ungit* of the dog? According to them it is a *dukah*[39]—the sap of a tree—which they burn and have their dogs smell. The dogs will then bite wild pigs and deer.

33. Now, these are all the charms of the Tiruray—all these herbs and various other kinds of *agimat.* They believe in them all, and their prayers are effective. If not, they will utter a prayer facing Tulus, or cast some spell, so that they will be effective.

34. Another charm is what they call a *bengat.*[40] What is a *bengat?*

It is like a poison, a spell cast upon a field where you have planted. The stomach of anyone who steals from that field, should he eat what he stole, will burst.

35. Now, the most terrible of their charms and prayers, which they say they believe and which they say is very effective, is what they call *lambus*. Various grasses, bones, and stones are wrapped and sewn into little cloth bags, and these are used for *ramut*. What is it that they call *ramut*? They say it is something that will kill anyone you hate, or that will make him sick. According to them, if someone says to his *lambus* or his *ramut*, "Go kill that person," that person, they say, will die.

36. Another of their charms[41] is what they call the *bolbol*. What is a *bolbol*? They are Tiruray whose bodies, they say, can fly when it is night time. Now, why do they set off to fly around in groups at night? What is their purpose in such night-flying? They say that they eat the bodies of their fellow men who have died. Moreover, if the *bolbol* hates someone he goes and spears him; the wound, however, is invisible. The person who was speared thinks that he is merely sick, but that is not correct. Someone who knows how to heal the sick will announce that he was stabbed by a *bolbol*.

One who knows how to heal can treat any sort of sickness. What are their medicines? Some herbs, which they apply to the painful spot on the sick person, or, similarly, some chew betel quid. The really laughable thing is that, while he is touching the sick person, he is murmuring something.

37. Now, they have still another superstitious custom. They place in front of their house four—sometimes two—*rangà*, which they use to offer betel quid to Tulus in hopes that Tulus will return their kindness, and that, thereby, the various sicknesses will not come near them.

38. They say that there is another charm of these people, which they know about and which they believe in; this is what they call *alamat*. What is it that they term *alamat*? It is something in their minds. There are, among them, people who can see the future and who know what will befall them. What will happen to them? Should they be about to die, they will be aware of the fact. Whatever evil should be coming to them, they will know about it. So, whatever happens to them, they are forewarned. Also, should someone

hate them, they know the plans of the enemy. Being able to suspect that something will happen to them along their way, they will not set forth.

39. Now, there is still another charm, which they call *sakabat*. What is that which they call *sakabat*? Even if someone is far away from those who would do him wrong, he can still hear about it—if he has a *sakabat*.

40. There is another superstition among these Tiruray for knowing signs of their coming fate, whether it is to be good, and of what will happen to them. How do they foretell their fate? They see in the lines on the palm of someone's hand what will happen to that person—whether good will come or bad, whether he will get *tamuk* or not, whether he will be very poor or very rich, very foolish or very wise. Everything! They will know it from one's palm lines. Similarly, they say that they will know whether they are to die by sickness, or by stabbing, or by whatever other cause of death. They say that they are able to know everything by means of those lines.

41. Moreover, beyond reading their palms, there is still another way of telling one's fortune. They measure their bodies.[42] From this, one learns about one's fate and about the character of one's companion, whether he is wise or foolhardy and what the future will bring to him.

42. I have still to tell you of another way these Tiruray have of telling the future, a way in which they also place great faith. They consult and heed this whenever they are going anywhere and whenever they must undertake some task. Now, what is the name of that sign? Here, I will tell you. Someone sneezes. If he has a trip to make, he will not go. He will just rest. Because, it is said, if one insists on proceeding, he will have an accident or something bad will happen to him. It is the same if the house lizard[43] should sing. Or, if anything in the house should break when people are going somewhere, they will not proceed. They will not do anything.

Now, it is the same with the bird they call the *lemugen*,[44] when it calls. Even if they are already along the way and the bird calls from a bad direction, they will go back. They will not proceed. (As I say, they really believe it.) And, according to them, there is also a good call. In telling the omen, they will point to the direction whence comes the bird's call. Here! I will tell you about their pointing the direction. If it calls from behind them, that is, from a branch at their back, they will not proceed. Now, if the bird's call is right in front of them, the more they will not go on farther, for they say that the *lemugen* is stopping them. They name these calls the *rigara sunur*. Regarding the good ways, or their other ways of pointing the call of this bird—I will not go on and finish telling about these. They really understand meaning in the direction from which the sound comes.[45] This bird has another call, which they hear as telling the truth. They call this *gerung*. They say that if it makes this call when one is doing something, it means that there would surely be some mishap were he to insist on continuing.

43. I will stop here telling about all the omens of the Tiruray. They are so many; I will not finish them all. There are too many! There are more than what I have described. Do you suppose that you could even count all those that are not here yet? But, you will learn about the rest as you are able to be together with the people.

V. Concerning Their Clothes, Weapons, and Adornment

44. I am astonished at all the things that I am telling you about the Tiruray! Now I will inform you regarding the way these people dress. (They are very poor.) They have different styles of dress. The men have three different manners of dress. Those called downstream people[46] all imitate the dress of the Maguindanaon—their trousers are long, the shirt style is that called *sinina* and *bagingubala*, which means just down to their waist. On their heads, they wear a bandanna, tied so that the corner sticks up. Their hair is long, not cut. The hair of both men and women is the same—long. Around their waist, they wear an *angkul*. What is this that they call an *angkul*? It is some cloth that is red, or perhaps spotted. And they also attach a handkerchief to it. These are their charms that I was telling you about before, which they attach to their body. They put a handkerchief over their shoulders and secure another one to the bandanna on their head.[47] Such are their clothes.

For beauty, they file their teeth and make them black by burning a coconut shell. While the shell is burning, they touch it to the blade of an old bolo and the soot which adheres to the bolo blade is what they call *fengileb*. Should their teeth break off, they put in wooden or brass "teeth."

45. Now here is what they do to their face. They shave the hair on their forehead and their eyebrows, and this makes them feel stylish. As for their eyelashes, they trim the tips.[48] For other adornment, both men and women melt wax in oil and then apply it to their lips, so that they will seem soft. They also rub it on their eyebrows to give their eyes a tantalizing appearance when they look at someone.

46. Here are their weapons: a kris, carried at one's side; a spear, held like a walking stick; a *fegoto*,[49] carried over one's shoulder; and a dagger, worn in one's waist. They also have a rounded shield, called a *taming*, and an elongated shield called a *kelung*.

47. Now, as to the men from the mountains,[50] here is their manner of dress. They wear short trousers. I have never seen even one of them wearing long trousers like the downstream people—even though they are all equally Tiruray. The cut of their shirt is the same. These mountain people are careless in their dress: As long as they have covered their body, that is enough for them; they are quite unlike the downstream people, who are very particular. They also wear a bandanna on their head, but they lack clothing compared to the downstream people.

Their weapons are: kris, spear, and bow and arrow. The latter inflicts a terrible death, because they put poison on the arrows.

48. Regarding the men from along the coast, their dress is like this: they wear G-string instead of trousers. Some wear trousers, but not many. Most wear the G-string. Their shirts have the same cut as those of the others, except that the coastal men have one different style: the shirt is sewn inside out. They too wear a bandanna, but they fold it and tie it around their head, for, like women, they wear their long hair knotted into a bun. Moreover, they use *kensal*, as do the women. What is it that they refer to as *kensal*? This is pinching the facial skin so as to cause blood-blisters. It is another part of their beautification. What is this beautification? Something which will improve their body in their eyes, in order to enhance their public appearance. They wear anklets around their ankles, and some also wear them around their knees. These are, however, unlike the women's anklets, which are very loose.

Men's anklets are quite tight around their ankles and knees.

49. They have something else which they never forget when they go out. They always carry a buri bag. If you inquire what they use that for, they use it to carry their betel chewing needs,[51] for these people all chew betel.

50. Their weapons are as follows: a *benongen* (which is like a *fegoto*, only a bit smaller) and a spear. Moreover, they all have a bow and arrow, even the children. The arrows are dipped in *kemendag*. Now, what is this *kemendag*? It is the poisonous sap of a tree. If even a little should enter a wound, it causes death. They say it is used for fighting.

I will turn again to telling how the Tiruray women dress. They wear a sarong which they speak of as their *emut*. It is woven of, and sewn with, abaca fibers. Their blouse has the same general cut as the men's, except that the women's blouse is form-fitting, whereas the men's is quite loose. Therefore, their breasts can easily be recognized (for the blouse is so tight) and the bulging is very clear.

51. Now, the other women's things: both wrists sport bracelets[52] and every finger is full of rings. They also wear a brass and cord belt, decorated with small jingle bells, and there are bells on their wrists. On their ankles, they wear brass anklet rings. Around their neck, they wear various necklaces of glass beads and colored crystals, and the *kemagi*, which is a necklace of gold. The edges of their ears are lined with little holes, in which they wear wire earrings, suspending small shell ornaments. In each ear lobe they have a large hole—you could put your big toe through it. In those holes, they wear large earrings, connected by a decoration which passes underneath the chin.

52. With regard to their other beautifications of the body, they cut their hair to short bangs at the forehead, which they press to make decorative blood blisters. They shave the edge of their eyebrows to thin them, and they cut straight their eyelashes.

53. Here is the way these people fix their hair. They wash their hair with grated coconut, and use a comb made of bamboo.[53] Women's combs are differently decorated, and they wear them in their hair.

54. Regarding their women, you will never see even a single one among them without a knife. Every woman will have a knife if she is going somewhere. Also, every Tiruray woman has a small basket, which she takes whenever she goes out.

55. Now, there is something I forgot to tell you about the people from along the coast. Their men—all of them—enlarge the holes in their ears and wear large pendulous ear hangings.[54]

56. All Tiruray women and some of the men wear *sayaf*.[55] Should you ask what the *sayaf* are made of, it is buri.

57. There are some things I forgot about the Tiruray women's way of wearing their sarongs. They have *saket*. They take a tuck in the upper edge of the sarong, and place it there around their waist. If you ask me what it is that they call the *saket*, it is the roots of the grass named *buruk*.[56] Now, if you further inquire why they do that, it has no significance. They merely do it so that when one sees them they seem attractive, with broadened hips and a small waist, as well as a pleasant odor.

I will also tell you, regarding these women, that it is there in their *saket* that they place their charms—their *lambus*—and the men do the same thing. They also use them as bracelets and necklaces.

I forgot to mention something about both men and women. They have charms which they eat, which are a whole different set from the others.[57]

VI. Concerning Killings and the Causes That Motivate Them

58. Now, I have already told my readers about the weapons of the Tiruray. I will now relate whether they are brave or cowardly, and I will tell about their way of fighting. Their customary way of fighting is *lemifut*.[58] What is this that they call *lemifut*? Or, rather, why is it that they *lemifut*? Is it perhaps that there is a long-standing grudge? No! *Kengasa ro fo!*[59]

When they see somebody having many belongings or lots of *tamuk*, or if they arrive at his house and he has no companions—even if there are many

184

there, but they feel them to be weak—they will murder in order to get that *tamuk*.[60] If there are lots of other belongings, the more the murderers are delighted .

59. Now, I will tell you, the reader of this writing, about the Tiruray, that among themselves the Tiruray seldom truly *lemifut*. Seldom only, for it is not their true custom to murder among themselves, except that they will fight each other if someone has done them an offense. When they really go in for killing is when troublesome Maguindanaon come up to the Tiruray areas. If the Tiruray see them, and if they have *tamuk*, they are apt to die for they will murder them. Besides, they hate them.

Now, why do they hate them so? Because some Maguindanaon are going too far in their behavior towards the Tiruray. So, what is this going too far which the Maguindanao do among the Tiruray? Listen, I will tell you. They demand tribute. They give the Tiruray a large bag and make them fill it with rice,[61] or they will mark someone's rice field and demand of the Tiruray all that is within their marks. When they have rice, or anything, in the mountains of the Tiruray, they make them carry it down to the Maguindanaon's home place.[62]

60. Now, about other things they do to the Tiruray. If they see them—or, if the Tiruray let the Maguindanaon see them—eating pork, they impose a fine. Those Tiruray are afraid of the Maguindanaon, and if they fine them, they give it. They give *tamuk*, just for eating pork, if they are seen by the Maguindanaon.

Why is it that they are afraid of the Maguindanaon? Are they so few in number perhaps? How few are they? Are the Tiruray people not numerous? Or, are they just afraid of the Maguindanaon? Are they not men? No. It is not that they are not numerous; they are quite plentiful. And it is not that they are afraid, and they say that they are manly. Well, what can the Tiruray people do? As I told you before, in the mountains their houses are not grouped but separated, far from each other. The men are in twos or threes. So, when the Maguindanaon arrive, they see the two men, and even if the two are full of anger, they cannot resist. The Maguindanaon number five or ten. Can they resist? No. Whatever the Maguindanaon want, they will just go along with them. So, the wicked Maguindanaon, seeing the Tiruray are not in force, but are merely a single isolated household, assume they will offer no resistance. They seize them, enslave them, and sell them. That is why the Tiruray abhor them. Their treating them so badly contributes to the Tiruray's killing of the Maguindanaon. It is, at least, part of it. But there is still another cause of the Tiruray's killing them treacherously—their *tamuk*!

61. Now, I will go on telling you the Tiruray customs in fighting—or whether they are brave or cowardly. I will tell you, therefore, that they are not cowardly, nor are they brave—they are in between cowardice and valor. They are a prudent people.

62. Now, the way they kill, if there is someone with whom they are angry or against whom they have a grudge, is this—they go after revenge. What is their revenge? When it is still daytime, they set out hiking to the place of the one they hate. Then, when they are at the place of the one they hate, and it is night, they come out. They go to shoot their bows and arrows or they may spear him as he sleeps. The avengers hide and do not want to be seen, for they do their killing by stealth. Once they have killed, they move away a bit—but they do not proceed to run home. They stay near the place of the one they have stabbed, in order to make sure from the sounds in the house whether the man died or not. When they hear someone shout out, "Who stabbed?" they, still being close by, will reply, "We did; we came to settle the *tamuk* of our friend, because we did not receive what we were entitled to."[63] That is the boastful reply of the avengers. So, then the killers go home, for they are satisfied.

When they are on their way home, already far from the scene of their revenge, they sing their *kerensiyow*. Now, what is this that they refer to as *kerensiyow*? They sing for their victim, so that Moferow[64] will open his window and look down to earth, so that he will open his door and allow the soul of that fellow to enter there. For that is the destination of stabbed persons. The purpose, they say, of their singing is to send the spirit of that person they stabbed to the right place, to the place of departed souls. Also, they say, the other significance of their singing is this: even if they have stabbed someone, they have no fault so long as they send his soul to the proper place. Their fault for what they have done is no more. It is already removed by their singing of that *kerensiyow*.[65]

63. Now, since I have told you already about the customs of these people

186

when they kill, I will tell you also the causes of their fighting each other: stabbing, using sorcery, killing one's wife for adultery, stealing, parental interference when children quarrel, teasing which goes too far, mockery, and farm work.

64. That is sufficient for me to tell you about the bravery of the Tiruray. Here I will tell my reader of another custom of this people. It is very different and frightening. It is not good to imitate it. Also, I think that no Christian person would do it. Why? What is this custom? Do you think it is a good one? It is frightening. Even if you only hear about it, it is painful to hear. How much more so, if you see it! What is it then?

They go to inform someone that they intend to drink a poison, which they call *tebeli* (it is a vine).[66] They commit suicide, in order to die. Sometimes, they jump into deep water. They cut their own throats, or, in various ways, they commit suicide that they might die.

Now, among the Tiruray, those that you always hear about committing suicide are the maidens and young men. Few married people kill themselves. You may ask me, why should the maidens and young men commit suicide? If one addresses them with obscenities, or should their name come out in scandal, they will really kill themselves if they cannot proceed at once to marry, for they are deeply humiliated by such things if they are still young and unmarried. They do not wish to talk about them.

Long ago, when the Tiruray were still unchanged, one who was still a maiden did not want to go near any man, but it was the same for a young man.[67] Do you think he would approach close to a maiden? But now, no more! The Tiruray have changed. Before their customs changed, the maidens could only be near a man if they were already married. And so with a young man; he could only draw near to a woman if they were married. Not the Tiruray of today. Even those who are still small are already acquainted with evil.

VII. Concerning Their Marriages

65. I will also tell you about the customs and arrangements regarding Tiruray marriage. The Tiruray customs are as follows:

If you have a son, and if you feel that you have ample *tamuk*, you go to arrange a marriage; that is, you go to the house of a man who has a maiden and the two of you discuss the matter. This is because they do not want their daughter to marry a man who has no *tamuk*. If you should ask me what the *tamuk* is for, it is used for the brideprice. If we were to compare it to buying and selling, it is what the man is using to buy the woman. But it is not really buying; the woman does not become their slave.

Once they are married, the couple stays with the elders of the man.

What I can say is that they have a very different way of marrying. Here is how the young man marries a maiden. The boy's father is the one who finds a girl for his son. (Among the Tiruray, that is the custom.) However, the man and the woman do not know that they are to be married. If they do not guard them carefully, when their names have not yet been announced as about to wed, they will commit suicide from shame.[68] So, only their parents discuss their plans; the girl and the boy do not suspect a thing. They will only learn about it when they are officially informed. Such is their custom regarding marriage.

Even should the boy not like the girl, they may still be married, for they will be forced to do so by their elders. In Tiruray custom, very few actually court each other.

Now, if there is no way to win the couple's hearts to each other—if they really do not care for each other—they will substitute a close relative of the same generation for the one who cannot come to care. If both the man and the woman do not give in and care, both are replaced. Their custom in marrying is very hard! If it is the man who does not care for his wife, the truth is that he must simply surrender his brideprice; he cannot get it back anymore. In such a situation, it is not the girl who does not care; it is the fault of the man. So, if there is no close relative of his to be set forth in his place as husband to the woman, the brideprice will be forfeited.

66. I will now return to what I was telling you earlier about their being informed that they are to be married. By custom, the man and the woman are always informed after it is dark, never in the daytime. They announce it to the man in the house of his *kefeduwan*.[69] If the bachelor who is to be married should ask why many people are gathered, they will tell him that it is for some other reason. The various *kefeduwan* present will be formally discussing many things, supposedly other than the wedding. The time when the fellow

wakes up to what is happening is when one *kefeduwan* says, "You, Sigayan; they have found a girl for you, a woman of Kafiton. The name of that girl is Ambug."[70] So I—having been told that I am about to marry—would begin to struggle. If no one holds me, I might strike someone, as I have been put to such shame (as they see it). But, it does not last long—not even long enough for someone to cook a shrimp![71]

67. The struggling was, really, just to observe the customs, for I liked that girl from the village. My reason in doing it was that I was all alone in being mentioned among all the people present. As soon as I got tired, I stopped. After all—imagine—there are sometimes five and sometimes seven men holding you! When I stopped struggling, I was in tears so they blew ginger into my ear. My anger came to an end while I was struggling, for I was securely bound and it was just too difficult to go on straining. While I was crying, they shouted at me, in the traditional way of such times.[72] One of the women shouts out, then everyone joins in and shouts along with her. (That is the way of the Tiruray wedding customs.)

68. Now, as for the woman to whom they will marry me, they formally announce our names to her the same night. Should my reader ask me what women customarily do when they receive the announcement, they also cry, for they are ashamed that it was spoken out among so many people that they were to be married.

69. I will now return to telling you about the man, and what happens once the announcement is finished. (It is usually night time when this occurs.) The following morning, the groom's kindred goes with him to the place of the girl. The groom, ever since his name was announced, has not been happy, and he keeps his head shrouded within his *emut*.[73] Never will he open it to permit his face to be seen. You would have to force him, to see his face, even when he is being dressed. They cannot get him to dress himself—that is the work of the other young men. Once they start to go, they have to drag the groom along—like a *wahwah*[74] with a broken leg! Not really wanting to go, he walks along very slowly. What several fellows do is to walk along with him, side by side, surrounding him.

Along the way, they play gongs until they reach the place of the girl's kindred. Also, all along the way, they continue to utter the traditional wedding shout to the groom. As I was saying before, when one so shouts to the groom, others also join in the shouting—and this is what they do, right up to the place of the girl's side.

Now, here is what they do with the groom when they are drawing near to their destination. They place a *dudum*[75] over him, made of a length of cloth. And all the many people in the group help the groom to take cover inside.

70. It is mid-afternoon when they come to the settlement of the girl's people. Now, once they have arrived there, do you suppose that they can immediately enter? Not yet, for at the boundary of the clearing there will be an *alang*—a barrier made of wooden posts stuck in on both sides of the trail with something tied across them. If a kris or a *fegoto* is not set there, the groom may not proceed. Only when there is a kris, for them to use in cutting the fence of the girl's kindred, then may they proceed.[76]

Then, they are all grouped there in the clearing. They do not immediately go up into the house.

Now, I will return to the way in which the man's side arrives at the place of the girl. What is that *alang* at their settlement? It is one way by which they are already asking for brideprice from the man's side. That, at their meeting, is the first one to be given.

71. I will now proceed with the account of the man's kindred being there in the clearing. Why is it that they do not immediately go up into the house? Because it is their custom that the bride's side will first bring the betel to chew, and, as some might be thirsty, they will also bring water to the clearing.

Why, moreover, should they tarry? Because they have something to do. They are first going to dance. The owner of the house—one of the girl's kindred—will perform the *keilawan* dance.[77] The men dance first, to the music of the *togò*,[78] holding a drawn *fegoto* in their right hand, and in their left hand they carry a decorated shield. As to their dress while dancing, they wear a sarong—not in the fashion of women, but rather *simful.*[79] Handkerchiefs are tied around both biceps, and another handkerchief is fastened around their sarong like a belt.

72. Now, when the bride's side has finished dancing, the men of the groom's kindred dance—in the same manner as the others had. When they are through, the women have their turn. They too dance to the music of the *togò*, played along with a pair of gongs to the melody known as "*Tebagen*."[80] You will really enjoy their performance—the *togò*, the gongs, and especially the sound of the women's movements with their ankle rings and little bells.

73. As to their dress for dancing, they wear a colorful, folded sarong crosswise over one shoulder, and, on each shoulder, a handkerchief.

Now, when their dancing is finished late that afternoon, the man's group prepares to go up into the house. Throughout the dancing, the groom had remained under his canopy. The woman's side cannot look at him. They can only see him in the morning, when the wedding ritual occurs. Up to that moment, they cannot.

74. I will now go on with what they do when they are about to go up to the house. They shout the traditional wedding cry to the groom. Then, the owner of the house also shouts it to their bride.[81] They give the shout twice to each of them.

Once this is all finished, they go into the house. Those of the woman's side—*kefeduwan*—say, "Come up." "Good," reply those on the man's side. So everyone is now actually up in the house.

What do they all do, once they are there? Nothing yet. They merely rest a bit, while the groom is enclosed in a little room.[82] Do you suppose you can look at him yet? You cannot! It is the same in the case of the bride. You cannot see her, for they have her in the *sibey*.[83]

75. At this point, I will tell anyone reading what I have written here that I am not now going on with the activities of those who have gone up into the house. At this point, I will go back and relate what the girl's kindred does when their daughter's hand has been asked in marriage.

Assuming that they consent to the marriage, they first construct a huge house, big enough to hold 200 persons when the wedding takes place. Once that is finished, they hurry their preparations.

When they have finished the house, they prepare the things needed for cooking—rice, coconut, salt, and spices. All of this they will cook to give to the man's side. With regard to their preparation of food, if, for instance, the wedding is to be tomorrow, they would cook now—all through the night. Suppose you ask them where they plan to put the food, knowing that they lack plates. Or, even if they have enough plates, still it is their custom to wrap the rice in banana leaves and put the bundles into baskets. They fill the baskets up with wrapped, cooked rice—numbering as many as more than 100. They also ready their *singà*.[84]

I mentioned that there are numerous baskets of bundled rice. They make an equal number of bamboo tubes filled with chicken broth. To prepare the chicken, they cook it whole in pots. Do you think that they first cut up the chicken? No. It would not be proper to cut it into smaller pieces, as the man's kindred might think that the woman's side did not cook the entire chicken. The correct package is one whole chicken with each basket of rice. Because of this, it is the custom that if one of the chicken's wings is missing from the basket, the woman's side must give the man's side one kris. It is the same with the chicken's neck; if it is missing the woman's kindred must surrender one spear.

76. Now I will go on with what I was telling you before, concerning the groom's going up into the house. After they have rested a while, here is what they do. The *kefeduwan* of the man's side will get all the baskets prepared by the girl's side. All in the groom's party are given baskets, one by one. These are the persons who help in giving the brideprice.

After they have finished eating, they all spend the night there in the house. They wait for the morning when they will wed the couple. All through the night, here is what they do: the *kefeduwan* talk together in *tiyawan*.[85] Some of the young men also converse with each other, by means of singing alternately, one after the other. What are they singing about? Is it addressed to Tulus? No, their singing does not concern Tulus. They are merely competing with each other in telling stories with hidden meanings. They are singing about all sorts of good things—or it may indeed turn to bad things. Anything they have heard may be put into the songs, and the one who knows this skill will be able to understand the message of the other singer, whether it is good or bad. It may be just this which some fellows come for—to seek out those who know how to do such singing. When one who knows how hears another sing, he answers it; for he knows what it means.

Now, I will tell anyone reading this, in case he is wondering, why it is the custom of these people, when they talk about things, to do it by this sort of antiphonal singing. It is because the singers are happy when many listen to them. Not everyone knows how to do it.

77. We will now leave the subject of such singing; that is their custom and that is what they do all the whole night at weddings. Moreover, even if it is not a wedding, if those who know how to sing this way meet each other in their houses, they sing together.

78. So, when daybreak has come, all those who went to eat chicken[86] give their *tamuk* to their *kefeduwan* to be given, for on this day it is turned over to the woman's kindred. When everyone who went to eat chicken has put down his contribution, that is the moment when it is given over.[87]

They say that if the girl is beautiful, they will give 400 plates plus five other pieces of *tamuk* as the brideprice. Now, they say that when the girl is homely, or has an ugly appearance, the brideprice is diminished from the homely down to the ugly. From four items according to them, to three, to two, to just one as the brideprice for those![88]

What are the items that these people give? Pay heed, I will tell you: plates, handkerchiefs, bandannas, blouses, trousers, waistbands, brass anklets, brass bracelets, brass betel boxes, sarongs, spears, krises, gongs, bead necklaces, horses, gold necklaces, carabao—all of these things are given as brideprice.

Now, when they have finished giving the brideprice, it is time for the actual wedding ceremony. What is the appearance of their wedding ritual? The mother of the bride prepares a betel quid and hands it to her daughter, asking her to give it to her groom. Then when they have finished chewing, the elders bump the couple's heads together. This is how Tiruray marry.[89]

Now, regarding their chewed quids, do you suppose that they will throw them away? No. They keep them until they die.[90]

That completes the wedding customs of the Tiruray.

VIII. Concerning Anniversaries of Weddings and Births

79. Now, I wish to tell my reader about another Tiruray custom with regard to those who are already married. When they have been married a year,

or when a child is born, there is something which will be done concerning them. They will have a feast called *sefeinem*.[91] The feast is given by the woman's side to the groom.

What is drunk? They call it *gimas*, and it is made from corn; it is to them a proper hard drink. It is really strong, and it makes one dizzy. They put it in a large jar, which they call a *biang*. It has handles, so when it is hoisted it can be held there.

Now, the *sefeinem* is just like the wedding feast. There is no difference. Of course, they do not do the wedding ceremony itself over again, but otherwise the two are just the same with regard to customs. The man's side will again give *tamuk*, as was agreed upon at the wedding feast. It is as though their *tamuk* were payment for the rice and chicken they eat! All remaining brideprice must be given at this time.

80. There is another custom among these people that has to do with marriage. I will tell you about it.

If a young man and a maiden to whom he is betrothed should become lovers, they will run away together. Neither their elders nor anyone else will know about it—only the couple. Their elders will only find out when someone says, "The lad, Sigayan, and the maiden, Ambug, the daughter of Mosulatan, have eloped."[92] Now, everyone will assume that they were probably lovers. They might report, "They ran to the *kefeduwan*, Bandara." In such a case, this Bandara, to whom they ran when they eloped, cannot turn them away. They become like his own children, and, having *tamuk*, he goes to their aid.[93]

81. These people have still another custom with regard to getting married. It is a bad custom, and I am ashamed to repeat what it is. This is also a way of running off, like the one I have just described to you, but there is a difference. Even though some maiden among them is not the lover of any young man, should some people meet her who have a young male relative, they may kidnap the girl for their young man. Although the girl will object, they will force her to go. Now, if the young woman refuses to walk, and if the kidnappers are many and can do it, they will drag her. And they will indeed be many, for it was their plan to take her with them. This is because many people have tried to arrange an engagement with her, but her kindred never permit it. Even when those going to make the arrangements have plenty of *tamuk*, still they will not give her up.

82. Now, therefore, what some Tiruray do who want her is wait for her somewhere. They will watch her pass by, waiting for her patiently by the place where people get water, or at some other place where those who want her have observed that she frequently goes.

Once they have hold of her—I have already said—they will carry her, not letting her walk. They pay no attention to her shouts. She grabs a hold of trees, because she does not want to go with them, but one of the abductors follows along behind chopping the trees off with a kris.

Let us turn now to consider the relatives or parents of the maiden. Once they know what has happened to their young woman, they will run after her fully armed. Now, they say in their hearts that they must be ready, for if they catch them, they will kill the maiden. In their minds, it is not the kidnappers who are at fault; they are angry at their young woman for going with them. Actually, she was forced and did not do it intentionally, but that is the thinking of the brothers and elders of the woman. So they run after her to kill her, for they say they were put to shame by her wanting to go along with what they understand to have been an elopement. (That is what the parents of the girl say.) If one really wishes to marry, and they feel it is like that, it is a very wicked girl who wants to go along.[94]

83. That is what they will say, if they are able to overtake them. Those, therefore, who abducted the maiden will be well prepared with *tamuk*. Then, even if they are chased, they have some to leave along the way, so the pursuers will not continue chasing them. What is this that they leave along their trail? Why should the chase after the maiden not go on? Because the first thing that they will come to is a naked spear stuck into the path. Now, suppose those chasing do not take that spear, but just leave it and continue their pursuit? They will then find a kris placed on the path. Do you think they will accept that? No! So they then come to a stack of one hundred plates, but again they pass it by. They come to a large Chinese jar, but still they proceed. So they come across a gong, with its hammer, laid upon the trail. Again they keep on going. Then they come to a bead necklace hanging along the path, but they pay it no heed. They just continue chasing, and come to a gold necklace of *furo teresang* type.[95] Still they continue running after the young woman. They have just not been convinced by all the *tamuk* which the kidnappers have strewn in their path. They soon come to a horse tied along the road, and an *emut* hanging nearby, and a special *emut*, and a brass belt, and a large brass

195

betel box, complete with all its various parts, but these people pay no attention to any of these things, for they pity their young woman.[96] They continue the chase, and reach a carabao tied at the side of the road. Now they have had enough. They do not go on chasing their maiden any more. They go home and inquire around about them, for they cannot disapprove of this man who has so much *tamuk* to leave along the way. The man would be dead who still does not agree.[97] Even if they did kidnap her, they can say, "Why do they not respect us?" and, "Is that not *tamuk* that we left for them along the way?" Then the ones who got the girl could say, "Take your maiden if you do not want the marriage, but you can just return all that *tamuk* doubled!"[98]

IX. Concerning Other Ways of Seeking a Spouse

84. Now, these people have still another marriage custom, which is funny, shameful and irritating. I will tell my reader about it. What is their other marriage custom? It is really strange.

If a young man sees a young girl who is attractive in appearance, well off, industrious, and talented, then he may want her and may go to her house, where he asks to marry her. Now, he is not alone in going to propose the marriage; he takes along some of his close kinsmen. These companions are the ones who speak out first. They say, "We have come here to your place in order to extend the size of your house." (So say those who went there to make the marriage, those who accompanied the young man.) "Here is the meaning of our coming here with our friend; he has come to marry your young lady. We brought with us *tamuk* for brideprice."

The parents of the girl do not reply; they are just silent, as are those who came with the suitor. That is the extent of what they reply: they are silent! Now, the answer of the girl's parents to such a suitor is to draw a kris and to try to frighten him by stabbing all around the place where the young man is sitting. If he is easily scared, he will run away. You might think that they would be likely to hit him and kill him, but no, they are just frightening him —and that is really the custom of all Tiruray. Everywhere around where the young suitor is sitting is cut to pieces, even the roof near his head.

This will only come to an end when a leader of the household, or one of the *kefeduwan* will tell the one slashing so angrily to stop, that he has done it enough. Otherwise would they just not stop?

196

Now, when this custom is all finished, what they do is have a *tiyawan*.[99] At this point, the girl's family will tell those who came with the young man whether or not they consent to the marriage. If they do, the brideprice will be given and the couple wedded that very afternoon.

If the parents of the girl do not want it, things become very difficult. How could it be otherwise, since the suitor has offered a substantial brideprice? If they really are determined to reject him, and do not double the *tamuk* he offered, it becomes very hard indeed. Oh yes, they will return to their home. But the truth is that someone may be missing![100] Were the disappointed suitors to stab someone under those circumstances, the girl's side would have no recourse, for it would be outside their rights.

If you ask what gives the young man's side the right to take revenge, they would say, "This is our right; the way we were treated when we went to marry! These people have scorned our *tamuk* and, besides, they have considered us as nothing at all, as so many idiots!" Those on the woman's side may indeed not be afraid, but those who went to propose marriage, even should they be cowardly by nature, would just forget their cowardice because of having been put to shame.

85. Now, having told my reader this people's custom when they marry—that of the young men's going to openly press their suit—I will also say that there is also such a custom for women.

86. A maiden among them may desire some young man. Even if the fellow has less love for her than so much urine, if the young girl is full of desire for him she may forget about her pride. Even though by nature maidens are very shy and customarily only marry when the elders arrange it properly, one may be unable to wait! She goes, therefore, to ask openly for the boy she loves, taking with her a bundle of *tebeli*.[101] If he refuses, she can commit suicide right there in his house.

Just as in the case of the young man's going openly, if the marriage is refused, *tamuk* must be given. If there were no *tamuk*, and if the boy really refused, the girl would surely kill herself.

Actually, that will never happen, because if he really feels that way, his elders will put forth another young man for the girl.

197

X. Continuing about Marriages

87. Now, since I have already told my reader about some Tiruray marriage customs, I will mention another way of marrying. It is very shameful to relate, for it is another bad custom of the sort Christian people would never have. Nevertheless, Christian Tiruray, in spite of the Fathers being here from the year 1862 to the year 1872, still follow their old customs.

Now, if the person who reads my writing should ask what this custom is, it is this: if a Tiruray couple are really faithful to each other, when God claims one of them, when one dies—especially when the wife dies first, and has living female relatives—one of them may marry her husband.[102] This is true even if she is still a little girl. She still becomes the widower's wife, and he must raise her from her childhood, if that is the only way. Even if the deceased wife's relatives do not personally wish it, the man's side would not permit them to reject the substitution, for they would take blood revenge.[103] If the woman who died has no appropriate relatives, then one half of the brideprice must be returned to the man's side. Likewise, if the husband died, and if he has an appropriate relative, the latter may marry his widow.

Why is it that they have such a custom? Because they are seeking to keep their brideprice alive. In this custom of theirs, although the brideprice was given long ago, still generation after generation they will chase after it. I think they would go on doing so right up to the end of the world. It is their custom, derived from the ancestors, to provide replacement spouses. So long as some relatives are still alive, they will always continue to do just that.

88. The Tiruray have still another abhorrent and shameful custom. Even bad Christians would not do such a thing, and yet there are Tiruray Christians right now who nevertheless still practice it. What is the custom? All right, here it is! Tiruray have—that is, the men only have—two, three, four, five, six, seven, eight, nine, or ten wives; if he is a good man, and can afford it, he might even have more than that. This is a worthy custom to them, one which earns praise.[104]

89. I have some more to tell the person reading this, of another Tiruray custom which is frightening and quite beyond the pale. Christians would not do it. Well, what is it? All right, here it is! They will elope together, even if

198

both are married, or if the man is single but the woman is married, or vice versa. They call this *selamfa*. They do not fear this custom, even though it is terrible. If no one will give the elopers sanctuary, they will both be killed and placed face to face on top of each other in a single grave.

90. Now, the Tiruray have another custom. If one sees that his wife is in love with some other man, he will really watch them, for if he is able to catch them both somewhere, he will stab them.

91. If the man is in love with another woman, and if his wife sees them, they will separate. Then it is only if the man gives more *tamuk* that they will not be divorced.

92. Suppose a married woman is being loved by another man, whom she does not love. If he touches her, he will be legally at fault and will be fined *tamuk*, for she will report him.

93. Now, the Tiruray have still another custom. If a young man touches a young maiden, the two will certainly have to marry, for among these people the young women do not want to be played around with. They are virtuous. They can only be with a man if he already belongs to them. That is why if a young man touches a girl, they must marry. Their custom is a good one.

XI. Concerning Births

94. Since I have already told my reader about Tiruray marriage customs, I will go on and tell about when they have children, and also about when they are still pregnant, and about what their customs are when they give birth.

95. By custom, when they are pregnant, it is bad to eat shrimp. For they say one will die in childbirth, because the child, in coming out, will imitate the shrimp in the water and will go backwards.
Similarly, in the case of a chicken's egg taken from inside a butchered hen, the pregnant woman cannot eat it. For the pregnant woman will be like that chicken whose egg was inside; it might be that she will be like that chicken and her child will not come out.[105]

199

96. Regarding their customs at the time of childbirth, they go inside a mosquito net. Some of the women who are helping the one giving birth are inside the net. There are some men—two, three, or four—and a midwife who stays near the feet of the parturient woman. I do not know what all she does, but she is the one who receives the baby.

If the woman is having a hard time delivering, they chew something and rub it on her stomach. I do not know what it is, perhaps some herb.[106]

Once the baby is out, they cut the umbilical cord and put it with the placenta into a basket, which they take to a *nunuk*[107] tree and hang on one of its branches. They do not throw them away, nor bury them.

The child is bathed at once.

Now, as to their helpers, they give them *tamuk* as payment for their fatigue.

97. I will also tell my reader of another custom of bad Tiruray women. If they feel that there is a child in their belly, they kill it by pressing, or else they drink a potion to prevent the child from developing.[108] This is also done when there is no fixed father.[109] Likewise, those who just do not want to have a child; they drink medicine. Those who drink a potion really do not have a baby.

98. Since I am telling the person reading this all about the customs of the Tiruray regarding births, I will go on now and tell about newly born children.

On the seventh night, they shave their hair. They leave a little hair on the top of the head, a little on the cowlick, and a little above each ear. The reason, they say, for leaving those patches of hair unshaved is so that there is a place for the child's soul to stay.[110]

99. Here is another of their customs having to do with babies. Every day they bathe the baby four times. Even if it is still pink,[111] and even if the sun is hot at noonday, they will bathe the child. They claim that it is a good habit to bathe it, in order to cool off the sweat and heat of the body.

That is also the custom of some older people. Even if it is noontime, once they feel the heat in their bodies, they immediately cool off by going to the river. Even more, if they are perspiring, they will not feel well unless they can take a bath.[112]

I will return to the things they do to the baby. They do not have the custom of dressing little babies. If the baby is still very small, they merely wrap it with cloth. Now when they have already grown a bit bigger, they will feel the need to cover up,[113] for they know what is proper, and they already feel embarrassment.

100. Now, regarding naming their babies, when they are still tiny, girls are called "new girl" and boys are called "new boy." This is not yet a real name, but is just their way of calling babies when they are still small. Once they are big, their names will be changed.[114] They are not named after the saints in heaven; they just get their names from the world. Look, it is like this. One of their names is Sigayan, which means "that on which falls the radiance of the sun."

101. I will tell you something else they do with their babies—they lay them down, or they put them to sleep, in a cradle made of a sarong suspended from the rafters. It moves softly up and down and sways back and forth, and into it they place the baby.

102. Having told you already what these people do with their babies, I will go on and say that they observe certain customs when they eat. They will mention the names of babies who are sleeping while their parents eat. They say, "Let's eat, Sigayan; there is plenty for you." The reason for doing this—as they tell it—is so that the soul of the sleeping child will not steal food from a *saitan*,[115] which, if he were to eat it, would make him sick.

XII. Concerning What They Do with the Sick and the Dead

103. Now, I will go on to tell my reader about when there are sick among these people. They have the custom, when they are tending or curing sick people, of putting *uwar* (a sort of rattan)[116] around the house. They use this to frighten the *bolbol*,[117] for it is the nemesis of the *bolbol*. *Uwar* is magical; it becomes a snake[118] and frightens the *bolbol*. As I mentioned a bit earlier, the *bolbol* are cannibalistic. They are people themselves but they eat people;

they eat the livers of sick persons. Now, some people can see *bolbol*, for they are said to be *bolbol*, too. These guard the sick, holding a kris. Then, when they see a *bolbol* below coming close, they draw their kris from its scabbard and stab him—to kill him for he is a cannibal.

Even me, I have seen how they do it. When my mother was sick, there was a person, a Tiruray, watching her at night and using my kris. (I had shined it up, so there was no rust.) I got it, and we inspected the blade first, in case you think he lied. He went down from the house, and not long afterwards came back up. While he was down, we heard a sound—for he had stabbed a *bolbol*. The house was destroyed, for the *bolbol* crashed against it, moving as though he were a large carabao. There was a sound like groaning down there. Then the person came up into the house, deeply disturbed and holding that unsheathed kris, which was flowing with blood. His body was also stained with blood. When I saw the blood dripping, I was afraid and I believed it.

104. Now, my reader should not imitate me in believing the foolishness of the Tiruray. The Christians say there is no truth to it, and it will just be a sin before Tulus. These people, believing such superstitions, see the *bolbol* because of the work of Damangias.[119]

Now, about their medicine for sick people, they use various herbs, and in treatment they chew them and rub them on. Some things are really laughable! One Tiruray curer touches the sick and, they say, gives a prayer by just moving his lips. They say that he is praying to Tulus, that Tulus should cure the sick fellow.

105. Now, as I am telling the customs of these people when they are sick, I will go on to describe what happens when there is a dead person among them. When someone dies, their custom is to weep and be very sad. After that, they will go into mourning for the dead individual.

106. The custom when somebody dies is this: the moment one loses one's breath, they bathe the body or at least wash its face. Then they immediately place a mirror near its head, for otherwise the *bolbol* would approach. (As I said before, they will eat the dead.) The reason is that when the *bolbol* sees the dead person, it sees two faces but only a single body. They say this will frighten it, and that is the purpose of the mirror.[120]

107. Now, there is a kris. If the dead is a grown male, they place a kris by his side. The purpose of that, they say, is that it is something of his. Even though he is dead, they can still see him when they see that kris.[121]

They put all the belongings of the deceased into their graves. They also put with them their spears, sarongs, trousers, shirts, bandannas, cloth belts and their brass betel boxes of various sizes, along with all their contents.[122]

108. When morning comes, they wrap the body in a mat, tying it up as one would a bundle of rattan. The sleeping sarong of the dead person is wrapped around the body, with its mat bound on outside of that. This is the way the dead are buried. Very few are placed in a coffin at death. They do not have the custom of using coffins.

109.[123] Now, that morning, while the body is still in the house, they cook a large meal, butchering chickens so that the people guarding will have a viand. When it is time to eat, when the food is ready, they never say to each other, "Come and eat," for to invite someone to eat food prepared on behalf of a dead person is considered very bad. The dead person may imitate them, and invite the living to die! (That is what they are trying to evade; hence their custom.) Thus, when they eat food prepared in the presence of a corpse, everyone in the house merely goes and begins eating without verbal invitation.

110. Once the various customs regarding the dead person are concluded, they will take the body to the grave. For a litter, they use two poles with crossbars where the body is tied. The size is measured so as to be just wide enough for the back of the deceased. Two persons carry the body.

By custom, the grave is dug very deep. Now, once they are already covering up the body, everyone who went along with the burial party helps in covering the grave—even if with only a single handful of dirt. The meaning to them of this custom is that they too will all die, and when someone dies, he should be buried.

111. When they have finished burying the body, they trace a mark around the grave with the back of a bolo. The significance of this is that if there is a *fagad*[124] who has come to eat the body, he will not be able to see it, for it will be magically shrouded in darkness.

203

112. They also erect a *feliyad*[125] made of dried grass—similar to the one used in hunting pigs—near the grave. They say that if a *fagad* comes to eat the body, he will not come near.

113. Now, that completes the description of graveside customs.

When they are going home from the grave, they have a custom that forbids treading on the heel of any companion. They do not want to step on anyone's heel, as it is considered to be a bad omen. Why? The point is that, should they accidentally step on someone's heel, while taking the body or while returning home, the dead will do the same thing. Every so often thereafter, someone will have to be buried—just because of walking on a companion's heel.[126]

114. Now, here are their customs upon arrival back at the house from the gravesite and for the next seven days. When it is late evening, they maintain a fire where the dead person will pass. If my reader should ask the purpose of this fire which they place there, it is so that the soul of the dead person will not get lost but can find its way home. It is said that when the dead one sees the fire he will say, "This is my house and my relatives and my elders."

According to these people, the soul of the deceased will not go on to its final resting place for seven days. It will stay near its relatives and elders, which is the reason for their customs over the seven days.

Each time they eat, they wrap up a packet of rice, about the size of a man's thumb, along with some viand. The spirit of the dead eats this, according to them.[127] So, their customs are fire and food wrapped in leaves. They hang packets of food from the outside wall of the house for seven days. Such are their customs.

115. When seven days have passed since the burial of the deceased, they no longer observe the custom of building the fire or of setting out food. They prepare a hearty meal to feed all those who have been gathered in the house, as well as others. That is their funeral feast; they go there to eat.

116. There is a laughable part of their customs in honor of the dead, which is embarrassing to relate. They prepare one roasted chicken and one pot of rice; two persons take these to the gravesite, and eat the food on top

of the grave.[128] They do not put any salt on this food which they take to the gravesite. Those who took the food there eat it. They do not take any water, and this is by custom. (I do not know why, nor do I know their reason for not eating salt.)[129]

117. They have a different custom when babies die. If the baby has teeth already, they place a knife with its body so that, using the knife, the baby can cut the *nunuk* bark in order to suck.[130] If the dead child is still without teeth, they put a ring in its mouth to act as its teeth in tearing the bark of the *nunuk*.

Regarding the dead baby's mother, it is her custom to draw milk from her breast and place it in a reed tube for her child to drink.[131]

The custom is not to bury the babies who die, but to hang their bodies from the branches of the *nunuk*.

XIII. Concerning Clearing the Land and Cultivation

118. Now that I have already told, here in my writing, all about the Tiruray customs, I will say that they have no other ones—except for their manner of working, their industriousness, and their way of making a living.

119. When it is time to work toward the planting of rice, these people will make a swidden in the virgin forest. They do not choose second growth forest if possible, as the trees are too small. What they much prefer is the virgin forest, where the tree trunks measure ten arm spans.[132]

120. What they do is to cut first the small growth in their plots under the big trees, then, when that is finished, they go through again and fell the large trees, using an ax about the size of the palm of one's hand. The large trees are not cut close to the ground; they erect a scaffold, upon which they stand while chopping.[133] The young men are the ones who do the felling.

121. Now, once they have finished felling the big trees, they slash the branches of the trees that have been cut down, so that the twigs all lie and so that when they burn everything will be well dried and the fire will consume

it all. When the slashed brushwood is well dried, they set fire to it and burn it. After the burning they pile and reburn the remaining twigs.

After they have finished burning the piles of unburned debris, that is the time they plant rice.[134] Their planting is strange,[135] for the men go ahead side by side poking holes, while the women follow with small baskets full of rice seed.

122. When the rice they planted has begun to grow and has become quite grassy, the women weed the swidden. Men do not help with weeding the rice; it is done by the women.

123. Now, when the end of the rice-growing season is near, they do not just immediately harvest. First they will burn a *dukah*[136] for its smoke, and cense one corner of the swidden. They bind one hill of rice, then get a single stalk out of the bound group and blow into it in the manner of a horn.

When this ritual is finished, they proceed to harvest. First, they set the rice to dry on the stalks. They do not gather the panicle bundles at once; they wait until they have a good number of them.

When the women go home, they take a little of the rice in their small basket, which they have filled up.[137]

They use their feet to shell the rice.[138]

In harvesting rice, they cut off the panicle well down on the stalk.

124. Now, if they want to taste the new rice, they will first toast it in a skillet, pounding the rice once it is toasted. The women are the ones who pound the rice, for that is properly their task. You will never see even a single man pounding rice or cooking food. Women are also the ones who work at the fire and go to get water. Even if it is quite far, it is the women who carry the basket full of bamboo tubes.[139] Likewise, they serve the meals and also keep in order all the things in the home.

When a married couple is hiking and they are carrying along something not overly heavy, it is the woman who will carry it. The husbands, you see, will not carry a thing. Suppose the woman is really feeling the weight of the load; do you suppose that he will relieve her? Not at all. Whether they are coming from far or near, it is only the woman who will feel the weight of their load.

125. Now, I will return to the subject of how they eat new rice. Some will toast it; some will boil it and then dry it. These people are really fond of eating newly harvested rice.

126. Their general custom is to eat twice a day. They normally do not eat early in the morning, but only—even if they have food—at noon and early evening.

As to what they eat, it is rice if there is any.[140] As a side dish, they always eat a vegetable, such as fruit from vines or the shoots of certain grasses. It is only rarely that they eat meat and fish, for they cannot afford it.[141] Thus they seldom have a very exciting side dish to the rice.

Now, it is not their custom to eat sweets after a meal. They do not eat any other snacks, no matter how much they may wish something to chew on.[142]

127. Now, it is their custom, when eating, to wash their hands first. Even if their hands are not dirty, they still wash them with water. That is their custom in eating; first they wash their hands.

128. They offer no prayers in connection with meals. They just eat! It is as though they were so many bugs, as though they had no souls. They just grab the food straightaway. They do not remember—they do not even know—that their food is given them by Tulus.

129. The customary way of eating is for the husband and the wife to eat together from a single plate.[143] Others may not join the couple in eating from their plate; it is the couple that is married to each other, and it would be bad manners. Even those who are siblings would look very bad to a stranger, should he see them eating from the same plate.

130. The only ones who may eat from a single plate are those who are husband and wife. When Tiruray eat, they do so one by one, though all share the same food.

131. Now, while they are eating, should someone come up to their house, they will invite him to eat. If he wants to join, they will serve him. One who is thus invited to eat may do so if he wishes. If not, he simply says, "No, thank you." That is all that is required.

132. If the first one to finish eating wants to stand up, he asks the others who are still eating, saying, "I will stand up now." Actually while others are eating, no one will stand up, for that is impolite as they see it. If people do stand up, and walk around the house while others are still eating, they will always ask permission. They will say, "Although you are still eating, we are getting up." Why is it that no one may rise while others are eating? Because it is not their custom to be bothered or disturbed while eating.

Now these people do not observe limits when they eat. Some are really greedy; even though they have had enough, they go on eating until every morsel has been consumed. They do not realize that eating too much is a sin to Tulus—as well as apt to make you sick!

133. I will go on and tell about the customs of this people with regard to sleeping. Each family—husband, wife, and children—has a single mosquito net and a single mat. Young boys and young girls sleep together, right near their parents.

134. Now, here is a custom I can tell you about, concerning their belief as to sleeping. When they dream while asleep, they believe their dream will come true. So, they will keep it in mind especially if it was a frightening dream—and they will try hard to evade whatever the dream warned them about. You see the foolishness of the Tiruray!

When someone has a dream at night while asleep, he will tell about it the following morning. Everyone will listen, and when he is finished relating his dream, he will ask his companions, "What does that signify?" Someone who knows says that it means this or that—there will be a sickness, or good is coming, or bad luck. I will not continue about this; it is no good.

XIV. Concerning Songs and Dreams

135. Now, they have still another custom at night when they have overnight guests. They do not go to sleep right away, out of fondness for this custom. It is telling folk stories. Those women who know how to tell stories will chant the epic of Lagey Lengkuwos, Metiyatil Kenogon, Bidek, and Bonggo[144]—who were all among the first people on earth. They say they are all spirits now, though. The people put trust in them, just as they trust for

good things from Tulus. But, actually, they are not really gods themselves. What the stories tell about is what happened to these people, when they were still on earth.

It is only the women who know about them; the men do not. Whoever does know about their ways will relate what happened to those first people, during the time they were still on earth.

The stories have been handed down from their forefathers.

136. Now, other folk tales are simply told in spoken words; they relate what went on among the first persons on earth, as well as stories about the world's first animals.

137. After that, the women chant and pose riddles; just fitting in the names of their companions!

138. Now, I will tell my reader about their fishing and their hunting for viands. For catching birds, they use snares or sticky tree sap. They also set rat traps—these people eat rats! For catching wild pigs, they set impaling spikes and tension-spring spear traps, they chase them with their bare hands, and they set log-fall traps. Another means of catching pigs is with dogs. Their dogs—even those with upright ears—are really ferocious toward wild pigs.

For fishing, they use their bare hands in the water, or they use spring-door fish traps—once a fish is inside it cannot get out—or various other woven basket traps. They use fish poles, fishing spears, hooks secured to posts, long lines with large hooks, and, in the ocean, nets. Their best way of catching fish is by poisoning the water with *tebeli*,[145] *gasi*,[146] *sedan*,[147] and *rembuwayà*.[148]

139. Now, I have still some more that I want to tell my reader. There is a custom among Tiruray, which they believe and which is true as far as they are concerned. It is this: they never laugh at anything an animal might do—and this is true of worms, in fact of any animate creature—for they will be *simbelowon*. What is this they call *simbelowon*? Their community will be treated very harshly. There will be heavy rain and strong winds, and the teeth of the lightning will bite! Now you see the silliness of the Tiruray! All these false notions—they cling to them in their customs. It is terrible.

140. Similarly, it is not good to speak to animals; for they say you will also

be *simbelowon*. No one, however, has ever experienced this aspect of their customs; they have just heard about it from the stories of the old folks. Once upon a time there were two persons—Kenogo Lagey and Kenogon by name—in a certain place. Kenogo Lagey went wild boar hunting with his dog. He caught a small pig, and then went home. But, his dog went ahead of him. When the dog arrived, Kenogon said to it, "Were you able to catch a pig?" The dog did not reply. Again Kenogon asked, "Were you able to catch a pig?" Three times she queried the dog. She just insisted on speaking to that dog, even though it was an animal and could not reply. I do not know how it was that it finally spoke. It answered the girl about its master, saying, "Yes, we got it, but"—this is how it said it—"you will never taste it; you will be punished severely."[149]

XV. Concerning Their Leaders and Their Mode of Self-Government

141. Now, since I have been telling my reader all the various customs of the Tiruray, I will go on to tell whether these people are all of equal rank. They are all ordinary people—nobody looks back at them[150]—but they do have an elder brother, whose standing they respect and who respects the standing of all of them. They call him their *kefeduwan*.[151]

Should my reader ask whether all *kefeduwan* are the same, they are not. There are some higher standing. Here are their *gelal*: Amirefes and Bandara. Now, the meaning of their *gelal* is as follows.[152]

If there is a *tiyawan* that cannot be readily decided,[153] once these two *kefeduwan*, Amirefes and Bandara, are involved it will be quickly finished.

Among the various *kefeduwan*, one is Bandara. If Amirefes is not present, Bandara takes his place. Another of the *gelal* is Masalikamfu. The meaning of this is that he owns all the Tiruray.[154]

142. These individuals that I have singled out—the Tiruray *kefeduwan*—have the highest standing among them. That is why I mentioned them one by one. They do not farm. Their work is just to settle the cases of their Tiruray companions. Nobody would refuse them by saying, "We do not like what you are asking," or, "We do not believe what you say."[155]

143. Now, the other *kefeduwan* are lower in rank than those, and they receive their *gelal* from the three I mentioned.

144. The titles of the ones given *gelal* of lower rank—all of whom are equal, each being the leader of one place are Kafita Watà, Datu Watà, Datu Watà Magalin, Ulubalang, Urangkaya, Kafitan, and Datu sa Falaw.[156] Each of them is the leader of some certain place.

145. Now, I will just bring an end here to my account of Tiruray customs. It seems to me that I have finished what I have to say. Perhaps I did not get to every single custom of the Tiruray; I may have missed just a few. But, in fact, I do not think there are any more at all.

146. I repeat again to my reader that, in what I have written, all the customs of the Tiruray were brought out. Perhaps I should not admit that I am the one who wrote all this—for I am myself a Tiruray. But I will admit it, and I will never feel ashamed toward all those who see it. Never mind. I do not care. It is all right—but I do consider myself like a crow that will call out its own name.[157]

It is as though an outsider were the one to tell all our customs—but the one who told them all was himself a Tiruray. [158] Well, I could not do anything about it. I was the first person to become a Christian, in the year 1863, so I know something of the teachings of the Jesuit Fathers. Therefore, they asked me to put down all our customs in this manuscript, and I was happy to do it.

I have, therefore, related them in their entirety, so that anyone who reads this will know all the customs—the good ones and the bad ones, too. And I say to you, in this regard, that whether or not they please you is to me a matter of complete indifference.

Amen. Jesus.

Notes

[1] d'Orleans (1870: 202-203), quoted in de la Costa (1965: 200-201).

[2] Tamantaka is the place, just north of Awang, across the Tamontaka River, near Cotabato City, where the Jesuit Mission was established and where the Tiruray "reduction" was attempted.

[3] Dulangan was the Tiruray term for the Cotabato Manobo, the tribe occupying the Cotabato Cordillera to the south of the Tiruray area. The term is derived from the name of a Manobo culture hero and its use by Tiruray is considered pejorative by Manobo and is deeply resented.

[4] The term *memilagé* refers to a group of people who today are more often called *balég* and who live in the boundary area between the Cotabato Monobo and the Tiruray. They are Manobo who have adopted Tiruray culture, but who speak the Tiruray vernacular with a marked accent.

[5] Tiruray settlements are characteristically named after some nearby river, creek or spring.

[6] *Marafati*: a type of pigeon (*Columbia livia?*).

[7] "Do not have bones" is a Tiruray expression meaning "do not have enough strength."

[8] The Tiruray sentence ends with the obscure expression *i na bingbing so*. *Bingbing* means to carry something with a handle, but neither I nor any of my Tiruray friends were able to guess its meaning here. Padre Bennasar renders the phrase, in his Spanish translation, as *por lo mucho que se mueven*, "for they move so much." Perhaps a contemporary idiom, now unknown, is involved.

[9] The lack of walling is defensive, so that the occupants can easily look out and shoot arrows, should raiders attack them.

[10] *Keroon*: the ubiquitous tropical grasses *Imperata cylindrica* (Linn.) and *I. exaltata* Brong. The Tiruray setting, of course, is the forest—rich with rattan—not the grassy lowlands.

[11] *Kureng*: "pot"; the *kureng* of today is of iron, but the word traditionally referred to clay pots obtained from Maguindanaon traders. The Tiruray themselves do not manufacure pottery.

[12] *Kaldero*: "large kettle," from the Spanish *caldero*.

[13]The Tiruray sarong (*emut*) is a loop of cloth which serves both as both as skirt and blanket.

[14]*Ubi*: "sweet potato" (*Ipomea batatas*, Linn.).

[15]*Beliyan*: the Tiruray shaman and religious leader. The Tiruray cosmos is populated by many spirit-people, and it is the special charisma of the *beliyan* that they can see and speak with them. To the ordinary person, the spirits are invisible.

[16]The *pandita*, in Maguindanaon social organization, is a man, well versed in the Koran, who serves as religious advisor to the district chief.

[17]Tulus, in Tiruray cosmology, is the creator and foremost of all the spirits. Padre Bennasar throughout translates Tulus as "God" (*Dios*).

[18]The Tiruray is unclear: "They do not realize that the *lakaliya* of God is everywhere around here." I have been unable to locate any Tiruray familiar with the term *lakaliya*. It may be a corruption of the Spanish *localidad*. My rendering of "habitation" is from the Spanish version of Bennasar: *que habite en toda la redondez de la tierra.*

[19]A *tenines* is a small house where the *beliyan* keeps his paraphernalia and where ritual rice is stored. In a footnote to his Spanish text, Bennasar misleadingly identifies the *tenines* as a chapel.

[20]Bennasar's translation specifies that the small bells are tied to the *beliyan's* legs and attached to his kris; he describes his shield as decorated with plumes. These details are all accurate, although absent from the Tiruray text. Bennesar had doubtless witnessed such dancing.

[21]*Fesayawan*: a well-cleaned clearing in front of a Tiruray house, where dancing, games and ceremonies are performed.

[22]*Rangà*: literally a "chicken nest." A *rangà* is made by making several short splits at the end of a length of bamboo, and tying them to funnel shape with rattan. A smaller version is used as the perch on which offerings are placed for Tulus or other spirits.

[23]The *togò belotoken* is an eight-string bamboo zither. The *togò tefuken* is a small drum, made of deer hide stretched over large bamboo, which is accompanied by gongs. The Tiruray text does not specify which type of *togò* is referred to, and either is possible in the context. Benassar's Spanish reads *tocar el tambor*, "play the drum," so the reference is presumably to the *togò tefuken.*

[24]Normally, the Tiruray play gongs in an ensemble of five persons, each with a single gong. Here the term used is *sesimfal*, which refers to a style of playing in which one person plays two gongs.

[25]It is not clear what constitutes Tulus' answer. I have asked many Tiruray about this passage, but none has ever heard of such a belief. The usual guess is that the answer must have been by rain, or a rainbow, or perhaps a beautifully colored sky. Bennesar's Spanish rendition says that God answers by playing another (*Dios contesta tocando otro*). This may have been the observation of Sigayan's *beliyan*.

[26]*Naraka*: the Malay term, from Sanskrit, for "hell" and used in this meaning by Philippine Muslims. The term is very uncommon in Tiruray, and is doubtless a borrowing from Maguindanaon usage. There is no place in Tiruray cosmology comparable to the Muslim or Western hell.

[27]Damangias is a spirit in Tiruray mythology who plays foolish tricks all the time. Bennasar generalizes the term and renders it as *demonios*, "demons."

[28]The name means "ancient heirloom."

[29]The personal names in sections 17-19 are all persons named in the great Tiruray epic chant, the *berinarew*, and are described as having gone up to the place of Tulus with Lagey Lengkuwos.

[30]Damangias is seen as the fountainhead of all foolishness.

[31]*Lambus*: any of several large-sized charms, frequently worn around the waist in the manner of a belt.

[32]*Agimat*: "talisman" or "amulet." Also the general term for protective charms.

[33]*Lateng*: A type of tree: *Trema orientalis* (Linn.).

[34]*Begongoh*: a medium-sized forest tree of undetermined species.

[35]The term used is *ketusen*, the general term for any sort of herb that is used as a medicine or charm. Sigayan uses the term more generally throughout these sections to mean "charm."

[36]*Felungkang*, used by Sigayan, is the Maguindanaon spelling; the general Tiruray word is *ferungkang*.

[37]The settlement of legal fines. *Tamuk* items include krises, spears, fancy bolos, brass betel boxes of various sizes and shapes, necklaces of several varieties, Chinese porcelain jars and plates, and, in the more acculturated

areas, horses and carabaos. See section 78 below.

[38]*Ungit*: a charm employed in hunting or fishing.

[39]*Dukah*: any of several kinds of charms that are made using the sap of trees. Often their use involves burning the charm, thus releasing a sort of incense.

[40]The *bengat* of today are typically inscribed with a curse, written in Maguindanaon. Tiruray say the *bengat* is not an indigenous Tiruray device, but has been borrowed from the local Muslims.

[41]"Another of their *ketusen* . . ." is the Tiruray text, a very curious statement as a *bolbol* is certainly not a charm, but a kind of flying witch. Bennasar translates it as *supersticiones ó tonterías*, "superstitions or foolishnesses," and apparently thought of *ketusen* as having this meaning as well.

[42]I was unable to find anyone who knew of this custom or who could clarify what is involved in "measuring" someone's body.

[43]*Terektek*: a common house lizard, *Hemidactylus frenatus* (Duméril and Bibron).

[44]*Lemugen*: a medium-sized forest bird, *Phapitreron leucotis* (Temminck).

[45]Sigayan's description of the good and bad directions for the *lemugen's* call does not jibe with general Tiruray custom, as I know it. At least in the Figel area, the call is a good omen if it comes from directly ahead of the hearer, from 45 degrees to the right or left of directly ahead, or from directly overhead. All other directions are understood as a bad omen.

[46]Awang people are also known as "downstream people." See footnote 50 below.

[47]Whatever this practice once was, it is unknown today.

[48]Their eyelashes are cut to a straight edge.

[49]*Fegoto*: a kind of wide-bladed kris.

[50]Awang Tiruray, like Sigayan, divide the tribe into three loose sub-groups: the *etew rotor*, "upper people" or mountain people, who all live in the interior among the hills; the *etew dawà*, "downstream people"—also called *etew inged*, roughly "town people" or *etew awang* "Awang people"—who live in the environs of the Pulangi River and its tributaries, at the northern foot of the mountains, including the Awang area; and *etew dogot*, "seacoast people," who live along the coast from the mouth of the Pulangi

to the Tran Grande River. In addition, those who live along the Tran are often called *etew teran*, "Tran people." The Awang people tend to consider all of the others as rude hicks.

[51]Areca nut, betel leaf, tobacco leaf, and lime. The "downstream people" also chew—as do all traditional Tiruray—but they use brass betel boxes, which they keep in the house or carry in a pocket.

[52]*Rintì:* a series of brass bracelets of increasing size, that extend from the wrist to about 20 cm. up the arm. These are still seen on rare occasions, but the custom of wearing them has largely fallen into disuse.

[53]Sigayan specifies the bamboo variety as *belotokan, Bambusa spinosa* Roxb.

[54]This custom has entirely died out today, but Bennesar comments in a footnote that anyone who had contact with the Tiruray will soon notice the effeminate character of the coastal men and their desire to wear female jewelry.

[55]*Sayaf:* a shallow conical sun hat.

[56]*Buruk:* "vetiver," *Andropogon zizanoides* (Linn.).

[57]There is a great variety of such charms, which includes ones believed to be contraceptives, abortants, aphrodesiacs, and so forth.

[58]*Lemifut* means "to murder"—often by going in a group against a single individual or else by killing from ambush. *Lemifut* is considered very wrong and foolish, and contrasts sharply with killing in revenge of one's honor, which is also wrong but thought to be quite understandable.

[59]*Kengasa ro fo!:* "It is their portent of death!" The phrase seems to make no sense here. Bennasar's Spanish translation says *por pura malicia*, "for pure malice," which makes sense in the context, but bears no resemblance to the Tiruray phrase.

[60]What Sigayan says here, if he means Tiruray, is simply not the case. It is not clear, however, in the text what he means. Later on, he refers such behavior to the Maguindanaon, and it seems most likely that he is already speaking of them in this paragraph. Apparently Bennasar raised the same question, as the following section greatly clarifies the situation.

[61]*Farey:* "paddy rice, not yet threshed."

[62]This sort of Maguindanaon behavior was less common in the Awang area than in the more isolated mountain and coastal settlements of Tiruray,

Manobo and Bilaan. Bennasar attributed this to mission influence, but it was doubtless due, at least in part, to longstanding relations between the Awang Tiruray and the Maguindanaon of the Cotabato City area.

[63]The reference to *tamuk* implies that the revenge killing here related is in connection with a brideprice violation, in which *tamuk* should have been, but was not, returned. See Schlegel (1970b: 119-151).

[64]Moferow is another name of the *segoyong sefebenal,* the spirit in Tiruray cosmology who presides over the place of souls who died by violence in matters of honor.

[65]The fault here referred to is, at least, shown to be understandable (*benal*). This does not mean that they are not still legally responsible for their killing.

[66]*Tebeli:* a poisonous plant, *Derris elliptica* (Roxb.). The statement is curious, as in Tiruray custom, at least as I know it, those intending to kill themselves never tell anyone beforehand. Perhaps the text is in error and should have read that "They never go to inform anyone that . . . ," but Bennasar translates the text as it is given.

[67]The word used for "man" here is *senangkadan,* possibly an old Awang word for bachelor or possibly a euphemism for penis.

[68]The text of this sentence is also obscure. Presumably the implication is that the couple would be mortally ashamed if they were to learn of the plans for their marriage prior to the official announcement of the night before.

[69]*The kefeduwan* is the Tiruray legal authority. This and the *beliyan* are the two principal leaders of the Tiruray.

[70]Sigayan is the Tiruray name of the author, José Tenorio being his Christian baptismal name. The woman, Ambug, of the village of Kafiton, which he uses in his example, is said by Bennasar in a footnote to have been a real person, but, curiously, not Sigayan's wife.

[71]This is one of many such common Tiruray expressions signifying a certain period of time.

[72]At several points in the marriage ceremonies, a traditional cry of "*u u feri*" is given. See sections 69 and 74 below.

[73]The *emut* is the sarong. Women use the *emut* as a skirt, and both men and women use it as their blanket at night. In the cool of the early morning, both men and women will drape the *emut* up over their heads for warmth, and this is the way the groom is described as wearing it here.

[74] *Wahwah:* a kind of bird, *Pitta* sp. (*steeri?*).

[75] *Dudum:* a cloth canopy held up at the four corners by poles.

[76] The kris, or some other suitable item of *tamuk*, must be given at this point by the groom's kindred to the bride's side. It is called the *alang* and is part of the agreed-upon brideprice. It is said, ritually, to be "for them to use in cutting the fence."

[77] Literally, the "human" dance, the *keilawan* is a kind of war dance. In a footnote, Bennasar states that it was popularly known as the "Moro-Moro dance." It probably was a borrowing from the Maguindanaon.

[78] The drum type of *togò*; see footnote 23 above.

[79] At least as the word is used today, *simful* is not quite appropriate here. *Simful* means that the sarong is wrapped G-string style around a man's waist. In dancing it is not worn this way, but rather sarong-style over the trousers and extending down only to the knees. This is termed *mentawih*, not *simful.*

[80] For *Tebagen*, instead of the customary five gongs being played by five persons, a single individual plays on two. This style of playing is called *sesimfal;* see footnote 24 above.

[81] The bride is at this time secluded in a special room or screened-off part of a room, called a *sibey*, set aside within the house for this purpose.

[82] Usually this is rigged on the spot by hanging several sarongs so as to hide the groom from sight.

[83] See footnote 81 above.

[84] *Singà* are large earthen pots, in which the viands are cooked, usually chicken.

[85] Tiyawan are formal discussions between *kefeduwan*, conducted in a highly metaphorical and round-about rhetoric.

[86] That is, the man's side.

[87] The brideprice is given in several installments, the first being at an important *tiyawan* between the two kindreds, when the total amount to be given is agreed upon. What is not given at that time is supposed to be given in the context of another *tiyawan* the morning of the wedding ritual, although frequently some undelivered balance is allowed to stand on past the wedding.

[88] Beauty is not the only, or even the main, consideration in bride selection or brideprice negotiations. Much more important are matters of good health and a pleasant, industrious personality. Perhaps the most signi-

ficant factor of all is the desirability of the girl's kindred as in-laws.

[89]The description of the wedding ceremony is given here in considerably abbreviated form. After the bride has been brought from the *sibey*, and the groom has been led to her side, both are seated on a pillow. A *kefeduwan* from each party then comes and stands in front of the couple—the *kefeduwan* of the man's side in front of the bride and the *kefeduwan* from the bride's side in front of the groom. As this takes place, the mother of each prepares a betel quid and passes it to the new child-in-law. The couple chew for a few moments, then place the chewed quids on a handkerchief. The two *kefeduwan* then move behind the couple and, while giving a speech of advice, comb the hair of their new in-law. A single plate is then brought in, containing some rice and a hard-boiled egg cut in two. The couple eat a bit of the rice and the egg, and the wedding ritual is complete. Henceforth, the couple is married. Old folks from Awang all concur that the mother does not, by custom, give the betel quid to her own child, as Sigayan describes it. They do agree, though, that the bumping of heads, which is not done today, was indeed once part of the Awang people's customs.

[90]The chewed quids are hardly kept. They are, by custom, wrapped in a banana leaf and hung from the rafters of the house where the wedding took place. The handkerchief in which they were placed is what is kept as a treasured memento of the ceremony.

[91]The name of the feast means, literally, "let them drink together." An Awang Tiruray custom, influenced by Maguindanaon culture, it is virtually unknown among Tiruray other than the "downstream people," none of whom traditionally drink any alcoholic beverage. Although, as the name suggests, drinking plays a role in the ceremonial, the *sefeinem* is structurally quite comparable to the wedding feast described above, in that the women's side feeds the husband's relatives, and the man's side gives brideprice. Properly, in Tiruray custom, the entire brideprice should be completed at the wedding feast, prior to the ceremony itself. However, in most cases, the *kefeduwan* in attendance permit the wedding to proceed, even though some unpaid balance remains. The giving of the last of this outstanding balance is the occasion among Awang Tiruray for the *sefeinem*.

[92]This is, again, only an example, and not an actual case.

[93]The runaways would actually only go to Bandara if he were a kinsman of one or the other.

[94]The text of this last sentence is quite unclear.

219

[95]Bennasar notes at this point that there are three types of gold necklace, classified according to their gold content, of which the *furo teresang* (literally "red sun") is of pure gold and the most valuable.

[96]Their anger toward the girl was based on their belief that she had gone freely with the kidnappers, that is, eloped. The anger turned to pity when they saw all the *tamuk*, all the cut trees, and realized that she had been forcibly abducted.

[97]The sentence is probably not to be taken literally, as Bennasar did in his translation (. . . *y es no, consintieran en este trance, alguno de ellos lo pagaría con la vida*); it is an idiomatic Tiruray expression with the idea of "How stupid can you be!"

[98]Their point would be that under the circumstances of their generous offerings of brideprice, refusal to agree constituted an insult worth a fine.

[99]See footnote 85 above.

[100]This manner of proposing a marriage, called *falunsud*, is a bizarre but recognized option in Tiruray custom. The girl's kindred is not free to simply reject the suit out of hand. If they do not want to accept, they must either give *tamuk* to the young man's party to cover the insult or face the possibility of revenge.

[101]See section 64 above.

[102]The replacement spouse must be of the same structural generation as the deceased person, even though her age may be quite different.

[103]That is, they would take revenge if the wife's kindred did not provide a replacement spouse and still retained the brideprice. If they returned all the brideprice or some properly negotiated portion, which need not necessarily be one half, there would, of course, be no question of revenge.

[104]Bennasar notes that this assertion puzzles him, as it is certain that the Tiruray do not permit polygyny and would seriously censure anyone who attempted it. It would seem that he was simply misinformed about the true situation. Polygyny, while never widespread, has always been practiced and respected, and it almost invariably resulted from their system of spouse replacement following the death of one of a couple. Awang Tiruray may have seen it partly as a matter of respect to have more than one wife, but for most Tiruray this is not much of a factor. It is simply the following of their logic of brideprice relations, given that being a single adult is, on the whole, economically unfeasible. Bennasar states that when there is a second woman she

is not called a wife but rather a concubine. This is also a mistaken understanding of the situation. The term in question is *duwoy*, which means "co-wife" and does not suggest a concubine of lower or unmarried status.

[105]The custom of not eating eggs taken from a butchered hen is followed by all men and women of childbearing age, and not just pregnant women.

[106]The particular herb used is chewed along with the betel quid, and the whole quid is then rubbed on the woman's stomach.

[107]*Nunuk*: "strangler fig," *Ficus benjamina* Linn.

[108]An herb, believed to act as a contraceptive by preventing the baby from forming in the womb of the mother.

[109]If the mother had slept with only one man, she could accuse him through Tiruray legal procedures. What is implied here is that she had been sleeping with several men.

[110]The belief is that if all one's hair should be cut, one's soul would escape through the bare scalp. The patches are left as tokens of a full head of hair.

[111]That is, newly born.

[112]Sigayan is not very admiring of self-indulgent people who jump into the river at noontime. Some Tiruray believe that the river belongs to the spirits at noontime and that humans should stay away.

[113]Literally, "they will feel the need to cover their little ones." This refers to the practice of older boys covering their genitals with the palm of their hand when bathing.

[114]There is no set time for giving the new name, and no ritual is involved. Usually, the name is given when the child is about a year old, but in some cases the original name sticks and the person is called "new boy" or "new girl" for life.

[115]See section 16 above.

[116]*Uwar, Flagellaria indica* (Linn.).

[117]See section 36 above.

[118]Kind of pun: the word for "snake" is *urar*.

[119]See footnote 27 above.

[120]The custom of placing a mirror by the body's head is Tiruray, but not the washing of the body. By all reports, even from Awang Tiruray, washing the deceased is a Maguindanaon Muslim custom.

[121]The kris is a sort of memorial heirloom, retained as a keepsake of the

dead person. When the deceased is a grown woman, a gold necklace is kept instead.

[122]This statement is puzzling as it goes directly against traditional Tiruray custom. The clothes are indeed buried with the body, but never any items of *tamuk*, such as spears or betel boxes.

[123]In Bennasar's version, an error in numbering begins here. Henceforth, the corresponding text in that version is numbered two less than in the present text.

[124]The *fagad* are a tribe of giant spirits, one of many such tribes in Tiruray cosmology. The *fagad*, also known as *busaw*, are fond of eating human beings whom they are said to hunt in the forest. They live in caves and are greatly feared.

[125]The *feliyad* is a spring-spear trap, one of many devices used by the Tiruray to hunt wild game in the forest; see Schlegel (1977, 1979). One erected by a graveside is not a real, functional one, but is merely a representation made of dried grass.

[126]This custom too derives from the idea of sympathetic magic. Just as someone in the burial party followed his companion too closely, so deaths will follow closely one after another.

[127]The general belief is not that the soul of the dead physically eats the food, but that it is shown respect and honor by being included in each meal.

[128]The number need not be limited to two. Generally four to six of the dead individual's close male friends and relatives go to the gravesite just before dawn of the seventh day.

[129]The salt would melt in the dampness of the early morning, and it is believed that as the salt melted so too would the relatives of the deceased "melt," i.e., die. With regard to not taking water to the gravesite, Sigayan is correct that this is the custom. I, too, do not know its meaning, nor could I find anyone who does.

[130]Infants who die while still nursing are not buried in the manner of adults. Their bodies are placed in a strangler fig (*nunuk*) tree; see footnote 107 above. The strangler fig tree is held, accordingly, in great awe and is seldom approached. It is believed that a tribe of dwarf female spirits live in those trees and care for the souls of the deceased children. The strangler fig has a white sap which resembles milk, and this is believed to be the nourishment of the

child's soul.

[131]This is done for seven days only, until the final ceremonies, and is equivalent to the food put out for the soul of a deceased adult. As with that food, this milk is not thought to be actually drunk by the dead child.

[132]Some of the larger primary forest trees are immense, but they hardly reach the size of circumference cited by Sigayan. The big dypterocarp trees generally have good-sized buttresses near the ground, and he may have meant that the trunks, including the buttresses, are that big around. A complete description of Tiruray shifting cultivation is in Schlegel (1977, 1979).

[133]The scaffolding is needed because of the large buttresses, mentioned in the previous footnote.

[134]Generally, a crop of corn is planted first in widely separated rows, and then rice is planted along with a variety of non-grains. Corn is, of course, not native to the Philippines, but was introduced centuries ago by the Spanish who brought it from the Americas.

[135]Sigayan probably means that the dibble system of swidden planting is strange in comparison to techniques used by lowland plow farmers.

[136]See footnote 39 above.

[137]Harvesting of rice or corn is regularly done on a share basis, the harvester receiving a set share of what she has cut.

[138]Threshing is done on a large woven mat.

[139]Water is typically carried in a stoppered bamboo internode.

[140]Some starch staple forms the basis for a Tiruray meal, whenever possible. If no rice is available, corn is the second preference, followed by various other roots or tubers.

[141]Bennasar notes at this point, quite correctly, that one should not conclude that the Tiruray lack dexterity in hunting and fishing; they are actually extremely skillful in both.

[142]By snacks, Sigayan probably means Western style cakes or candies, such as he may have known in the home of Padre Bennasar. The Tiruray do eat a variety of wild fruits and occasional cooked starches, such as the toasted new rice mentioned above, as between-meals snacks.

[143]Sigayan says that they "eat together *sefelang*," which means off a single plate or a single banana leaf. In Tiruray custom, everyone must have his or her own plate (or leaf) with the exception of married couples and small chil-

dren. It is not the case that married couples will always eat this way, but that no other adults ever will.

[144]See sections 17-19 above.

[145]See footnote 66 above.

[146]*Gasi:* a croton oil plant: *Croton tiglium* (Linn.).

[147]*Sedan:* a tree: *Lepisanthes schizolepis* Radlk.

[148]Species unknown.

[149]This story is an often-told folk tale, usually ending with the boy returning to find Kenogon dead, struck by lightning. The prohibition involved in *simbelowon* is against ridicule of any kind, whether directed toward animals or human beings. Speaking to dumb animals, or picking up their front feet so as to "dance" with them, are commonly cited examples of what the Tiruray consider ridicule.

[150]"Nobody looks back at them" is an idiomatic expression meaning no one exerts any special care over them.

[151]See footnote 69 above.

[152]A *gelal* is a title given by Maguindanaon leaders to Tiruray leaders in recognition of trade-pact agreements. The last sentence of the paragraph is evidently a false start; Sigayan does not go on to tell the meaning of the *gelal*, but rather to describe the effectiveness of Amirefes and Bandara.

[153]See footnote 85 above.

[154]What Sigayan means here is very unclear. Perhaps the sense of "owns all the Tiruray" is that the *Masalikamfu* title belongs to some sort of native military commander or civil official. Bennasar notes at this point that he suspects "*Masalikamfu*" to be a corruption of the Spanish *maestro de campo*, "a title with which the ancient Spaniards honored certain natives for their loyalty to our flag and for their assisting with their people in the conquest of these lands."

[155]Tiruray culture does not institutionalize power into any personal role, so, unlike the Maguindanaon leaders, Tiruray *kefeduwan* are not able to give indiscriminate or arbitrary orders. Their position of respect and authority is based solely upon their reputation for skill in settling disputes through *tiyawan*.

[156]The titles listed here by Sigayan are traditional and prominent Awang area *gelal*.

[157]Sigayan is worried over whether he should put his name to his writing. In the Tiruray language, the crow is known by the onomatopoetic name, *uwak*.

[158]Here Sigayan is concerned about having told so many unfavorable customs (that is, to the Spanish priests) along with the good ones. His final word on this is the delightful last sentence of the document, prior to the Amen!

Key to Orthography

In presenting Tiruray terms in this volume, I have used the following symbols to represent the six vowel phonemes and the 16 consonant phonemes of the language. See Schlegel (1971a: 6-8) for a fuller discussion of Tiruray phonology and orthography.

Vowels

i	voiced, high close, front, unrounded
é	voiced, mid open, front, unrounded
e	voiced, high close, mid, unrounded
a	voiced, low open, mid, unrounded
u	voiced, high close, back, rounded
o	voiced, low close, back, rounded

Consonants

Voiceless stops:

t	alveoloar, lightly aspirated
k	velar, lightly aspirated
`	glottal (inscribed over preceding vowel)

Voiced stops:

b	bilabial
d	alveolar
g	velar

Voiceless fricatives:

f	bilabial
s	alveolar, grooved
h	velar

Voiced nassals:

m	bilabial
n	alveolar
ng	velar

Others:

l	voiced, alveolar lateral
r	voiced, alveolar vibrant (trilled fluctuates freely with flapped)
w	voiced, nonsyllabic bilabial (vowel)
y	voiced, nonsyllabic palatal (vowel)

The high front and back vowels have been interpreted as the vowels *i* and *u* respectively, when they occur as syllabus nuclei and may take stress. When they occur in consonant position they have been interpreted as *y* and *w*.

This orthography was first suggested by Ursula Post of the Summer Institute of Linguistics.

A note on pronunciation. Primary stress falls on the penult or antepenult of polysyllabic bases, except when the vowels of those syllables are shortened, in which case the stress falls on the ultima. Two reduplicated identical closest syllables in a base receive equal primary stress. In the case of words of four or more syllables, secondary stress falls on the second syllable prior to the primary stress. In Tiruray, stress is non-contrastive and is not indicated in the orthography.

With place names, I have used this orthography for places which do not regularly appear on maps (e.g., Kabàkabà), but have used the conventional spellings for places which have them (e.g., Upi instead of "Ufi").

References Cited

Angeles, de los, Francisco
    1964   *Mindanao: The Story of an Island.* Davao City: San Pedro
                Press, Inc.

Berger, Peter
    1977   *Facing Up to Modernity.* New York: Basic Books.

Berger, Peter and Thomas Luckmann
    1966   *The Social Construction of Reality.* Garden City: Doubleday.

Camus, Albert
    1946   *The Stranger.* S. Gilbert (trans). New York: Random
                House. (Original: *L'Etranger.* Paris, 1942.)

Conklin, Harold
    1952   *Outline Gazetteer of Native Philippine Ethnic and Linguistic
                Groups.* Mimeographed.
    1955   *Preliminary Linguistic Survey of Mindanao.*
                Philippine Studies Program, University of Chicago.
    1957   *Hanunóo Agriculture: A Report on an Integral System of
                Shifting Cultivation in the Philippines.*
                Forestry Development Paper 12. Rome: Food and
                Agriculture Organization.

Corte, de, Felipe
    1887   La Isla de Mindanao y lo que contiene. *Boletin de la So-
                ciedad Geografica de Madrid.* Vol. 22, pp. 351-352.

Costa, de la, Horacio
    1968   *Asia and the Philippines.* Manila: Solidaridad Publishing
                House.

Dalton, George
    1972   Peasantries in Anthropology and History. *Current Anthro-
                pology.* Vol. 13, nos. 3-4, pp. 385-415.

Food and Agriculture Organization

1957   Shifting Cultivation. *Unasylva.* Vol. 11, pp. 9-11.

1962   Calcium Requirements. *FAO Nutrition Report Series.*
        No. 30. Rome.

1965   Protein Requirements. Joint FAO/WHO Expert Group.
        FAO Nutrition Meetings Report Series. No. 37. Rome.

1970   *Amino Acid Content of Foods and Biological Data on Proteins.*
        Nutritional Studies. No. 24. Rome.

Food and Nutrition Research Center

1964   *Handbook 1: Food Composition Table.* Manila: National
        Institute of Science and Technology, National Science
        Development Board.

Geertz, Clifford

1958   Ethos, World View, and the Analysis of Sacred Symbols.
        Antioch Review. Winter 1957-1958, pp. 421-437.

1964a   Ideology as a Culture System. *In* D. Apter, ed., *Ideology
        and Discontent.* New York: The Free Press.

1964b   The Transition to Humanity. *In* S. Tax, ed., *Horizons of
        Anthropology.* Chicago: Aldine.

1966   Religion as a Culture System. *In* M. Banton, ed.,
        Anthropological Approaches to the Study of Religion.
        London: Tavistock Publications.

Hart, H. L. A.

1961   *The Concept of Law.* Oxford: Clarendon Press.

Intengan, C. L.

1970   Recommended Dietary Allowance for Filipinos.
        Philippine Journal of Nutrition. Vol. 23, pp. 1-17.

Kroeber, Alfred L.
    1948   *Anthropology.* New York: Harcourt Brace.

Majul, Cesar.
    1973   *Muslims in the Philippines.* Quezon City: University
              of the Philippines Press.

Matawaran, A. J., C. G. Gersavasio and A. B. de Gala
    1966   Preliminary Report on the Average Height and Weight
              of Some Filipinos. *Philippine Journal of Nutrition.*
              Vol. 19, p. 29.

Montano, Joseph
    1887   Excursion al interior y por el oriente del Mindanao.
              Boletin de la Sociedad Geografica de Madrid, Vol. 23,
              p. 41.

Moore, Grace Wood
    1972   Review of *Tiruray Justice: Traditional Tiruray Law and*
              Morality. Journal of Asian Studies. Vol. 31, no. 2,
              pp. 466-468.

Orleans, d', Ferdinand-Philippe-Marie
    1870   *Lucon et Mindanao.* Paris: Michel Lévy.

Saleeby, Najeeb Mitry
    1905   *Studies in Moro History, Laws, and Religion.* Manila:
              Bureau of Printing.

Sartre, Jean-Paul
    1964   *Nausea.* L. Alexander (trans.). New York: New Directions.
              tions. (Original: *La Nausée.* Paris, 1938).

Sawyer, F. H.
    1900   *The Inhabitants of the Philippines.* New York: Scribner.

Schlegel, Stuart A.

1967a   Repercussions of Naive Scholarship. The Background of a Local Furor. *Philippine Sociological Review*. Vol. 15, nos. 3-4, pp. 108-113.

1967b   Tiruray Constellations: The Agricultural Astronomy of a Philippine Hill People. *Philippine Journal of Science*. Vol. 96, nos. 3-4, pp. 116-142. Reprinted in edited and expanded form as Schlegel (1987).

1970a   *The Customs of the Tiruray People*, by José (Sigayan) Tenorio. Translation of Tenorio (1892) from theTiruray and Spanish and annotated by S. A. Schlegel. *Philippine Studies*. Vol. 18, no. 2, pp. 364-428.

1970b   *Tiruray Justice: Traditional Tiruray Morality and Law*. Berkeley, Los Angeles and London: University of California Press.

1971a   *Tiruray-English Lexicon*. Berkeley, Los Angeles and London: University of California Press.

1971b   Tiruray Morality. *Philippine Sociological Review*. Vol. 19, nos. 1-2, pp. 99-130.

1972   Tiruray-Maguindanaon Ethnic Relations: An Ethnohistorical Puzzle. *Solidarity*. Vol. 7, no. 4, pp. 25-30.

1975   *Tiruray Justice: Traditional Tiruray Morality and Law*. Quezon City: Institute of Philippine Culture, Ateneo de Manila University. Paperback reprint of Schlegel (1970b).

1976   From Tribal to Peasant. The Tiruray Example. *Studies in Third World Societies*. Vol. 1, no. 1, pp. 73-95.

1977   *The Subsistence Economy of the Tiruray of Mindanao, Philippines*. Quezon City: Rizal Library, Ateneo de Manila University.

1979   *Tiruray Subsistence: The Transformation from Shifting Cultivation to Plow Farming*. Quezon City: Ateneo de Manila University Press.

1981a   Tiruray Traditional and Peasant Subsistence: A Comparison. *In* Olafson, Harold, ed., *Contributions to the Study of Philippine Shifting Cultivation*. Laguna: Forest Research Institute, University of the Philippines, Los Baños.

1981b   Tiruray Gardens: From Use Right to Private Ownership. *Philippine Quarterly of Culture and Society.* Vol. 9, no. 1, pp. 5-8.

1984   The Anthropologist as Outsider. *Philippine Quarterly of Culture and Society.* Vol. 12, no. 1, pp. 57-66.

1987   The Traditional Tiruray Zodiac: The Celestial Calendar of a Philippine Swidden and Foraging People. *Philippine Quarterly of Culture and Society.* Vol. 15, pp. 12-26.

Schlegel, Stuart A. and Helen Guthrie

1973   Diet and the Tiruray Shift from Swidden to Plow Farming. *Ecology of Food and Nutrition.* Vol. 2, pp. 181-191.

1980   Diet and the Tiruray Shift from Swidden to Plow Farming. *In* Robson, J. R. K., ed., *Food, Ecology and Culture.* New York: Gordon and Breach Science Publishers. Reprint of Schlegel and Guthrie (1973).

Schutz, Alfred

1962   *Collected Papers.* Vol. 1. The Hague: Martinus Nijhoff.

Sherman, Peynoyer L.

1903   *The Gutta Percha and Rubber of the Philippine Islands.* Manila: The Philippine Islands Bureau of Government Laboratories (Publication 7).

Spencer, Joseph E.

1966   *Shifting Cultivation in Southeastern Asia.* Berkeley, Los Angeles and London: University of California Press.

Stone, Julius

1961   *The Province and Function of Law.* Cambridge: Harvard University Press.

Tenorio, José (Sigayan)
    1892   *Costumbres de los Indios Tirurayes, traducidas al Español y*
            anotades por un misionero de la Compañia de Jesus.
            Manila: Amigo del Pais.

Thomas, David and Alan Healy
    1964   Some Philippine Language Subgroupings: A Lexicostatis-
            tical Study. *Anthropological Linguistics.* Vol. 4, no. 9,
            pp. 21-33.

Turner, G. S.
    1903   Tirurayes. *Census of the Philippine Islands.* Washington:
            United States Bureau of the Census.

Wickberg, Edgar
    1965   *The Chinese in Philippine Life, 1850-1898.* New Haven:
            Haven: Yale University Press.

Wilson, Colin
    1956   *The Outsider.* New York: Dell.

Wood, Grace L.
    1957   The Tiruray. *Philippine Sociological Review.* Vol. 5,
            no. 2, pp. 12-39.

Yudkin, J.
    1969   Sucrose and Heart Disease. *Nutrition Today.* Vol. 4,
            pp. 16-20.

leadership roles. *See* authority, legal; shaman

Lebak (town), 6, 104, 106

legal leader. *See* authority, legal

legal system, traditional, 9-10, 12-14, 27, 29-30, 49-50, 53, 82-84, 86, 93-96, 99, 128, 132, 161, 178, 180, 184-188, 192-199, 214-218, 220-222

Lick Observatory, University of California, Santa Cruz, 70

location of Tiruray, 4, 55-56, 129, 172

logging, 88, 100, 132, 140

Luckmann, Thomas, 54, 166, 229

Maguindanao (province), 1

Maguindanaon (ethnic group), 5, 6, 17-24, 85, 87, 93, 96, 100, 111, 129, 140, 174-175, 181, 185-186, 213-217, 219, 221, 224; relations with Tiruray, 6, 19-22, 85, 87, 96, 111, 140, 185-186, 217, 224; trade with Tiruray, 6, 19-22, 85, 111, 224

Majul, Cesar, 16, 25, 233

Malay Peninsula, 136

Malaysia, 147-150

Manila, 77

Manobo (ethnic group). *See* Cotabato Manobo

marketing, 7, 8, 56, 58, 65, 82, 85, 93, 104, 106, 111

marriage arrangement and ceremony, 20, 93, 130, 139, 187-199, 217-221

Martin, Mamerto, 2, 172

Matawaran, A. J., 231

Mateber River, 106

Methodist Church, 87

migrants, Tiruray, 134

Mirab (village), 2, 90

missionary work, 87, 99, 127, 129-130

"modernity," 164-165

money, traditional Tiruray use of, 82, 104, 111

Montano, Joseph, 25, 233

Moore, Grace Wood, 96, 233, 234

morality, 4, 12, 26-53

"mountain people," 182, 215

music, 15, 175, 192-193, 208-209, 214, 218

musical instruments, 175

Muslims, 5, 17-25, 77, 85, 100, 147-151, 171, 213-214. *See also* Islam; Maguindanaon

mythology. *See* folk stories

national language, 95

Negritos (ethnic group). *See* Semang

neighborhood, 8, 78-84, 89-91, 100-101, 109; traditional definition of, 78-80; peasant definition of, 89-91, 101, 109

Nuro (town), 87, 90, 106

Olafson, Harold, 97, 232

omens, 64-65, 180-182

Orleans, d', Ferdinand-Philippe-Marie, 212, 231

Outlook Magazine, 127, 128

ownership, 8, 33-34, 72-75, 99, 102

peasant society, definition of, 76-77

Philippine government, 85, 88, 100, 132

plow farming. *See* subsistence system (peasant)

polygyny, 9, 11, 81, 92, 198, 220-221

population of Tiruray, 5, 85, 89, 100, 129; population density, 85

areas, 134; neighborhood, 89-91, 101; professionals, 15, 128-129, 132, 134; settlement system, 85, 89-91; shift to from tribal, 76-94; smoking, 7; tenancy, 9, 89-94, 101, 111; use of alcoholic beverages, 7; use of public schools, 11, 95. *See* subsistence system (peasant)

Tiruray (traditional), 1, 4-24, 26-53, 55-70, 72-75, 77-87, 89, 93-96, 99, 100-105, 107-127, 129-133, 137-140, 147-150, 161, 171-224; abortion and contraception, 200, 216, 221; absence of institutionalized power, 83, 86; actual pronunciation of name, 4; adaptation to forest, 4; arrangement of marriage, 27, 83, 93; aversion to violence, 29-30, 45-46; "Awang people," 19, 21-24, 171-224; babies, treatment of, 200-201; basket weaving, 15; betel quid, use of, 7, 20, 183, 190, 216, 219, 221; birth customs, 221; calendar (star), 7, 55-70, 109; charms, 176-181; child-rearing, 11-12; clothing, 181-183; "coastal people," 182-184; "common sense," 28-29, 30, 50; comparison with peasant subsistence system, 107-109, 112-126; contraception, 200, 216, 221; cooking, 7, 173, 191-192, 203-207; cosmology, 13, 55-70, 186, 214; "custom," definition of, 26; death customs, 202-205, 221-223; diet, 58, 96, 103-104, 110, 112-126, 223; division of labor by gender, 8, 11, 102-105, 206; "downstream people," 19, 21-24, 171-224; dress, 6, 190-192; early men-

tion in literature, 127-128; eating, 207-208, 222; effect on author, 3-4, 162, 165; egalitarianism, 13, 139, 210; epic chant, 214; ethnic neighbors, 5, 18; exogamy, 83; facial decoration, 6, 181-183, 215; feuding, 10, 12, 49, 161; fishing, 7, 8, 56-58, 65, 69, 82, 103, 137, 209, 223; folk stories, 17-24, 39-40, 43-44, 59-65, 70, 99, 175-176, 208-210, 224; food, 7, 58, 96, 103-104, 110, 112-126, 129, 174, 223; gardens, 72-75, 111; gathering, 7, 8, 55-58, 65, 69, 82, 103; hair style, 130, 181, 183, 221; healing, 13-14, 139, 179, 201-202; house construction, 6-7; household, 9, 78, 80-82; houses, 172-173, 212; hunting, 7, 8, 56, 57, 65, 69, 80, 82, 103, 136, 209-211, 222-223; incest, 128; isolation of, 78, 132; land tenure, 8, 72-75; language, 2, 5, 18, 234; legal system, 9, 12-14, 27, 29-30, 49-50, 53, 82-84, 86, 93-96, 99, 128, 132, 161-162, 178, 180, 184-188, 192-199, 214-218, 220-222; location, 4, 55-56, 129, 172; marketing, 7, 8, 56, 58, 65, 82, 104, 111; marriage arrangement and wedding customs, 130, 187-199, 217-220; military alliance with Maguindanaon, 21-22; money, means of obtaining, 82, 104, 111; money, use of, 104; morality, 12, 26-53; "mountain people," 182; music and dance, 15, 175, 208-209, 214, 218; musical instruments, 15, 175; naming customs, 221; neighborhood, 78-84, 100; neighborhood, definition of,

78-80; ownership as right of use, 8, 33-34; 102; personal property, 173; persons with legal authority, 12-13, 15, 19-20, 43, 50, 82-83, 89, 93-94, 130, 132, 188-189, 191-194, 196, 210, 217-219, 224; polygyny, 9, 11, 81, 198, 220-221; power, absence of institutionalization of, 83, 96; pregnancy and birth, 199-201; relations with ethnic neighbors, 19-22, 87, 96, 129, 140, 185-186, 217; residence, 95, 172, 188; rituals, 14-16, 65-67, 80, 84, 94, 110, 130, 139-140, 193; sacred meal, 14, 66-67, 80, 84, 94, 110, 139-140; settlement system, 8-9, 78-82; settlement, 8-9, 80-82, 172-173, 212; shaman, 12, 13-14, 64, 82-84, 89, 93; 94, 132, 139, 162, 174-176, 213-214, 217; sharing, 80, 223; shift to peasantry, 4-7, 9, 11, 13-15, 52, 56, 85-96, 99-101, 104-111, 119, 131-134, 140; signs and omens, 64-65, 180-182; sorcery, 179; spirits, 13-14, 64, 83-84, 130, 139-140, 162-163, 175-176, 201, 213, 217, 221-222; trade with coastal market, 82, 104; trade with Maguindanaon, 6, 19-22, 85, 111, 224; "Tran Grande River people," 216; understanding of "human nature," 12, 28-31, 45-46, 50, 160-162; weapons, 182-183; zodiac, use of as calendar, 7, 55-71, 109. *See also* subsistence system (traditional); swidden cultivation
Tiruray Cooperative Association, 90
Tiruray Mountains. *See* Cotabato Cordillera

Tiruray Welfare Association, 128, 143
"town people." *See* "Awang people"
trade, 6-8, 19-22, 56, 58, 65, 82, 102, 104, 106, 111, 148-149, 224; pacts with Maguindanaon, 19-22, 85, 111, 224; ritual for establishing with Maguindanaon, 19-20; with market, 7, 8, 56, 58, 65
Tran Grande River, 78, 92, 100, 129, 172, 215
"Tran Grande River people," 216
tribal society: definition of, 76-77
Turner, G. S., 128, 134, 234
Tuwol (neighborhood), 43

United Church of Christ in the Philippines, 130
University of Chicago, Department of Anthropology, 172
"upper people." *See* "mountain people"
Upi Agricultural School, 86, 99, 129
Upi Valley, 86, 99, 100, 106, 132
Upi (town), 1, 86, 87, 129, 133; police, 93; road from Cotabato City, 6, 86, 90, 99; Agricultural School, 86, 99, 129
use-right, 8, 33-34, 72-75, 92, 102

Vasilevskis, S., 70
vengeance. *See* revenge

Weekly Graphic, 128
Whitmarsh, Phelps, 127
Wickberg, Edgar, 25, 234
Wilson, Colin, 158, 166, 234
Wood, Grace L. *See* Moore

Yudkin, J., 234

Zamora, Mario, 76
zodiac, 7, 55-71, 109

Typeset by GIRAFFE BOOKS using
12 pts AGaramond for the text
and 14 & 18 pts Bodacious for the titles.

GIRAFFE BOOKS are published exclusively by
Gloria F. Rodriguez